Race and Politics in
School/Community Organizations

GOODYEAR EDUCATION SERIES

Theodore W. Hipple, Editor
University of Florida

Change for Children
Sandra Nina Kaplan, Jo Ann Butom Kaplan,
Sheila Kunishima Madsen, and Bette K. Taylor

Crucial Issues in Contemporary Education
Theodore W. Hipple

Elementary School Teaching: Problems and Methods
Margaret Kelly Giblin

Facilitative Teaching: Theory and Practice
Robert Myrick and Joe Wittmer

The Future of Education
Theodore W. Hipple

Open Sesame: A Primer in Open Education
Evelyn Carswell and Darrell Roubinek

Popular Media and the Teaching of English
Thomas R. Giblin

Race and Politics in School/Community Organizations
Allan C. Ornstein

School Counseling: Problems and Methods
Robert Myrick and Joe Wittmer

Secondary School Teaching: Problems and Methods
Theodore W. Hipple

Solving Teaching Problems
Mildred Bluming and Myron Dembo

Teaching, Loving, and Self-Directed Learning
David Thatcher

Will the Real Teacher Please Stand Up?
A Primer in Humanistic Education
Mary Greer and Bonnie Rubinstein

Allan C. Ornstein
Loyola University of Chicago

Race and Politics in School/Community Organizations

GOODYEAR PUBLISHING COMPANY
Pacific Palisades, California

Library of Congress Cataloging in Publication Data

Ornstein, Allan C.
Race and politics in school/community organizations.

(Goodyear education series)
1. Negroes—Education. 2. Schools—Centralization—
United States. 3. School integration—United States.
I. Title.
LC2801.076 1974   370.19'31   73-86433
ISBN 0-87620-774-3
ISBN 0-87620-773-5 (pbk.)

Current Printing (last digit):

10 9 8 7 6 5 4 3 2 1

ISBN: 0-87620-773-5 (paper)
        0-87620-774-3 (case)

Library of Congress Catalog Card Number: 73-86433

Y-7743-1 (case)
Y-7735-7 (paper)

Printed in the United States of America

Ricky and Cheryl.....

happiness and health in their
adventures with life.

Ricky and Cheryl.....

happiness and health in their
adventures with life.

Contents

Preface

Although no social scientist is supposed to hitch his work to a set of biases, he cannot escape from them; they are inherent in his work. Similarly, no reader can be totally objective, and the way he reacts to the data in this book or, for that matter, in any social science book, will reflect his biases. To assume that neither the author nor the reader has values would be to deny that the social sciences are human activities. Social scientists and readers of the social sciences are people, and where there are people there are values.

The natural sciences operate on the principle of the uniformity of nature, but in the social sciences there is considerable disagreement concerning the explanation of human nature and social behavior. Facts about people do not speak for themselves; they must be interpreted in a frame of reference. It is this frame of reference, which is both conceptual and value-ridden, which leads to disagreement. Disagreement in the social sciences is a sign of health and vigor, not an invitation to confusion or belittlement. A social science is an adventure in human events, and ideas and theories develop through discussion and debate. The realm of debate, however, is less extensive in race relations than in most other topics in the social sciences because of the sensitivity of the topic. It would be most dangerous, most disastrous, if we were to achieve a mechanical uniformity in discussion of race, or if we were to remain too intimidated to discuss related issues frankly. An atmosphere of freedom must exist if the social sciences are to flourish; avoidance of discussion of certain topics or repressive control of ideas through subtle or overt methods would be foreboding to the academic world and could possibly lead to the imposition of dogma.

I expect some readers to be hostile toward this book because I am questioning many communal and ideological beliefs and calling to account the vested interests of many groups. I hope serious students who read this book will find in it the bases for legitimate discussion of the issues.

Race and Politics in
School/Community Organizations

chapter 1

Organizing the Schools and the Community

This chapter discusses methods for organizing schools and communities. It deals with three alternative models for the schools: administrative decentralization, community participation, and community control. It also examines three alternative models for the community: social planning, locality development, and social action. All six organizational approaches reflect various methods for distributing decision-making authority and power. As the discussion evolves, a metropolitan orientation is advocated, not only for schools and communities, but also for all social systems. This orientation proposes that the schools and the community—banks, libraries, railways, communication centers, and the like—can be discussed together because all are fundamentally bound with one another within a metropolitan area.

Alternative Methods for Organizing Metropolitan Schools

As the characteristics of the metropolitan population have changed, the problems confronting the schools, and especially the inner-city schools, have increased. Nonwhite students, most of whom are from lower-income groups, have become the majority in many city school systems and particularly in the elementary schools. At the same time, outmigration of blacks to the suburbs has begun, and some suburban and county school systems are beginning to experience the problems once considered to be characteristic of only city schools.

Critics have focused on the city schools, however, contending that the nonwhite students bring to the schools a culture and set of values different from the white middle-class life style upon which the school systems have been based and that the schools still reflect the traditional culture. In the

1

few school systems that have exhibited change and a sensitivity that reflects a pluralistic society, the critics further contend, these alterations have resulted mainly from political pressure and community organization, and especially from black politics and black organizations. Where these changes have occurred, however, there has been concurrent concern among some educators that black power is duplicating the errors of white racism and ethnocentrism. There is also growing apprehension that an increasing number of blacks are no longer committed to educational change within the existing structure and that they are not only questioning but are also opposing its legitimacy.

From the concept of black power, demands have evolved for community control of the schools, that is, policy-making in education by parents and community representatives. In their influential book on *Black Power*, Carmichael and Hamilton (1967) reject the notion of a black-white partnership on the grounds that it is a myth. They urge blacks to organize on their own terms and to use "the black community as a base of organization to control institutions in that community." This includes gaining "control of the ghetto schools" and taking control away from the professional and white educators because, they allege, these people "bring with them middle-class biases, unsuitable techniques and materials, [which] are, at best, dysfunctional and at worst destructive" to black children (pp. 166–67). Similarly, McCoy (1969) claims that blacks must lift "the yoke of oppression off [their] backs" (p. xi). Across the country, the black community is voicing "its contempt for white American institutions that are keeping black people in a sophisticated form of slavery" (p. xii). Continuing the rhetoric, he concludes that the black community must gain control of its schools and "destroy its traditional paternalistic dependency on the white community" (p. xiii). More recently, Banks (1972*ab*) states that blacks are resorting to "aggressive actions" in order to take control of their schools. He argues that these actions are liberation tactics and denounces teachers' rights as a racial euphemism for preventing blacks from gaining control of their schools. And Fantini, Gittell, and Magat (1970) assert that control of the schools by blacks and other minorities is necessary to enhance their children's education and their "own power [and] destiny without the white man's intervention." To support their liberal proposition, the authors refer to a black caucus statement that rejects participation by whites, "even those whites who have been . . . allies" (pp. 94–95).

This increasing pressure, often accompanied by violence by the militant members of the black community and compounded by criticism of the Establishment by liberal educators, has played a part in forcing school authorities to decentralize many city school systems and to increase community involvement in the schools. This black-liberal demand for change—whether legitimate or not, whether based on education or on political ideology—seems to have a counterpart (mostly arising for other reasons) in some suburban and county schools, and many school systems in these areas also have decentralized and increased community involvement. What have emerged, then, are the following (not mutually exclusive) administrative-community alternatives for governing metropolitan schools: (1) administrative decentralization, (2) community participation, and (3) community control, with either the second alternative (participation) or the third (control) usually accompanying the first (decentralization). We will briefly define and preview these three administrative-community organizational models.

1. *Administrative Decentralization.* Administrative decentralization is common in metropolitan school systems that have 50,000 or more students. A school system may stop with decentralization or, as it usually does, proceed to increase community participation. In only two cases, New York City and Detroit, have the state legislatures enacted some form of community control.

With administrative decentralization alone, the locus of political power remains in a single, central administration and board of education. In one form of decentralization the bureaucracy is divided into field or administrative units, and sometimes these units are further subdivided. In still another, more traditional, form of decentralization, the school system is divided into attendance units, usually with one (or possibly more than one) high school serving as the focal point of the unit, which includes the elementary and middle or junior high schools feeding that high school. In each form of decentralization there is usually a field administrator (such as an area or district superintendent) who is responsible for the schools within his unit.

In theory, breaking down the bureaucracy into field or administrative units brings the central administration closer to the schools and the community and results in better communication. Influence is shifted from the central office to the field administration to the extent that services and departments are transferred from the central office to the field. Field administrators and school principals are empowered to make some decisions formerly made at the central office. Accountability is still directed upward, not toward the community, although the field administrators presumably are sensitized to residents within the boundaries of their units. Since the professionals and school board members retain power, most school people prefer this kind of organization.

2. *Community Participation.* Although decentralization need not lead to increased community participation, it usually does. Under this policy, decision-making authority and power still remain with the professionals, especially those at the apex of the administrative hierarchy. Community participation usually results in the formation of *advisory* committees and groups beyond the usual PTA and other parent-voluntary groups.

Such advisory committees are comprised of various combinations of representatives of such elements as parents, community residents who do not have children attending public schools, teachers, administrators, students, and local business, political, religious, and social organizations. They may operate at any of the various levels of the school system—the local school, the field unit if the schools have been decentralized, or the central office—making recommendations and serving as liaison between the community and the schools. Committee members are usually appointed by the school principal, if the committee is operating on the individual school level, or by the field administrator or central office administrator, depending on whether the committee is operating on the field or on the central level; however, a few school systems encourage local election of members of these advisory committees. Community participation is usually accepted and supported by teachers, administrators, and school board members, as well as by many minority parents and community leaders; however, it is rejected by some critics of the teachers and schools because it does not transfer authority and power to the community.

3. *Community Control.* Demands for community control are often made by persons in the black community (not only with regard to the schools but also with regard to other social institutions such as the political system, economic system, law enforcement agencies, social welfare agencies, and health clinics). They claim that the schools have been unresponsive to the needs and interests of black children. Because, they claim, the professionals have failed to educate these children, first most of the liberals and black militants and now a growing segment of the black moderates blame the Establishment and its "caretakers" and argue for a chance for members of the community to succeed—or fail—on their own terms. The usual procedure is to advocate the decentralization of the schools within the existing framework; such decentralization facilitates community control or at least brings about greater community input. But, although some form of decentralization can make community control possible, the decentralization process does not necessarily lead to actual control of the schools by the community.

Community control refers to legal provision for an elected local school board that functions under specific guidelines and in conjunction with the central board of education. It means a sharing of decision-making authority and power between the local and the central school boards. Community control of the schools carried to the fullest extent implies total governance by the community, or by so-called representatives of the community, over personnel (hiring, firing, and promoting), curriculum (course electives, textbooks, and evaluation), student policy (student-teacher relationships, discipline, and testing), and financing (federal funding, allocation of money, and determination of the budget). In short, the powers of the professionals and central school board members are abridged, actually transferred to the community. This curtailment is spurned by most teachers and administrators, especially by those whites in ghetto schools who fear reverse discrimination, increased preferential hiring and promotion of blacks, and even loss of their own jobs.

We can view the three alternative models as representing two options: either administrative decentralization and community participation or administrative decentralization and community control. Most professionals advocate the first option because their authority and power remain less subject to scrutiny. Many liberal educators and black militants, and an increasing number of other minority groups, prefer the second option, which connotes a shifting of political control to a *few* (but not necessarily representative) members of the community.

Status of administrative-community organization of metropolitan schools

To obtain data on the status of the three alternative means of administrative-community organization, Ornstein (1973*a*) surveyed the school systems in which 50,000 or more students are enrolled. Out of 77 school systems having this number of students, 62 (82 percent) responded to the survey.[1] Three other school systems (Baltimore City, Prince George's County, and Denver) have been added to the tabulation on the basis of another study (Ornstein 1974). The 65 school systems are listed in descending order of size according to student enrollment figures in table 1.1, which shows the extent to which each school system has decentralized and whether it is experiencing community participation and/or control.

Of the 65 school systems listed in table 1.1, 39 had decentralized and 8 were considering doing so. In addition, one school system (Clark County) had changed from centralization to decentralization then back to centralization. More large school systems than smaller ones had decentralized. For example, 18 of the 21 school systems with 100,000 or more students had decentralized or were considering it, whereas only 29 of the 44 school systems with between 50,000 and 100,000 students had decentralized or were considering doing so.

The great majority of the school systems started the decentralization process in or after 1967. Even the larger school systems that had already decentralized in previous stages had more recently implemented major decentralization plans. Six school systems (Philadelphia, Milwaukee, Denver, Jefferson County (Colorado), Minneapolis, and Austin) reported decentralization based on attendance and feeder patterns (movement by students from elementary and/or junior high school or middle school to senior high school). Two school systems (Indianapolis and San Francisco) had decentralized only the elementary schools, and one school system (Minneapolis) had decentralized only the inner-city schools. The Cincinnati schools had decentralized into separate elementary school and high school districts. Many terms were used to describe the decentralized units, including *district, area, zone, region, complex, cluster, unit,* and *pyramid*; the first two terms were used in 80 percent of the decentralized school systems. In five systems (Chicago, St. Louis, Indianapolis, Seattle, and Minneapolis), the decentralized unit was subdivided into smaller units.

The number of decentralized units ranged from as few as one area and two pyramids in Minneapolis to as many as 32 community districts

Table 1.1

STATUS OF ADMINISTRATIVE DECENTRALIZATION, COMMUNITY PARTICIPATION, AND COMMUNITY CONTROL IN SCHOOL SYSTEMS WITH A STUDENT ENROLLMENT OF 50,000 OR MORE STUDENTS

School system	Setting City	Setting Suburban	Setting Rural	Enrollment	Admin. decent. Yes	Admin. decent. No	Studying decentralization	Studying further decent.	Year decentralized	Number of units and decentralized unit term(s)	Number of students in decentralized units	Community participation None	School level	Decentralized level	Central level	Community control Yes	Community control No
New York City	X			1,200,000	X				1969[a]	32 community districts	20–38,000		X	X	X	X	
Los Angeles	X	X		621,230	X				1971[a]	12 areas	52,000±/area			X	X		X
Chicago	X			558,825	X				1968[a]	3 areas; 27 districts	154–216,000/area; 20,000±/district		X	X	X		X
Philadelphia	X			290,000	X			X	1968[a]	8 districts[e]	18–42,000		X				X
Detroit	X			277,540	X				1971[a]	8 regions	26–40,000		X	X	X	X	
Dade County, Fla.	X	X	X	240,000	X				1965[a]	6 areas	31–48,000			X	X		X
Houston	X			225,000	X				1971	6 areas	34–40,000		X				X
Baltimore	X			190,735[b]		X		X[c]					X				X
Hawaii	X	X	X	181,585		X							X				X
Prince George's County, Md.	X	X	X	162,830[b]	X			X	n.d.	3 areas	50,000±		X	X	X		X
Dallas	X			155,000		X	X[c]								X		X
District of Columbia	X			140,000		X	X[c]								X[d]		X
Memphis	X			139,115	X				1971	4 areas	33–40,000		X	X	X		X

Locality	Population		Date	Organizational units	Ratio
Fairfax County, Va.	136,000	X	1967	4 areas	34,000±
Baltimore County, Md.	132,000	X	1965	5 areas	25–30,000
Milwaukee	129,000	X	1967	14 clusters[e]	2.5–8,500
Broward County, Fla.	129,000	X	1968	5 areas + 1 complex	25,000±/area
Montgomery County, Md.	126,620	X	1971	6 areas	14.5–27,500
San Diego	125,000[b]	X			
Duval County, Fla.	109,795	X			
St. Louis	104,000	X[f]	1968[a]	5 districts; 10 units	17–23,000/district
Indianapolis	97,880	X	1969	3 regions; 10 areas	5–9,000/area
Boston	97,000[b]	X			
Jefferson County, Ky.	96,200	X	1956	5 areas	16–23,000
Atlanta	96,000	X			10,000±
Denver	94,840[b]	X	n.d.	9 areas[e]	
Pinellas County, Fla.	88,000	X X[c]			
Fort Worth	86,000	X X[c]			
Orange County, Fla.	86,000	X X[c]			
Nashville-Davidson County, Tenn.	85,290	X X	1966	3 districts	24–31,000
San Francisco	80,455	X[f]	1971	7 zones	5–6,000
Charlotte-Mecklenburg, N.C.	79,875	X X[c]			
Cincinnati	79,000	X	1973	4 elementary districts; 2 secondary districts	12,000±; 15,000±
Anne Arundel County, Md.	77,000	X	1973	4 areas	20,000±
Clark County, Nev.	76,200	X[g]			
Seattle	74,300	X	1970	2 regions; 11 areas + 1 central area	33,000/region; 6,000±/area

Table 1.1 (cont.)

School system	City	Suburban	Rural	Administrative decentralization Yes	No	Studying decentralization	Studying further decent.	Year decentralized	Number of units and decentralized unit term(s)	Number of students in decentralized units	None	School level	Decentralized level	Central level	Community control Yes	Community control No
Jefferson County, Colo.	X	X	X	X				73,980	1971	9 areas[e]	5–14,000		X	X			X
San Antonio	X			X				73,825	1969	3 areas	24,500±		X	X	X		X
Pittsburgh	X			X				70,000	1969	3 areas	17–33,000		X		X		X
Tulsa		X			X			70,000					X	X	X		X
Portland, Ore.	X			X				69,000	1970	3 areas	21–25,000		X	X	X		X
Buffalo	X				X	X	X[c]	68,345[b]					X		X		X
Palm Beach County, Fla.	X	X	X	X			X	68,200	1969	4 areas	17,000±		X				X
Kansas City, Mo.	X				X	X[c]		68,000						X	X		X
East Baton Rouge Parish, La.	X	X	X		X			67,500					X				X
Mobile	X	X	X		X			66,000				X					
Brevard County, Fla.	X	X		X				62,795	1969	3 areas	12–26,000		X	X	X		X
Omaha	X	X	X		X			62,715					X				X
El Paso	X			X				62,580	1972	3 areas	18–25,000		X	X			X
Granite, Utah		X		X				61,980	1971	3 complexes	18–26,000		X	X	X		X
Minneapolis	X			X[h]				61,580	1967	1 area; 2 pyramids[e]	10,000±/pyramid		X	X	X		X

8

City	1)	2)	3)	Enrollment[b]	Dec.	Year[a]	No. of units/areas	Population/area			
Oklahoma City	X			60,340	X	1971	3 regions	20,000±	X		X
Oakland, Calif.	X			60,000	X				X	X X	X[i]
Greenville County, S.C.			X	57,525	X	1972	4 areas + 1 experimental area	13,000±/area; 5,000/ experimental area		X	X
Wichita	X			57,220	X				X		X
Jefferson County, Ala.		X		57,000	X				X	X	X
Austin	X			56,000	X	n.d.	11 clusters[e]	5,000±	X X	X X	X
Fresno	X			55,750	X	1973	6 areas	5–12,000	X	X	X
Polk County, Fla.	X	X	X	55,000	X	n.d.	4 areas	14,000±		X	X
San Juan, Calif.			X	54,000	X				X	X	X
Akron	X			53,990	X				X	X	X
Dayton	X	X	X	53,000	X	1971	3 units	16–20,000		X X	X
Kanawha County, W. Va.	X	X	X	52,000	X					X	X
Garden Grove, Calif.	X	X		51,445	X	1970	3 areas	15–19,000		X[j]	X
Norfolk, Va.	X			51,000	X						X

9

Notes: Respondents were given the opportunity to check the table for accuracy and suggest revisions if necessary.

For purposes of the survey: 1) *Administrative Decentralization* connotes breaking down the central bureaucracy into smaller field components and reducing the administrative span of control by transferring some administrative functions and responsibilities from the central office to the field or decentralized level; 2) *Community Participation* refers to advisory input of local parent and/or community groups beyond the usual PTA and parent-advisory organizations; and 3) *Community Control* refers to legal provisions for an elected local community school board which shares decision-making authority and power with the central school board or has total jurisdiction in specified school matters within their boundaries.

a = The school system has decentralized in stages with the specified year representing the latest major administrative/community change.

b = Source for student enrollment is based on 1971–72 data. All other figures represent the 1972–73 student census.

c = Considering administrative decentralization, and if implemented, community participation will most likely be included at the decentralized level. Included are 1) Baltimore City, tentatively 6–9 areas with 20–30,000 students/area; 2) Dallas, some departments and services are already decentralized, other plans are undetermined; 3) District of Columbia, plans are undetermined; 4) Pinellas County, tentatively 3–4 areas with 22–30,000 students/area; 5) Orange County, plans are undetermined; 6) Charlotte-Mecklenburg, plans are undetermined; 7) Buffalo, tentatively 5 districts with 12–15,000 students; and 8) Kansas City, Mo., plans are undetermined.

d = A few model city and experimental schools also have community participation at the school level.

e = Based on feeder schools to a high school.

f = Decentralization is limited to the elementary schools.

g = The school system was decentralized between 1964–68 with 5 zones and approximately 15,000/zone. Returned to centralization.

h = Decentralization is limited to the inner-city schools.

i = One of the 92 schools of the system has a local community-controlled school board.

j = Community participation at the central level is in process of being implemented.

n.d. = No date indicated.

© 1973 by Allan C. Ornstein

in New York City. The most frequent numbers of decentralized units were
three units (in 13 school systems) and four units (in 7 school systems). The
approximate number of students per decentralized unit ranged from as few
as 2,500 to 8,500 in Milwaukee to as many as 154,000 to 216,000 in Chicago.
The most common size was between 15,000 and 25,000 students. This corresponds somewhat to the ideal size of 25,000–30,000 recommended by
Havighurst and Levine (1971), the 12,000–40,000 suggested by the New York
City Mayor's Advisory Panel (1967) (in what is commonly referred to as the
Bundy report), and most closely to the 20,000 figure suggested in the Passow
report (1967). These numbers of students per unit represent recommendations
of the proper size to carry out administrative functions, work with the community, and grow with relative efficiency and sufficient resources.

Only two school systems (New York City and Detroit) reported
some legalized form of community control. A far more frequent form of
citizens' involvement was community participation. Sixty-two school systems
reported some form of community participation; the type most frequently
mentioned was at the school level (51 responses) and the second most frequently mentioned was at the central level (43 responses). Ironically, eight
school systems that reported having decentralized did not indicate community
participation at the field level.

Arguments for and against community control

There is not much controversy over administrative decentralization because
most people, including teachers and administrators and their critics, tend to
accept this alternative. Many professional educators see a need for it because
their school systems are so large and favor it because they still retain control
of the schools; the critics accept it because they view it as the first stage of
community control. The controversy, then, is about whether the schools
should go beyond administrative decentralization to community control and
about which group, the professional educators or community, will have the
power and authority to run the schools.

The issues related to community control have been examined in
depth by Fantini et al. (1970), Gittell and Hevesi (1969), Levin (1970), Ornstein (1972b, 1974) and Sizer (1968). This book summarizes and extends
their data and presents a different approach to the study of the underlying
issues. A debate between the proponents and the critics of community control is presented in table 1.2. In the first part of the table, critics' reasons for
opposing community control are listed in the first column with proponents'
corresponding responses being given in the second. In the second part of the
table, the proponents give their arguments for community control and the
critics respond. Thus, each group is given the opportunity both to advocate
and to defend its position. The reader can sum up the arguments for and
against community control and reach his own conclusions.

Table 1.2

**A DEBATE BETWEEN THE CRITICS AND THE PROPONENTS
OF COMMUNITY CONTROL**

PART I

Arguments against, by the Critics	Responses by the Proponents
1. Community control will impede integration.	a. Integration connotes white assimilation. b. The schools in most cities are more segregated now than prior to the Supreme Court decision in 1954. c. Most whites and many blacks do not want to integrate.
2. Community control will balkanize the cities.	a. Most cities are already balkanized.
3. Community control is a scheme for alleviating pressure from the black community.	a. The parents are motivated to action because their children are failing in school. b. They will be motivated to seek high-quality education for their children.
4. Parents and community residents (especially those in low-income areas) are too inexperienced and inept to deal with complex educational issues.	a. As for inexperience, train the incoming local school board members. b. As for ineptness, this is insulting. How do we know this, if these people have not had the opportunity to run the schools.
5. Community control will destroy the merit system.	a. Competitive examinations are white-oriented. b. There is no proof that those who pass the examinations are "fit and qualified" for their jobs. c. Maintain the list of eligibles and permit the local school boards to select personnel from the list.
6. Community control will weaken teachers' unions.	a. They are already splintered by political and racial issues in most cities. b. The unions are already weakened, not by community control but by depleted school budgets, the citizens' revolt against higher taxes, and the surplus of teachers.
7. Community control is a distraction from the greater need for money to educate children, and especially ghetto children.	a. This is only one method of reform. b. We can implement community control and still seek increased finances.
8. Community control will enhance black racism.	a. What about 400 years of white racism? b. Black children need an education that will help them cope with white discrimination.
9. Community control will lead to rejection of white participation.	a. White personnel who are sensitive to the needs and interests of black children will be encouraged to remain in ghetto schools.

Table 1.2 (cont.)

PART II

Arguments for, by the Proponents	*Responses by the Critics*
1. Community control will make teachers and administrators accountable to the people.	a. It will lead to vigilante groups (as in New York City and Detroit).
	b. It is questionable whether parents and community representatives can objectively assess the performance or the output of teachers and administrators, since the experts in the field of testing and evaluation find it difficult if not impossible to evaluate teachers and administrators with reliability and validity.
	c. Many community representatives have already reached the conclusion that the professional educators are the only ones responsible for students' failure; other influences such as the home, community, and students themselves must be taken into consideration.
2. Community control will lead to educational innovation.	a. The local school boards will concentrate their interest on politics and issues of self-interest and ideology.
	b. Innovation is based on pilot testing and evaluating programs; community control has not been sufficiently pilot-tested or evaluated.
3. Community control will lead to greater parental and public participation.	a. The majority of people, including parents, are indifferent to educational issues—or at least do not participate in school meetings or vote on educational issues.
	b. Politically oriented groups, ranging from black militants to white segregationists, will gain control of the schools for their own purposes (as in New York City and Detroit).
4. Community control will enable local school boards to hire qualified principals and superintendents (on the basis of their ability to relate to ghetto children and serve as models).	a. This will lead to increased ethnic and racial favoritism in appointing and promoting administrators (a pattern which is already evident in many city school systems).
5. Community control will enhance flexible hiring and promotional practices and will attract teachers and administrators with more initiative and imagination.	a. Flexibility connotes that competitive performance, experience, and objective tests can be replaced by patronage, nepotism, and pork barrels.
	b. Initiative and imagination are difficult to define; they mean different things to different people and, to some, euphemisms for reverse discrimination.

Table 1.2 (cont.)

Arguments for, by the Proponents	Responses by the Critics
6. Community control will raise student achievement.	a. There is no proof that this will happen; we should pilot-test this assumption before we make massive changes. Achievement may remain the same or even decline with community control. b. There is no evidence that black teachers and administrators can do a better job in raising achievement among black students, as indicated by school systems in which there is a majority of black teachers and administrators (e.g., black schools in the South and in Washington, Philadelphia, St. Louis, Baltimore, Gary, and Newark).
7. Community control will promote self-government by blacks as well as by other minorities.	a. This is a return to the myth of "separate but equal." b. This will foster white ethnicity and backlash. c. Inherent in this concept is the surrender of the suburbs to white domination while blacks obtain control of the ghetto—a ghetto depleted in finances and saddled with decay, drug addiction, violence, crime, traffic congestion, pollution, population density, etc.
8. Community control will lead to educational reform.	a. This thwarts future possibilities for school desegregation, which should be the immediate goal for educational reform. b. Despite the present shortcomings of the federal government, it is recognized as the only institution with the strength, expertise, and financial resources to reform schools and society. (In the past, virtually all major social reform—in education, welfare, housing, health services—has been initiated by the federal government.)

SOURCE: Allan C. Ornstein, "The Politics of School Decentralization and Community Control," a report to Dan Walker, Governor of the State of Illinois, August 1972a, pp. 6-8. © Copyright 1972 by Allan Ornstein.

The politics of community control

The main concern of the advocates of community control has very little to do with children's welfare or education, although they argue that their ultimate concern is for the children. The crux of the matter is largely political power—which group will control the schools—and related issues of self-interest and group ideology. Indeed, the administration of the schools is largely political (who makes what decisions) and linked to economic considerations (not only who gets what jobs in the future but who gets what jobs now). As Goodlad (1971) points out, "Schooling is conducted within a framework of power and struggle for power. It is no more protected from the abuse of power than are political enterprises" (p. 16).

Under the banner of educational reform, many minority group leaders are advocating a political ideology that corresponds with black power and control of local institutions such as the public schools. As Billings (1972) states, the "conflict over community control . . . of schools represents nothing more or less than a struggle of power between blacks and whites" (p. 277). Carmichael and Hamilton (1967) claim that control of the schools must be taken away from whites and that blacks must gain "control of the public schools in their community: hiring and firing, . . . determination of standards." They argue that "it is crucial that race be taken into account in determining policy," and with questionable logic they claim that this policy is not reverse racism but "a method of emphasizing race in a positive way" (p. 167). In this connection it should be noted that almost all demands for community control are accompanied by demands that professionals be held accountable. For many of these proponents of "reform," accountability has very little to do with good teaching and administrative abilities; they consider it to be a potential weapon that can be used by local community boards against specific groups or individuals—to hire, promote, and discharge on the basis of color rather than merit. In fact, many black spokesmen are now claiming that, because of their background and biases, whites are unable to relate to blacks and are unqualified to teach blacks (and, for these reasons, are unable to dispense social and community services in black communities). The political and economic implications of this logic will be clear to readers. Race and ideology have never been recognized as elements that enter into the definition of good teaching or administration. Yet today they are considered by blacks as assets of blacks to be capitalized on and as liabilities of whites to justify excluding whites from black communities and the educational, social, and cultural services in black communities. Although most school officials do not subscribe to this logic, their recent actions in schools and colleges across the country show that they surrender to such racial and ideological demands to keep peace and avoid the risk of violence by black militants.

Today's increasing black militancy also makes highly questionable whether incompetent black teachers and administrators can and will be held accountable in the same way as are whites, or whether such blacks can be held accountable at all. Not only has it become a political liability to question the formal qualifications of blacks, but affirmative action programs now urge the lowering of standards for minorities. As black militant ideology intensifies and as governmental goals and timetables continue to be transformed into quotas and reverse discrimination, it is likely that heredity (color and race) will become more important than competence. The net result may be that only white teachers and administrators will be held accountable or, at best, that community-controlled (and even central) school boards will apply a double standard in judging the performance of black educators and white educators.

In New York City and Detroit, where community control exists, local power groups and militant leaders have fought over procedures and issues in appointing and discharging administrators, sometimes with little regard to legality. Racial quotas (preferential quotas for blacks and other minorities) have been publicly announced in at least 2 of the 32 New York City community districts and three of the eight Detroit regions, and it is common knowledge that many of the other decentralized units are employing quotas without publicly acknowledging the fact. In each of these school systems, candidates who have recently obtained their teaching licenses have been placed on waiting lists while unqualified people off the streets have been hired to staff classrooms. Ideology is a factor too. Not only are militant groups forcing the resignation of many elected community board members in each of these school systems, but also there are allegations in New York City and Detroit newspapers that black militants are fighting with and threatening the lives of black moderates. Furthermore, there is testimony that elected school board members in both school systems direct questions at supervisory candidates contrived to find out where they stand on political issues.[2]

When we talk about community control, we are also talking about licensing procedures, what will determine fitness to perform professional tasks competently, and what power groups will establish professional performance standards. In the name of equal opportunity for teaching and supervisory jobs, the National Teachers Examination and English grammar qualifying tests have been dispensed with in many large school systems, and in other school systems the qualifying examinations have been attenuated. In New York City and San Francisco the NAACP has successfully argued that supervisory tests do not measure "merit and fitness" for the jobs involved and that the test questions are culturally biased. The NAACP fails to admit that some groups are better achievers or more educated than others; it fails to point out why there is less reason to eliminate merit examinations in the medical and legal professions. In Chicago a different testing procedure has evolved to mollify blacks. The Chicago school board recently changed the principal's examination by awarding as many as ten extra points for special services, which heavily favors the black candidates, and by replacing most of the questions on science, mathematics, and English grammar with questions on human relations and education. One might contend that the ten service credits are valid predictors of job success, that they are similar to veterans' credits in civil service examinations, or that human relations questions are more "relevant" to job requirements than a knowledge of the rules of grammar. Or one might claim that the extra points are necessary to enable blacks to compete with whites on cognitive examinations; further, that, because the substituted questions are soft in content and geared to help minority groups pass the examination, they serve to create administrative jobs for blacks and thus help quell the demand for community control.

In short, when we talk about the politics of community control, we are talking about which teachers and administrators will be hired and promoted and which will be fired in a period when, according to Bard (1972) and Ornstein and Talmage (1973), such jobs are difficult to come by. Moreover, these observers point out, there is an increase in the number of black "acting principals" and newly assigned superintendents in inner-city areas and an increase in competition among whites for administrative jobs in the outer cities and suburbs. We are also talking about big money—who gets jobs ranging in salary from $25,000 to $40,000. According to Greene (1970) we are referring to hundreds of jobs in each school system which will become "patronage plums" (p. 7). For Billings (1972) and Sizemore (1972) the talk is about a conflict between blacks and whites and which group will run the nation's largest school systems. According to Hamilton (1968) community control means the power (of the community) to make economic decisions and gain economic control of the schools and then the use of the schools to gain control of other institutions in the cities. It also connotes racial militancy and ideology. All of these factors combined have very little to do with education, with whether children can add a set of numbers or read the words in their textbooks. What these political-economic-racial-ideological factors do is to foster rhetoric and educational sloganeering or, even worse, conflict and educational irresponsibility.

The situation is perhaps summarized best by Kenneth B. Clark (1972a), the noted black psychologist and one of the original supporters of administrative decentralization. (In New York City where he resides, decentralization also connotes community control, since both alternatives were and still are usually debated simultaneously and as one "reform" measure.) Clark states:

> Those involved in decentralization [and community control] have forgotten what the purpose was. The purpose was not a struggle for power or control. The purpose was to try to find some way in which the quality of education provided a particular school child could be increased. . . . The evidence does not now add up to any indication that decentralization is making for a better break for our children in the schools. If we find that we're wasting time and that people are going to squabble and fight and . . . neglect the children, then we [should] try to find other ways in which the children will be given priority [pp. 1, 26].

And elsewhere Clark (1972b) reports:

> School decentralization has been a "disastrous" experience in which the basic issue, teaching children, has been substituted by selfish forces. . . . These forces include the radical politics of small local groups [p. 7].

On the basis of the foregoing data and above discussion, it seems that most metropolitan school systems have implemented various forms of administrative decentralization and community participation. It also seems that individuals and groups who advocate community control are apparently not convincing many school administrators, school board members, and state legislators. Many of the advocates appear to be writing from a New York City perspective, which probably does not represent the rest of the country. In fact, the New York school system is often considered atypical because of its size, ethnic diversity, teacher militancy, and special governance problems. Those educators and community leaders who argue for community control appear to represent a provincial and political viewpoint and are probably misleading the educational field about the merits of community control. Other than New York, only Detroit has responded to the advocates of community control. A number of zealous educators and community leaders (most of whom are outside the public schools) repeat the oversimplified statements and slogans for community control, but the number is small (yet vocal) and the officials who run the schools, despite the continuous pressure for community control, have managed for the greater part to maintain control of the schools.

The administrators, school board members, and political legislators running the various school systems seem relatively familiar with events in New York City (and in Detroit, to some degree) and recognize that community control may have increased racial hostility and segregation. Moreover, community control has not yet accomplished what the advocates claimed. Instead of innovation there has been increased rigidity in rules and in supervisory relations with teachers; instead of the entire community, including the silent but majority voice of the parents, local school board members seem to represent selected and well-organized agencies; instead of there being increased student achievement, reading scores have declined in both the New York and the Detroit school systems since community control was legislated.[3] (These reading scores may not be correlated with community control, but the advocates have generalized that community control would enhance student achievement.) As for other large school systems such as those of Los Angeles and Philadelphia, many organizational policy reports have clearly specified that community control has potential for more harm than good, and nearly every report on administrative-community guidelines (in most of the school systems listed in table 1.1) has clearly reaffirmed that policy making should remain in the hands of the central school board.

Alternative Methods for Organizing Communities

In this section we attempt to achieve greater conceptual understanding of the three aforementioned models of the schools by extending and relating the discussion to three models of community organization. The idea is to note the parallels of organizing schools and communities.

The three models of community organization frequently used by urban planners, social workers, and sociologists are termed:

1. *Social Planning.* This approach emphasizes processes for solving social problems and requires professional experts to plan, coordinate, and implement necessary changes and reforms. Community involvement varies with each situation, but it does not play an essential part; the community serves more or less in some advisory capacity. This approach resembles the concept of administrative decentralization in school organization.

2. *Locality Development.* This approach is designed to improve the entire community through active participation by a wide range of community residents and representatives. Democratic procedures, voluntary cooperation, and self-help are emphasized. The purpose is to enhance community self-development with assistance from professional advisors and workers. To some degree, this method corresponds to the school concept of community participation.

3. *Social Action.* This strategy stresses a disadvantaged and even oppressed subgroup; it makes demands on the larger society, considers conflict as a chief means for implementing change, rejects professional leadership, and seeks a redistribution of power. In terms of school organization, this community approach resembles the concept of community control.

Morris and Binstock (1966) outline similar community organizing concepts; they do not use names or terms to distinguish their three different approaches but merely refer to them as "general types." For our purposes, we will call them Dimensions A, B, and C.

A. This framework of action "tries to alter conditions by changing the policies of formal organizations." It attempts to modify and adjust "the quality, the accessibility, and the range of goods, services, and facilities for people."

B. This type "seeks to alter human attitudes and behavioral patterns through education . . . and a number of other methods for stimulating self-development and fulfillment." It stresses civic leadership and massive community programs, facilitated by "material resources and technical assistance."

C. This type attempts "to effect reforms in major legal and functional systems of society. It relies upon political agitation . . . and a host of other instruments to cope with powerful trends and developments" (p. 14).

On the basis of Rothman's (1968) data, we can combine Dimension A with Social Planning, Dimension B with Locality Development, and Dimension C with Social Action. Although these combined approaches are not "pure" community organizational models, their respective variables or characteristics are relatively valid; they do discriminate within the categories outlined in tables 1.3 and 1.4. The categories are somewhat arbitrary, yet it is possible to gather specific characteristics or items into general clusters. With caution, then, we can make certain generalizations for purposes of conceptualizing the three different approaches for treating community organization.

The practice variables or characteristics of the three organizational approaches (listed in table 1.3) can be exemplified by the literature. As an example, for Dimension A, the Social Planning approach, the themes of problem-solving and change techniques are exemplified in Meier's (1968) concept of people and social systems interacting to form a transaction system.

> The strength of the linkages between transactions provides the best foundation for forecasting trends and long-range developments.
>
> Balancing one category of transactions against another requires some fundamental conceptualizations of the [environment].
>
> Affluent societies are those that have succeeded far better than the average in reducing the frequency of erring transactions" [pp. 1304–07].

The medium of change, another practice variable, is illustrated by Parsons' (1951) analysis of social systems as a

> plurality of individual actors interacting with each other in a situation which . . . is defined and mediated in terms of a system of culturally structured and shared symbols [pp. 5–6].

Both Parsons (1960) and Udy (1965), in their classic texts on how organizations interact with the community or environment, envision technical people developing a new product or training recipients, and managers controlling, coordinating, and directing the various organizational functions. (In schools, teachers represent technical personnel, administrators represent managers, and students represent products or recipients.) Both the technical and managerial personnel are aware of the community for purposes of arresting the universal entropic process, that is, the disorganization or death of the system. In other words, the organization (which may be the school) must consider community factors for purposes of adjustment and survival.

Table 1.3

THREE MODELS OF COMMUNITY ORGANIZATION ACCORDING TO SELECTED PRACTICE VARIABLES

Practice Variables	Dimension A Social Planning	Dimension B Locality Development	Dimension C Social Action
1. Goal categories of community action	Problem solving with regard to substantive community problems (task goals)	Self-help, community capacity and integration (process goals)	Shifting of power relationships and resources; basic institutional change (task or process goals)
2. Assumptions concerning community structure and problem conditions	Substantive social problems: mental and physical health, housing, recreation	Community eclipsed, anomie; lack of relationships and democratic problem-solving capacities: static traditional community	Disadvantaged populations, social injustice, deprivation, inequity
3. Basic change strategy	Fact gathering about problems and decisions on the most rational course of action	Broad cross section of people involved in determining and solving their own problems	Crystallization of issues and organization of people to take action against enemy targets
4. Characteristic change tactics and techniques	Consensus or conflict	Consensus: communication among community groups and interests; group discussion	Conflict or contest: confrontation, direct action, negotiation
5. Salient practitioner roles	Fact-gatherer and analyst, program implementer, facilitator	Enabler-catalyst, coordinator; teacher of problem-solving skills and ethical values	Activist-advocate: agitator, broker, negotiator, partisan
6. Medium of change	Manipulation of formal organizations and of data	Manipulation of small task-oriented groups	Manipulation of mass organizations and political processes
7. Orientation toward power structure(s)	Power structure as employers and sponsors	Members of power structure as collaborators in a common venture	Power structure as external target of action: oppressors to be coerced or overturned
8. Boundary definition of the community client system or constituency	Total community or community segment (including "functional" community)	Total geographic community	Community segment
9. Assumptions regarding interests of community subparts	Interests reconcilable or in conflict	Common interests or reconcilable differences	Conflicting interests that are not easily reconcilable: scarce resources

20

Table 1.3 (cont.)

Practice Variables	Dimension A Social Planning	Dimension B Locality Development	Dimension C Social Action
10. Conception of the public interest	Idealist-unitary	Rationalist-unitary	Realist-individualist
11. Conception of the client population or constituency	Consumers	Citizens	Victims
12. Conception of client role	Consumers or recipients	Participants in interactional problem-solving process	Employers, constituents, members

SOURCE: Adapted from Jack Rothman, "Three Models of Community Organization Practice." In National Conference on Social Welfare (ed.). Social Work Practice, 1968. *New York: Columbia University Press, 1968. Pp. 24–25. Reprinted by permission of the publisher.*

Table 1.4

THREE MODELS OF COMMUNITY ORGANIZATION ACCORDING
TO SELECTED PERSONAL ASPECTS

Personal Aspects	Dimension A Social Planning	Dimension B Locality Development	Dimension C Social Action
Agency type	Welfare council, city planning board, federal bureaucracy	Settlement houses, overseas community development: Peace Corps, Friends Service Committee	Alinsky, civil rights, black power, New Left, welfare rights, cause and social movement groups, trade unions
Practice positions	Planning division head, planner	Village worker, neighborhood worker, consultant to community development team, agricultural extension worker	Local organizer
Professional analogues	Demographer, social survey specialist, public administrator, hospital planning specialist	Adult educator, nonclinical group worker, group dynamics professional, agricultural extension worker	Labor organizer, civil rights worker, welfare rights organizer

Except for the dimensional categories, A, B and C, the data is based on Rothman (1968).

SOURCE: Adapted from Jack Rothman, "Three Models of Community Organization Practice." In National Conference on Social Welfare (ed.). Social Work Practice, 1968. *New York: Columbia University Press, 1968. Pp. 24–25. By permission of the publisher.*

In this connection, control of community programs by "grass roots" activists who lack technical and managerial expertise is considered dysfunctional to social planners. Hence, Moynihan (1969) claims that one reason for the failure of community action programs in the 1960s was that the practitioners who eventually gained control of these programs were grass roots activists (he referred to them as opportunists) who lacked not only social responsibility but also planning and managerial skills. In education, a similar theme is advanced by Havighurst (1968 b) and Moseley (1972); they feel that professional educators are best qualified to serve their clients or students; that the antiteacher, antiadministrator rhetoric distorts reality; and that community activists are detrimental and disruptive to the educational process. (Havighurst feels they are irresponsible, and Moseley calls them outlaws.)

For Dimension B, the Locality Development approach, the general theme is expressed in Ross's (1955) assumptions that:

> man is being overwhelmed by forces of which he is only dimly aware, which subjugate him to a role of decreasing importance. . . . Aspects of this central problem are the difficulty of full expression of a democratic philosophy and the threats to the mental health of individual members of societies [p. 84].

The practice variables regarding the interests of the community (and its groups and factions) and the concept of public interest can be reconciled through rational persuasion and communication, as expressed by Biddle and Biddle (1965):

> There will always be conflicts between persons and factions. Properly handled, the conflicts can be used creatively.

> Although the people may express their differences freely, when they become responsible they often choose to refrain in order to further the interest of the whole group and of their idea of community [p. 61].

In terms of education, one of many practitioner roles is envisioned by Levine (1972), who establishes the concept of the ombudsman, "whose job is to investigate citizen perceptions of unjust or ineffective government," improve school-community communication, help correct school-community dysfunctions, and "process information and grievances which employees feel unable to raise through regular channels" (p. 370). The conception of public interest in education is also outlined by Ravitz (1971):

> The school must work closely with parents regarding the mutually-agreed upon aims and values of education and the best ways to teach children.

If people are to become concerned citizen participants in
educational affairs, the school must become a stimulating,
provocative, available place for both children and adults
for every neighborhood [p. 190].

In Dimension C, the Social Action approach, we note that the role
of the practitioner is that of agitator, skilled in organizing masses. Confrontation tactics, including conflict and direct action, are emphasized. As Alinsky
(1946) explains,

A people's organization is a conflict group. This must be
openly and fully recognized. Its sole reason for coming
into being is to wage war against all evils which cause suffering and unhappiness. . . .

A people's organization is dedicated to an eternal war. . . .
A war is not an intellectual debate, and in war against
social evils there are no rules of fair play. . . . [pp. 153–55].

Elsewhere Alinsky (1967) argues that, in order to gain power from the "haves"
of the system, the "have nots" must be willing to wage war, and "in war the
end justifies almost any means" (p. 111). In war and politics, ethics and
morality "must be elastic (and secondary) to stretch with the times," and the
major question is whether the means will work. "A means which will not
work . . . is nonsense" (p. 112). He concludes:

The means and ends moralist must be seen for what he is,
a supporter of the status quo and an enemy of change; his
inaction is action in support of the prevailing authorities
and practices [p. 123].

Granted, means and ends are subjective and depend on one's political position
and biases; but Alinsky's tactics can lead to increased backlash, counterviolence by the power group, and a worsening of the position of the disadvantaged group. Regardless of these possibilities, such tactics have for the
greater part been adopted and modified by black militants.

In the Social Action group, the power structure variable is viewed
as an external target of action, a circle of exploiters who need to be limited
or removed by the client group, their oppressed victims. Sizemore (1972)
illustrates these concepts as she argues for community control of the schools.
She outlines two groups: A, representing power and utilizing exploitative
tactics, and B, representing the powerless and oppressed group who need to
be liberated from A.

The B group must establish organizations and institutions
which permit the oppressed to carry on the "critical and
liberating dialogue which presupposes action" [p. 283].

Considering that education is not neutral, she concludes that the B group must gain complete control of the schools, not for educational purposes per se but to maintain

> solidarity against oppression, enhance the myths, rites, and rituals which preserve this solidarity . . . and produce ideologies that make liberation possible [p. 283].

Hamilton (1968) also points out that the disenfranchised group needs to organize to gain political and economic power. He views the school as the focal point of the community and gaining control of it as extremely important, even though gaining such control has little to do with improving education. His view of the client variable also connotes a fellow partisan.

> The school . . . should become the center of additional vital community functions. Welfare, credit unions, health services, law enforcement, and recreational programs—all working under the control of the community. . . .
>
> [This] plan envisions the local school as a central meeting place to discuss and organize around community issues, political and economic [p. 683].

In general, the Dimension C, Social Action approach regards such professionals as teachers and social workers as outsiders and with contempt; they are considered as "foreigners" (Whyte 1943), "caretakers" of the system (Gans 1962), defenders of the status quo who do the "dirty work" of administering the lives of the community (Rainwater 1965), and "bureaucrats" who follow the rigid rules of the system (Rogers 1969). And today, if the professionals are white and working in the black community, they are often considered to be "racists" (Carmichael and Hamilton 1967), "oppressors" (Sizemore 1972), and "colonializers" (Blauner 1969). The idea is that these professionals are to be held accountable to the community, with the sometimes unstated but implied warning that accountability will be used against them. In still other instances, the point is made clear that they will simply be put out of their jobs and run out of the community.

Social Planning and the Evolving Metropolitan System

The social planning approach, besides being related to the concept of administrative decentralization, is linked to the concept of metropolitanism in the schools and society. In simple terms, the metropolitan area consists of a city and its surrounding suburbs. Havighurst and Levine (1971) define as a metropolitan area a city of 50,000 or more with those contiguous counties and/or suburbs which are economically and socially linked to the central city. They estimate that in 1968 there were 233 such metropolitan areas in the United

States, comprising 127 million people, or 65 percent of the population; they ranged in size from Meriden, Connecticut, with about 55,000 to New York City and its surrounding area with approximately 15 million people.

In theory, the city serves as the focal point, upon which people are dependent for various jobs and services. In reality, however, because of a significant population shift since the 1950s—in effect, an outmigration of the stable middle class to the suburbs—the suburban population is increasingly less dependent on the city for work, recreation, education, and other services—as sectors of the economy follow the population trend to the suburbs. Nevertheless, the process of action and planning, as well as the functions of quasi-public and private organizations that operate within the metropolitan area, require that people consider the concept of metropolitanism. Metropolitan development and cooperation is now in its infancy, still unperceived by most laymen. As Havighurst (1968*a*) points out:

> Metropolitanism may be a state of mind as well as an action process. . . . The metropolitan mind is not characteristic of many people as yet. For them, the metropolitan area tends to be an *unperceived community,* quite different in their minds from the perceived communities of the church, the organization in which they work, and their local school district [p. 6].

To understand social change and the need for social planning in the metropolitan area, it is important to conceive of the various social systems and subsystems (organizations and departments), how they function, and how they routinely interact. For example, the water department is a subsystem within the public service system, and it cooperates with various departments in the health maintenance system to purify the water we drink. The transportation system comprises several different subsystems, including the rail transit, and highway departments, which must work in coordination with other subsystems in the housing and economic systems. Imagine, for example, a morning traffic jam (transportation system) in a large city and how it affects the people leaving their homes (housing system) for work (economic system).

For our purposes, the educational system consists of many private and public schools, from nursery schools to universities and adult schools. The neighborhood school is but one of the subsystems within the educational system. The educational system needs to make better use of the resources of the other social systems and their subsystems. For instance, it needs to make better use of museums, libraries, playhouses, and art galleries, all of which are part of the cultural system. The schools also need to make better use of the resources of banks, businesses, industries, stores, and the like, all of which comprise the economic system. When planning a new school, the board of education must consider the various social systems—the housing system (projected student enrollments), transportation system (how students will travel to school), the recreational system (existing or planned parks and playgrounds nearby), the political system (will favorable legislation be forthcoming?), and others.

In short, we can conceive of the residents of a metropolitan community as carrying out their daily affairs through a variety of interacting social systems and subsystems organized to make contributions to the people of the area and society in general. The relationships and interactions of the educational and other systems and subsystems are depicted in figure 1.1. The *general environment* represents the larger society and consists of four major trends—political, economic, social, and scientific—which influence the immediate environment. The *immediate environment* represents metropolitan society or the metropolitan area and consists of 16 social systems and their interacting subsystems. The *focal environment* represents the specific social system and related subsystems which is the target for discussion. For our purposes the focus of attention will be the educational system and the neighborhood school.

It is pointed out in chapter 6 that for the last 15 years special emphasis has been placed on the inner cities and inner-city schools, often at the expense of the outer cities and suburbs. This coincides not only with the nation's interest in meeting the needs of the poor and the minority populations but also with the prevalent disregard of metropolitan society in favor of urban society. Having an urban view often means having a city or, more precisely, an inner-city perspective. As groups continue to polarize, and as most cities and suburbs become segregated as a result of population trends, the need to depolarize and integrate schools and society becomes increasingly evident if we are to function as a viable society. There is need for a realistic political and economic policy that is just and fair for all groups and reduces inequalities. This is to be combined with a metropolitan perspective in education, one that reduces the black-white crisis and breaks down the escarpments between the cities and the suburbs, one that recognizes the importance of every student regardless of race or class and of every school system regardless of setting or size. In a guest editorial for the *Kappan*, Ornstein (1973b) points out:

> If we are to save the cities, if the nation is to continue to prosper, if we are genuinely to integrate our schools and society, if minorities are to find new ways to work with the larger community on a more equal basis without surrendering their own identities, if we are to recognize the diverse needs of the various groups, if the American twentieth-century concept of a nation of many nations is to work, then we as educators should start thinking in terms of metropolitan educational development and cooperation—and this concept should be extended to other social systems such as housing, transportation, and welfare.
>
> To think only in terms of community control is to invite further balkanization of the cities and a counterfever of

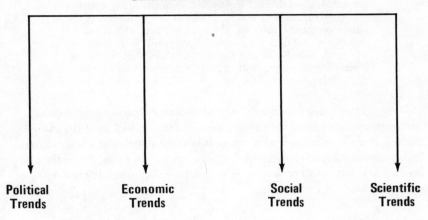

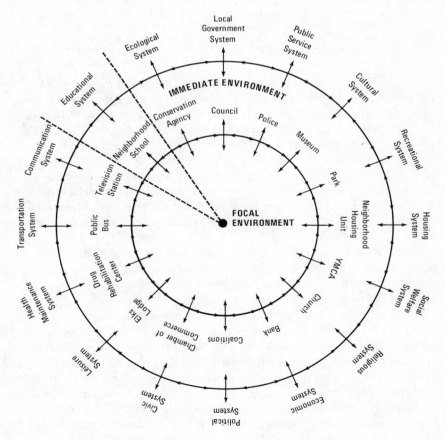

white ethnicity. To think only in terms of cities and suburbs is to invite the building of higher walls between
municipal governments. Both types of thinking produce
polarization. Inherent in the first concept is the continuous ghettoization of blacks; inherent in the second is the
surrender of the suburbs to whites while blacks obtain
control of the decaying cities. Both result in a rising level
of social, economic, and political conflict that raises the
possibility of violence at the city-suburban boundaries
[p. 712].

Attempting to solve the educational problems of urban America
without consideration of the suburbs and counties, as well as of the various
social systems in metropolitan areas, is at best naïve; yet, ironically, we have
been following this circumscribed route for the last 15 years. For example,
the two major issues in education appear to be school financing and desegregation. Thus,

No solution to these [two] problems can be found unless
we consider both the city and its surrounding areas. Similarly, to discuss the educational system without considering the other social systems in the metropolitan area is
also simplistic and senseless [p. 712].

What we need is a reorientation from an urban to metropolitan
perspective, together with practical strategies and research designs that enable
us to consider educational problems with a broader and more comprehensive
view. We want programs and policies which consider students of all cultural
groups and geographical areas, and the numerous and different schools that
house these students. We need to consider the whole equation, not a portion
of it, in trying to find solutions to our problems. We need the same kind of
comprehensive view in dealing with problems that affect other social systems.
What we must try to do is define those important variables and suitable policies which are rooted in a multi-stage, multi-social system if we are to restore
balance to the unwieldy, colossal metropolis.

At this point it is important to note that the Social Planning approach attempts to analyze the complexities and processes of the entire
metropolitan order. (Within this framework, the educational system is only
one social system of many to consider within a greater framework.) The approach includes several different types of planners and policy makers, each
trying to work out problems and achieve goals in relation to the various social
systems. The planners have different motivations and interest considerations:
personal, group, and professional. Nevertheless, their planning is generally
based on reason and hard data, not emotion or rhetoric. These people are
not agitators but analysts. Although their planning sessions may involve a
conflict of interests, they do not resort to overt confrontation or violence.
Decisions are made by gathering facts and through the democratic process of

compromise and consensus. Social planners recognize the needs and concerns of various interest groups, but their goal is the greatest good for the greatest number; demands of a minority group rarely prevail.

The democratic system is simply not able to respond to a situation in which the majority is unwilling to take actions that a minority insists on. Campbell (1970) points out that minorities should be allowed to make their wishes and needs known through the rights of free speech, free press, and assembly, but that this does not necessitate the adoption of policies to coincide with their interests or meet their demands. What do minorities do in this case? How do they work within the political system? How do they work with social planners? Besides having the advantage of appealing to the concepts of equality and justice and besides appearing as the underdog, they have the opportunity to join and work together with other groups such as civil rights organizations, women's groups, and labor unions. Thereby they can create a stronger bloc and a plurality or even a majority program that is diversified to meet the needs of many groups. And recent political, economic, and social trends indicate that blacks have been successful in doing this.

The procedures used by social planners involve management planning and research. For example, Meyerson and Banfield (1955) list four general methods of social planning:

1. Analysis of the situation—in which the conditions, favorable or unfavorable, are assessed in terms of ends and the alternatives of action leading to the ends also are assessed;
2. End-reduction and elaboration—in which the planners decide on and develop the urgent and feasible ends;
3. Design of course of action—which involves a detailed account of the means to be employed in carrying out actions and alternative actions; and
4. Evaluation of consequences—which includes reporting and assessing the anticipated (sought) and unanticipated (unsought) results. (In general, the more elaborate the end system the less feasible it will be to attempt to attain all the anticipated ends.)

A similar set of procedures has been developed by the International Conference of Social Work (1965); it includes:

1. Descriptions—based on data;
2. Objectives—implying a course of intended actions;
3. Arbitration of objectives—determining preferences;
4. Determining action—searching for the best alternatives and routes to be taken and putting means and resources into operation under timetable conditions;
5. Guidance and control—maintaining coordination and monitoring tasks; and

6. Evaluation of results—assessing what has been achieved and what still needs to be achieved.

The conference also recognizes the need for "the widest possible participation of individuals, groups, organizations, local and national bodies . . . at different levels" in devising and carrying out plans. However, it rejects the idea of one group shouting down other groups or having its interests met at the expense of those of the majority; it concludes that there is need for "preventing usurpation of power by one group" (p. 16).

In the broad sense, the aim of social planning is to promote the general welfare. It considers the metropolitan cosmos to be a social organism or organic whole—a system of closely related parts which includes individuals, groups, and social systems. It considers public and private interests and the public at large, and how they interact to form the whole. At present, the potential for social planning has not been fully developed, as indicated by the fact that existing relationships within the metropolitan cosmos are somewhat disjointed and that sometimes there is lack of cooperation and harmony among the various social systems. That improvements have been slow is not necessarily the fault of social planners but results from their relatively recent arrival on the scene.

In the future, social planners will need to consider the multiple interrelations and interactions of the various components comprising the metropolitan order; this is a complex task and calls for sophisticated research and development, as well as a systems-analysis and management-control approach to assessing the various input factors. Bundy (1970) writes, "There is the pressing need for broad-gauged analysis of information to identify simple correlations between independently observed and measured phenomena"; for testing our hypotheses and ecological models "to improve our powers of prediction, to spur our defensive and preventive view of our environment" and its interrelating social systems and subsystems. We need to know "the complex interrelationships of the parts of man-made or natural systems, and the cause of equilibrium or instability" (p. 56). Similarly, Bryson and Ross (1973) point out that no one factor can account for the seriousness of our predicaments or the solution to our problems. The complex nature of our society requires that we at least consider a threefold equation: people $\times$ resources $\times$ technology. If 100 people per square mile use 100 bottles per year, and 70 percent of the bottles are thrown away, then the bottle pollution "is 100 (people) times 100 (bottles) times 70 percent, or 7,000 bottles per square mile per year" (p. 21). In attempting to deal with bottle pollution, do we reduce the number of people, the number of bottles they buy, or the proportion that is discarded? In addition, if we consider aluminum cans, our throw away habits become even more expensive: a ton of aluminum costs approximately 56,000 kilowatt hours to mine and refine—which adds to the energy crisis—not to count costs of fabrication, depreciation, and transportation. We can apply this equation to almost all problems facing the metropolis, from teaching children how to read to solving the problem of poverty. This equation can be used along with an interdisciplinary social science and interdisciplinary social system approach. In planning for social change, we might consider the following.

1. The responsibility for planning belongs to and should be assumed by regularly constituted agencies and authorities at the level proper for each of the social systems involved.
2. The planning procedure should be carefully formulated, unified, and carried out within prescribed guidelines.
3. Planning should be considered as a continuous process requiring constant adaptation to meet emerging needs and problems.
4. Planning should involve the participation of various interest groups and organizations.
5. Planning should recognize local needs but be carried out to improve metropolitan development and cooperation, as well as to meet state and national interests.
6. Provisions for planning should be coordinated within the organic whole of a given area.
7. Research and development, as well as evaluation, should be utilized in all stages of the planning.
8. Planning should be realistic, but not needlessly limited to avoid conflict.
9. Planning should consider the past, the needs of the present, and—most important—the demands of the future.
10. Planning should be geared toward perpetuating and improving society.

As urbanization increases, so will the complexity of planning and coordinating the various components. Future planning will probably involve the simultaneous action of separate agencies from various social systems which together should have a greater total effect than the sum of the individual effects. We will increase our potential to plan effectively by having several individuals with different professional backgrounds modify one another's opinions; this should increase our overall efficiency for coping with the future—including the future of education. In the same vein, there will be greater need for assembling data and developing the innovations and prototypes required to improve the interactions of the metropolitan order. Similarly, there will be greater interlinking of individuals, groups, and social systems. We will need to deal with increasing overlap, duplication, and bureaucracy. We will need to be more sophisticated in thinking in terms of cost-effectiveness, individual versus social benefits, and human resources versus physical considerations—and will need to give great attention to our actions and alternative actions. We will have to deal not only in multiple relations but also in multiple cause-effect relations. For example, when X

occurs, what will happen to the other components of the metropolitan system? Indeed, we will require a computerized approach to provide us with knowledge and efficient metropolitan models. We must begin *now* to assess the various options, arrangements, and styles; to transform data into conceptual models to help us make interpretations and prudent choices, take defensive measures, and store up for future use energies that are now being depleted; to develop the best possible network of interrelations and quality of life, now and for the future. Lindsay (1968) sees as one potential application of systems analysis the creation of "a model or series of models from which one can draw information useful in generating or modifying urban programs" and describes one such model as follows:

> For example a population model of a city would include
> a statistical sample of all the families in the city, incorpo-
> rating such factors as age, number of children, type and
> location of housing, income characteristics, type and lo-
> cation of employment, expenditure patterns, and probable
> medical requirements. Such information can be made dy-
> namic in the sense that future projections can be formu-
> lated as each individual grows older, leaves the family and
> school, marries, starts a family, changes location of living,
> or progresses upward on the employment ladder. A
> variety of alternative assumptions can be fed into the
> model and tested for effects on the community. Changes
> in education level, for example, will subsequently result
> in employment and upgraded economic status [p. 1223].

Michael (1968) points out that, as we obtain the data and make choices, certain value assumptions will be operating.

> What are to be the measures of costs and benefits? What
> range of economic and social variation is to be considered?
> . . . What goals for the plan are revealed by the methods
> for ranking the options generated by the computer-
> manipulated data? . . . To what extent is the computer-
> ized option-generating model to operate within the
> constraints of the private enterprise value system? Is an
> assumption made that inequities for 4 percent of the tar-
> get population are acceptable, but unacceptable for 5
> percent? Will monitoring the plan in action require data
> about people presently considered private? [p. 1186].

The whole concept of values can be illustrated by the process of deciding where to locate a new factory or business center. What group will benefit by the new jobs it creates? How will other groups and other communities be affected? Is business being expanded at the expense of creating traffic problems and polluting the air? Do the economic gains of a few people, or even of a sizable group within the community, justify the additional traffic congestion and pollution that the whole community and perhaps surrounding communities will have to deal with?

Similar value-based questions can be asked about almost all changes that affect the metropolis. For example, where do we build new schools when limited money is allocated for them? There are many schools in the outer city and modest suburbs that are dilapidated, as are many inner-city schools. Where do we build new swimming pools? Children from the $5,000-$10,000 family income bracket also perspire in the summer. Where do we build new libraries? Certainly, there is greater need to provide books for inner-city children than outer-city or suburban children. But where will the books be used the most? These are value-based questions and lead to value-based answers.

It is quickly apparent, however, that no adequate methodology exists for determining values, yet values of individuals and groups often divide us and can lead to opposing schools of thought and political ideology. This is where we can get into disagreement—and that is why a social planning approach, one that is rational and fair, should be used to help solve the metropolitan juggernaut. On the other hand a provincial or less cosmopolitan method, one that is based on raw politics and power, can be dangerous and can increase polarization. An approach based on violence, or the threat of violence, may eventually lead to counterviolence, and to the destruction of the metropolis.

Conclusion

Formerly disenfranchised groups and their supporters demand a new set of priorities, partly on the basis of justice (or, more precisely, a sense of justice), partly on the basis of expediency, and partly on the basis of political ideology. The poor, and particularly blacks, are demanding new programs and policies to assist them—now. They are speaking up and demanding, sometimes through the traditional political process and sometimes through violence. The rhetoric of reform advocates a community control policy that focuses on the schools as the institution by means of which to organize the community for control of other institutions. This policy rejects the middle-class professionals. The technical assistance of these people, rather than being welcomed by the black community, is often rejected as being irrelevant, racist, and antithetical to the interests of blacks. This rejection not only leads to separatism and subsequent polarization but also ignores the metropolitan perspective.

Reformers tend to use the catchall approach of calling every social, political, and economic problem a problem of the cities (ignoring the suburbs) and especially of the inner cities (ignoring the outer cities). Similarly, problems are often considered as being the problems of a particular social system without regard to its interrelationships with other social systems. There is need, then, to redefine our problems in terms of a broader metropolitan base and to cast them into manageable units that consider the transactions and aggregates of the various social systems and link social policy to long-range developments and the future.

Notes

1. Five additional school systems completed and returned the survey questions but were omitted because each had fewer than 50,000 students. One such school system was Louisville with 49,645 students. Twenty-one of the 68 schools in Louisville established elected neighborhood school boards or local mini-boards in 1972. Another 20 elected neighborhood school boards were established in 1973. At the present, the school system has proceeded beyond community participation but without legislative amendments to the school law and without specific guidelines for community control. Although there is the possibility of community control in some schools, the community has not yet fully realized its potential decision-making authority.

2. Concerning New York City see *New York Times*, July 23, 1970, August 15 and November 15, 1971, April 20 and August 8, 1972; Bard (1972); Feldman (1972); Moseley (1972); Ornstein (1974) and Shanker (1971*a*, 1971*b*, 1972*a*, 1972*b*, 1972*c*, 1972*d*). Pertaining to Detroit see *Detroit Free Press*, March 26, 1972; *Detroit News*, March 3, 10, 14, 23, 28, 29 and April 4, 19, 1972; *Northeast Detroiter*, April 20, 1972; *Redford Record*, January 10, 1972; *Summaries of Regional Board Meeting Minutes* (1971–72), and Grant (1971).

3. Ibid.

References

Alinsky, Saul D.
    1946 *Reveille for Radicals.* Chicago: University of Chicago Press.
    1967 "Of Means and Ends." *Union Seminary Quarterly Review* 12: 107–24.
Banks, James A.
    1972*a* "Imperatives in Ethnic Minority Education." *Phi Delta Kappan* 53:266–69.
    1972*b* "Racial Prejudice and the Black Concept." In *Black Self-Concept*, ed. J. A. Banks and J. D. Grambs, pp. 5–35. New York: McGraw-Hill.
Bard, Bernard
    1972 "The Battle for School Jobs: New York's Newest Agony." *Phi Delta Kappan* 53:553–58.
Biddle, William W., and Loureide J. Biddle
    1965 *The Community Development Process.* New York: Holt, Rinehart & Winston.

Billings, Charles E.
1972 "Community Control of the School and the Quest for Power." *Phi Delta Kappan* 53:277–78.

Blauner, Robert
1969 "International Colonialism and Ghetto Revolt." *Social Problems* 16:393–408.

Bryson, Reid A., and John E. Ross
1973 "Hercules vs. the Hydra." *Saturday Review,* April 28, p. 21.

Bundy, McGeorge
1970 "Charting the Complexities." *Saturday Review,* April 4, pp. 56–57 ff.

Campbell, Alan K.
1970 "Breakthrough or Stalemate? State Politics." In *The State and the Urban Crisis,* ed. A. K. Campbell, pp. 196–209. Englewood Cliffs, N.J.: Prentice-Hall.

Carmichael, Stokely, and Charles V. Hamilton
1967 *Black Power.* Vintage ed. New York: Random House.

Clark, Kenneth B.
1972*a* News article in the *New York Times,* May 8, pp. 1, 26. © 1972 by The New York Times Company. Reprinted by permission.
1972*b* Quote in the *New York Times,* December 3, p. 7. © 1972 by The New York Times Company. Reprinted by permission.

Detroit Free Press
March 26, 1972.

Detroit News
March 3, 1972.
March 10, 1972.
March 14, 1972.
March 23, 1972.
March 28, 1972.
March 29, 1972.
April 4, 1972.
April 19, 1972.

Fantini, Mario D., Marilyn Gittell, and Richard Magat
1970 *Community Control and the Urban School.* New York: Praeger.

Feldman, Sandra
1972 "The UFT and the School Conflict." *United Teacher,* April 23, pp. 1–8.

Gans, Herbert J.
1962 *The Urban Villagers.* New York: Free Press.

Gittell, Marilyn, and Alan G. Hevesi, eds.
1969 *The Politics of Urban Education.* New York: Praeger.

Goodlad, John I.
1971 "What Educational Decisions by Whom?" *Science Teacher* 38: 16–19 ff.

Grant, William R.
1971 "Community Control vs. School Integration—the Case of Detroit." *United Teacher,* November 7, pp. 1–4.

Greene, Jay
1970 Quote in the *New York Times,* October 18, sec. 4, p. 7.

Hamilton, Charles V.
1968 "Race and Education: A Search for Legitimacy." *Harvard Educational Review* 38:669–84.

Havighurst, Robert J.
1968*a* "Introduction." In *Metropolitanism: Its Challenge to Education,*
ed. R. J. Havighurst and D. U. Levine, pp. 3–12. National Society
for the Study of Education, Part I. Chicago: University of Chicago
Press.
1968*b* "Requirements for a Valid 'New Criticism.'" *Phi Delta Kappan*
50:20–26.
Havighurst, Robert J., and Daniel U. Levine
1971 *Education in Metropolitan Areas.* 2d ed. Boston: Allyn & Bacon.
International Conference of Social Work
1965 *Social Progress Through Social Planning: The Role of Social Work.*
Report of the Pre-conference Working Party to the Twelfth Inter-
national Conference of Social Work, Chalkis Greece.
Levin, Henry M., ed.
1970 *Community Control of Schools.* Washington, D.C.: Brookings
Institute.
Levine, Daniel U.
1972 "Organizing for Reform in Big City Schools." In *Inquiries into the
Social Foundations of Education,* ed. A. Lightfoot, pp. 364–71.
Chicago: Rand McNally.
Lindsay, Franklin A.
1968 "Managerial Innovation and the Cities." *Daedalus* 97:1218–30.
Mayor's Advisory Panel on Decentralization of the New York City Schools
1967 *Reconnection for Learning: A Community School System for New
York City.* New York: Ford Foundation–Praeger.
McCoy, Rhody
1969 "Introduction." In J. Haskins, *Diary of a Harlem Schoolteacher.*
New York: Grove Press.
Meier, Richard L.
1968 "The Metropolis as a Transaction-Maximizing System." *Daedalus*
97:1292–313.
Meyerson, Martin, and Edward C. Banfield
1955 *Politics, Planning and the Public Interest.* New York: Free
Press.
Michael, Donald N.
1968 "On Coping with Complexity: Planning and Politics." *Daedalus*
97:1179–93.
Morris, Robert, and Robert H. Binstock
1966 *Feasible Planning for Social Change.* New York: Columbia Univer-
sity Press.
Moseley, Francis S.
1972 "The Urban Secondary School: Too Late for Mere Change." *Phi
Delta Kappan* 53:559–64.
Moynihan, Daniel P.
1969 *Maximum Feasible Misunderstanding.* New York: Free Press.
New York Times
July 23, 1970.
August 15, 1971.
November 15, 1971.
April 20, 1972.
August 8, 1972.
Northeast Detroiter
April 20, 1972.

Ornstein, Allan C.
1972*a* "The Politics of School Decentralization and Community Control."
A Report to Dan Walker, Governor of the State of Illinois. Chicago.
1972*b* *Urban Education: Student Unrest, Teacher Behaviors, and Black
Power.* Columbus, Ohio: Merrill.
1973*a* "Administrative/Community Organization of Metropolitan
Schools." *Phi Delta Kappan* 54:668–74.
1973*b* "Toward a Metropolitan Orientation." *Phi Delta Kappan* 54:
649–50 ff.
1974 *Administrative Organization of Metropolitan Schools.* Metuchen,
N.J.: Scarecrow Press.
Ornstein, Allan C., and Harriet Talmage
1973 "A Dissenting View on Accountability." *Urban Education* 8:
133–51.
Parsons, Talcott
1951 *The Social System.* New York: Free Press.
1960 *Structure and Process in Modern Societies.* New York: Free Press.
Passow, A. Harry
1967 *Toward Creating a Model Urban School System.* A Study of the
Washington, D.C., Public Schools. New York: Teachers College,
Columbia University Press.
Rainwater, Lee
1965 "The Revolt of the Dirty-Workers." *Trans-action* 5:2.
Ravitz, Mel
1971 "Urban Education: Today and Tomorrow." In *Urban Education in
the 1970's,* ed. A. H. Passow, pp. 177–93. New York: Teachers
College Press, Columbia University.
Redford Record
January 10, 1972.
Rogers, David
1969 *110 Livingston Street.* New York: Random House.
Ross, Murray G.
1955 *Community Organization: Theory and Principles.* New York:
Harper & Row.
Rothman, Jack
1968 "Three Models of Community Organization Practice." In *Social
Work Practice, 1968,* ed. National Conference on Social Welfare,
pp. 16–47. New York: Columbia University Press.
Shanker, Albert
1971*a* "Decentralization II: The New York Experience." *New York
Times,* August 15, sec. 4, p. 11.
1971*b* "Decentralization: Have the Claims Proved Valid?" *New York
Times,* November 28, sec. 4, p. 9.
1972*a* "A Quarrel with Quotas." *New York Times,* July 16, sec. 4, p. 5.
1972*b* "School Decentralization: A Troubled Picture Emerges." *New
York Times,* May 14, sec. 4, p. 9.
1972*c* "A Threat to Human Rights Confronts Us Again: Ethnic Quotas
vs. Individual Merit." *New York Times,* February 20, sec. 4, p. 9.
1972*d* "A Time for Action Against Disruptions in the Schools." *New
York Times,* March 26, sec. 4, p. 9.
Sizemore, Barbara A.
1972 "Is There a Case for Separate Schools?" *Phi Delta Kappan* 53:
281–83.

Sizer, Theordore R.
   1968 "Report Analysis: Reconnection for Learning." *Harvard Educational Review* 38:176–84.
Summaries of Regional Board Meeting Minutes. Detroit: Office of School
      Decentralization, Board of Education of the City of Detroit,
      January 1971–June 1972.
Udy, Stanley H., Jr.
   1965 "The Comparative Analysis of Organizations." In *The Handbook of
      Organizations,* ed. J. C. March, pp. 678–709. Chicago: Rand
      McNally.
Whyte, William F.
   1943 *Street Corner Society.* Chicago: University of Chicago Press.

chapter 2

The Misunderstandings of Community Control and Community Action

This chapter is divided into three parts. First we explore some of the misguided notions and assumptions about community control; in doing so we examine some problems related to this trend. Next, we analyze the effects of governmental regulations—the rise of quotas—in school and community organizations. Then, we discuss community action programs. The reader should relate these programs to the models of community organization presented in the first chapter, particularly the Social Action approach. To fully comprehend both community control and community action, the reader should recognize that both trends are highly political. In the past, professionals have made decisions regarding schools and community programs. The professionals in both social domains are now being threatened and in some cases coerced by the emerging power wielded by community organizations and activist groups. These new actors on the educational and community scene have shown a determination to challenge the traditional system, even at the expense of breaking the law. We now turn to some of the misunderstandings related to community control of the schools.

The Fallacies of Community Control

From the last quarter of the nineteenth century to the early twentieth century, many large American cities were divided into separate school districts or local community boards with extensive decision-making power over local schools. As cities grew the schools were consolidated, thus creating unified school districts. Even when the schools in a city were gradually brought into one large, centralized system, that system usually had a weak central school board and strong local school boards, because of local ward and community politics. In major cities the newly created central boards exercised general supervision of the schools, but power and authority over personnel, curriculum, and finances still remained in the hands of local influentials. To obtain a teaching job, and especially to be promoted or hired as principal, or to get a contract to build a school or repair the windows, it was important to know the local alderman or councilman. As Lyke (1970) contends, many local school boards were illiterate: some board members were corrupt; most were pawns or representatives of the political machine and used their influence for personal and partisan gain.

By the turn of the century reformers saw the need to strengthen the central school boards and to eliminate, as much as possible, political and ethnic influences from the schools. Local school boards were gradually abolished, partisan favoritism was minimized, and uniform standards in personnel, curriculum, and financing were adopted. The reformers recognized that it was impossible to eliminate politics completely from the schools; their purpose was to minimize it, to adopt central and higher, nonpartisan standards, and to curtail the dominance of local group interests. As professionals gained control of the schools, they managed to eliminate most of the local political influence and corrupt practices.

Today there is a counteracting trend in many large cities to return to political and ethnic influences over local schools. The thought for some community-oriented reformers is to decentralize the schools, that is, to weaken the central school boards and restore and strengthen local school boards. Under the guise of community control, there is a growing attempt to weaken the influence of the professional reformers, to substitute for their input that of local political and community groups, and to eliminate civil service examinations and uniform standards—in short, to restore patronage and partisan influences, as well as ethnic and racial favoritism, in local school practices. Those who advocate this policy present the following arguments.

1. All-black schools, controlled by blacks, will lead to quality education for black children and youth

This is simplistic rhetoric, if not pure rubbish. There is sufficient evidence to indicate that the school output depends largely on a single major input, namely, the characteristics of the entering students and their families. This conclusion dates back to the pioneering investigations of social stratification which deal with white students (Hollingshead 1949; Warner, Havighurst, and Loeb 1944) and is borne out by the more recent, classic studies that include, or deal mainly with, minorities (Coleman et al. 1966; Jencks et al. 1972).

Liberal and black reformers often refuse to admit that the students' input is crucial in determining student output; rather they direct the blame toward the teachers and schools. In particular, the liberal-black community claims the problem lies with the "racism" of teachers and the institutional "racism" of the schools (Banks 1972a; Gittell 1970; Hamilton 1968). This argument contradicts the empirical data on the importance of student input and is based mainly on rhetoric and unproved assumptions; in effect, it leads to political ideology and strengthens demands by militant groups for community control of the schools and for making teachers accountable to the community. This argument also coincides with the growing trend of driving white teachers and administrators out of ghetto schools and creating jobs for blacks (Banks 1972*a*; Bard 1972; Moseley 1972).

Black militants go so far as to denounce integration because it connotes that blacks can learn only in the presence of whites (Hamilton 1968; Wingate 1967; Young 1969). According to Clark (1968) the assumption that all-black schools, controlled by blacks, will lead to quality education represents a pathetic wish for a separate and superior school system. Actually it is a return to the "separate but equal" system of education. That this doctrine results in inferior education has been well documented since the 1954 *Brown* decision by the studies of the 1967 U.S. Commission on Civil Rights and the research by Katz (1964, 1968, 1969) and A. Wilson (1963, 1968, 1971).

Furthermore, there is no evidence to support the assumption that black schools staffed and controlled by blacks will be more efficient in educating black students (Bard 1972; Clark 1968; Katz 1968). Black teachers and school administrators in the southern segregated schools seem to have a neutral effect on black student achievement. Black students who come out of southern schools are just as educationally crippled as those from schools in northern ghettos, where whites occupy most of the teaching and administrative positions. This is also true of the school systems of such cities as Chicago, Baltimore, Detroit, Gary, Newark, Philadelphia, St. Louis, and Washington, D.C., where there is a large or a predominant number of black teachers and administrators. Regardless of their role models, black students do not achieve any higher in those school systems than they do in the ghetto schools where there is a large or predominant number of white teachers and administrators, as in the ghetto schools of such cities as Boston, Cincinnati, Los Angeles, Milwaukee, and New York.

2. The solution of ghetto problems depends upon knowledge that can be obtained only by living in the community

This contention has many derivatives: gut experience is more important than professional experience, race is more important than formal qualifications, only blacks can coordinate local agencies in the black community, and only blacks can "solve" the black problem. All these allied claims are based on assumptions, intuition, and rhetoric. Moreover, these claims are used as arguments for the creation of jobs for blacks in almost all fields—education, social work, community service, health maintenance, business, and so on. This strategy is perhaps needed to solve the War on Poverty, but we should be honest about our hidden agendas. We may create jobs, but it is doubtful if this will improve the quality of education, social work, etc.

Analysis of complex problems is usually not understood by laymen (Sizer 1968), much less by those who lack a formal education. Finding solutions to the problems of a school system, whether on a local or a central basis, calls for professional and technically competent people, not someone who is merely vocal or considers himself to be an "expert" because of gut experience. Participation of the community is important so long as the community is truly represented; however, ultimate solutions to problems lie with the professionals and also involve the support of the local, state, or federal government. In the long run, the problems of the ghetto, including the schools, cannot be solved without a wide range of professionals from various agencies and governmental groups, nor without support from the larger political and economic systems.

When Hamilton (1968) points out that the professionals are no longer considered "relevant" to the black community because their expertise is based on middle-class criteria, or that the professionals are "racist," he is using a ploy to discriminate against whites and implying that race will be used to judge who gets the jobs in the black community. In *Black Power,* Carmichael and Hamilton (1967) flatly state that the middle-class professionals are no longer welcome in the black community. They contend that new hiring standards must be adopted by the black community, standards that stress race and de-emphasize formal qualifications. The importance of the issue is indicated by the claim (Billings 1972) that the learning industry is second only to the defense industry in terms of generating employment. Education, if not yet the dominant institution, is fast becoming the major source of employment in American cities. Blacks intend to gain political power over the schools, as well as control of related jobs by creating new standards of expertise. Perhaps this trend is inevitable—simply reflecting the rise of one ethnic group and the decline of power of another group in our big cities—which whites will have to get used to.

There is nothing wrong with wanting blacks to obtain good employment. Nevertheless, the method some blacks advocate is based on a form of reverse racism. If blacks can implement racial practices and new qualifications, then it follows that the white majority should not be condemned as "racists" for not hiring blacks who do not have formal qualifications. If black institutions seek to hire only blacks, and if predominantly white institutions continue to be forced by the federal government to hire representative quotas of blacks, sometimes regardless of formal qualifications, then we can expect to find an increasingly large share of formally qualified and professional whites underemployed and unemployed. In fact, this trend is already apparent.

3. Community control is a form of "grass roots" democracy; it stands for representative and participatory democracy for the poor

The argument goes that if people can elect representatives to city councils and the Congress they should have the right to elect school board members.

This is true if you want to make schools more political than they are already and to open them to the type of ward corruption and favors found in machine politics. The argument also goes that if middle-class suburban parents have the opportunity to elect school officials, then the parents of the poor and the ghetto-dwellers should have the same right. This assertion connotes that people are interested enough to go to the polls and elect school officials. This is simply not true (as we will discuss later in this chapter in greater detail); rather, it is the representatives of organized pressure and political groups who turn out to vote (Mayer 1969; *New York Times*, August 15, 1971; Ornstein 1974). Moreover, blacks and other minorities turn out to vote less than do whites in school and political elections (Grant 1971; *New York Times*, April 29, 1973). An important interaction variable with race seems to be class; the poor do not go to the voting polls in the same proportion as working and middle-class groups.

There is also research (Boyd 1972; Boyd and O'Shea 1972; O'Shea 1972) indicating that people who live in middle-class suburbs and do vote for school officials limit politics and patronage in education, whereas in lower-class areas, schooling becomes linked with machine politics, ethnic favoritism, and patronage. For example, in New York City the merit system and civil service examinations, which have limited politics and patronage in the schools and maintained standards for hiring school personnel, seem to be on the way out. In that city, the local communities now hire their own personnel; thousands of teachers and administrators without licenses have been hired while licensed candidates have been waiting, some for several years, for employment (Bard 1972; Moseley 1972; Shanker 1972b). In addition, the central school board has issued to unlicensed personnel "certificates of competency" (a form of patronage) for "coordinators," "assistant directors," and "instructors," with 1973-74 salaries ranging from $9,400 to $25,710. In the 1970-71 school year, when community control first started in New York City, 812 "certificates of competency" were issued; in the 1971-72 school year the number jumped to 1,842; in the 1972-73 school year the number rose to more than 2,500. No formal test is required; Shanker (1972b, 1973b) points out that it is increasingly important now to know someone to get hired[1] and Bard (1972) indicates that the point has been reached where there is buying and selling of jobs. In Detroit, the situation does not appear as much out of control, but there are reports that ineligible personnel are teaching in the classrooms while licensed teachers remain unemployed and that the regional school boards have ignored the eligible lists in hiring school administrators (*Detroit Free Press*, March 26, 1972; *Detroit News*, March 29, 1972; Ornstein 1974).

The potential for conflict is also evident where all the poor are not of the same ethnic group, and the growing hostility between blacks and Puerto Ricans in New York City is exemplified in the bitter and overt conflict in school and poverty programs. According to Herman Badillo (1967), the Puerto Rican-born president of the Bronx, community control events have turned into a winner-take-all political campaign in which the black and Puerto Rican groups are vying for power over the programs.

Ideally, community control means that parents and residents have the opportunity to run the schools in their community. Sounds great, doesn't it? Yet in New York City and Detroit, where community control has been legislated, analysis of voting for local school boards indicates that some of the boards represent groups that have gained control of the schools for their own self-interest and do not truly represent the community (Grant 1971; *New York Times*, August 15, 1971, April 29, 1973). In a sense, community control is a substitute for the ward system or Tammany Hall, which was noted for its political corruption and ethnic favoritism. There is little romanticism or "grass roots" democracy in such machine politics, nor is there romanticism in the politics and corruption of the Harlems of America, according to Clark (1965) and Featherstone (1969).

To preserve their power and prevent a complete upheaval within the system, many power brokers on local and state levels have capitulated to the demands for community control in New York City and Detroit and are experimenting with the idea in various other large cities. Such capitulation represents a fraudulent solution to appease black militants at the expense of other groups including the majority of black moderates (Sizer 1968; Sowell 1973) and a cheap accomodation to a small group of militants who do not necessarily represent the majority of the community (Ornstein 1972*b*).

A Harris poll taken in 1968 found that, whereas 35 percent of the black community approved, 47 percent disapproved the black-controlled local board in Ocean Hill–Brownsville because of its militant stand. During the summer of 1968, 2,000 community people signed a petition demanding new elections for the local board, twice the number of people who voted the previous summer for members of the board. Since 1970, when community control was enacted in New York City, black militants and black moderates have been squabbling and fighting; assaults, threats, and vandalism of local school board property have often been reported by the *New York Times*. Shanker (1972*b*) describes incidents in Community Districts 1, 4, 6, and 23, which are plagued by violence in the schools and fights between "community" groups over power, jobs, and money. He adds that there is the flagrant violation of the personal rights of parents, teachers, and administrators. Similarly, Clark (1972*a*, 1972*b*) has condemned community control because of continuous and sometimes violent political fights among community interest groups. In Detroit, Regions 2, 3, 6, and 8 seem to be plagued by fighting between militants and moderates, and there are constant charges that the regional school boards, black or white, do not represent the community (*Detroit News*, March 14, 1972; *Michigan Chronicle*, February 5, 1972; *Redford Record*, January 10, 1972).

The cause of democracy is not helped by the creation of power vacuums into which extremists can move; the evidence continues to mount up that once these extremists move in, teachers, administrators, and black

and white moderates in the community are harassed (Moseley 1972; Moynihan 1969; Shanker 1969, 1972b). Furthermore, blacks cannot criticize this
harassment without being denounced as "Toms" (Moynihan 1969; Rustin
1969; Sowell 1973). More and more, the majority voices of black moderates
are being muffled. Indeed, participatory democracy is not served by such
slogans as "Power to the People." In the name of the people, a group within
the governmental framework can move against the institutions that are hall-
marks of democracy. One who fails to grasp such implications does not know
twentieth-century history; he is unfamiliar with the slogans akin to "Power to
the People" employed by the Communist and Fascist movements in Europe
in their overthrow of democratic institutions.

4. The community has the right to hold professionals accountable for educating their children

This statement assumes that the community, or any group, can adequately
and objectively judge the performance of teachers and administrators. The
political and racial implications of this assumption were examined in the preceding chapter; here we will extend the discussion.

The statement also connotes that student achievement, or lack of
achievement, is mainly related to professional performance and, according to
Fantini (1968), that when students are not reading at grade level their parents
have "a right to question professional performance, since the schools are supposed to educate everyone" (p. 162). Surely most people agree with the basic
notion that each person should be held accountable for his work. But try to
translate this concept into specifics, however, and you have trouble. Try to
translate theory into practice, and you have more than just politics and racialism possibly quackery and chaos. Ornstein and Talmage (1973a) ask:

> How can we safeguard teachers from being scapegoated?
> Dare teachers and administrators state the simple truth:
> the students and community must also be held account-
> able? Can school people and schools solve all the ills of
> society? Is not student failure among poor and minority
> groups a symptom of these social ills? [p. 141]

Before we march in many directions, singing the latest tune of education's
critics, how do we answer those vital questions, as well as the following ones
by Ornstein (1972a)?

> Where does accountability begin and end (in the class-
> room, at the state level)? Who should be held account-
> able—and for what, and to whom? Who determines who
> will be held accountable? Who determines the respon-
> sibilities or criteria of effectiveness that will be measured?
> Who evaluates these criteria? [Are the evaluators them-
> selves honest, or are they concerned with politics,
> ideology, or providing certain answers that will secure

them next year's evaluation contract?] How are the results to be measured? How is each participant's contri-
bution determined? [p. 45]

Too quick adoption of the concept of accountability, coupled with
failure to work out problems inherent in the concept, may lead to educational
hokum and add another dismal failure to a long list of reform-minded failures.
Even worse, it may lead to a scheme to fix the total blame on educators and
punish them for students' poor performance. What many educators object
to, even fear, is the oversimplified definition of accountability as being the
sole responsibility of the teacher or principal.[2] Many different kinds of
people have various impacts on student learning, and they too must be held
accountable if we are to employ a constructive model. They include not only
teachers and administrators but also parents, community residents, school
board members, taxpayers, government officials, members of state departments of education, and, most important, the students themselves. A student's health and physical condition, cognitive ability, motivation and
self-concept, family background, and age—all these affect his learning.

Not only are numerous test hazards, such as chance variations,
guessing, regression effects, change of raw scores to grade equivalents, and
validity,[3] inherent in measurement of performance, but there is also the temp-
tation to teach what is being measured. As Grobman (1972) asserts, "If mem-
ory is measured but inquiry-oriented exploration is not, if rote learning is
measured but building healthy self-concept is not, it is clear where the teaching emphasis will be" (p. 65).

Accountability presumes that the schools know how students learn.
The trouble is, we have several competing ideas that introduce further difficulty into relating learning to accountability. These competing ideas range,
on one hand, from Bereiter and Englemann's (1966) drill approach, which
tends to encourage student anxiety and discourages impersonal relations, and
Skinner's (1963) notion of breaking down learning into behavioral conditioning and motivation and programmed learning to, on the other hand, the progressive philosophers who frown upon drill and behavioral conditioning and
treat learning in terms of developing the whole child and teaching broad concepts. Also implicit in the idea of accountability is the expectation that
available tests can measure learning with sufficient precision. As we have
discussed, this is not true; moreover, many of the things we are concerned
with, such as conceptual thinking, creativity, and human learning, we do not
know how to measure. As Krathwohl (1972) points out, "Measures must be
carefully taken and sophisticated techniques used" if we are not to be misled
by use of simple pre- and post-tests "to evaluate effects of treatment" (p. 4).

But we are not heading in the direction of research and development
of means of measurement; in fact, most of the advocates of community control and accountability reject the social scientists who are involved in such efforts. Many liberal educators reject them as "caretakers" of the Establishment,

and black educators in increasing numbers look upon them with suspicion
and distrust and condemn them for being victimized by their white, middle-
class culture and biases. You cannot have accountability both ways. Yet first,
the community control advocates claim they want to use test procedures to
validate accountability while they disregard the cautions of social scientists in
the field of testing; then, they dismiss the data forthcoming from tests as
being "culturally biased" when such disregard serves their ideological purposes.

5. Community control will not lead to vigilante groups or violence directed toward whites

The tactics and strategies of community control are based on confrontation
and conflict; they are rooted in the black-power philosophy of (1) Marcus
Garvey, who preached a race war in which blacks would ultimately win;
(2) Frantz Fanon, who analyzed the Algerian liberation movement and advocated violence as psychologically healthy and tactically sound for the oppressed; and (3) Malcolm X, who preached the need for blacks to rid themselves of the white oppressors. According to Blauner (1969), King (1967),
and Ladner (1967), many black-power advocates quote and are influenced by
the claim of these philosophers that violence is necessary to bring about liberation. Brown (1969) urges blacks not to sing songs or write poems about
black pride or black being beautiful but to sing and write about confrontation, saying,

> Violence is as American as cherry pie . . . and the vio-
> lence is a necessary part of revolutionary struggle.

> Power, indeed, must come from the barrel of a gun. We
> can no longer allow threats of death to immobilize us. . . .
> I say to America, Fuck it! Freedom or Death [pp. 144–45].

And Lester (1968) warns white America that it is doomed:

> We will destroy you or die in the act of destroying.

> The race war, if it comes, will come partly from the
> necessity of revenge.

> Black power . . . will not be denied. America's time is
> not long and the odds are on our side.

> There are no crowds, to mourn, to weep. No eulogies to
> read. . . . There is no time, for . . . everything must be
> scoured clean. Trash has to be thrown out. Garbage
> dumped, and everything unfit, burned [pp. 137–43].

Among the artists featured in recent black expositions in San Francisco and
Chicago of new black art forms and social and political ideas were young
black poets who urged blacks to pick up guns and kill "whitey" (*Chicago
Tribune,* September 28, 1972; *New York Times,* September 24, 1972).

Whereas in previous analyses racial subordination in the United States was explained in terms of caste and class processes, the ideology of community control and black power outlines a "colonial" analogy where the whites exploit the land and labor and the "oppressed" must rise up in revolt and gain control of their institutions, including the schools. In fact, Carmichael and Hamilton (1967) and Fantini, Gittell, and Magat (1970) suggest gaining institutional control as a viable policy because other routes have in the past been blocked. Similarly, Blauner (1969) views the riots of the 1960s as a preliminary, if not primitive, form of mass rebellion against the white "colonialists." In other words, in the strategy of violence even rioting is legitimatized as being a necessary part of the revolution.

One can argue that these concepts are purely intellectual, that the riot phenomenon has passed its peak, and that even the Black Panthers are using ballots instead of bullets. Nonetheless, violence is still evident in many city schools where some militant black youth and even some adults are harassing and assaulting white teachers and administrators. The situation has reached crisis proportions in the community-controlled schools of New York City and Detroit. In New York City, the *Saturday Review* (February 19, 1973) and the *New York Times* (November 5, 1972) report that more than 500 teachers and administrators are mugged and assaulted in ghetto schools each year and that many other incidents are not recorded by the city school board. To combat the growing violence in New York City schools, the United Federation of Teachers (UFT) has announced a $5,000 reward for anyone who provides information leading to the apprehension and conviction of a person who assaults a teacher; and the Board of Education has announced that 5,000 special guards are to be assigned to the schools. In Detroit, the number of attacked teachers average 25 per month and the *Summaries of Regional Board Meetings Minutes* (1971-72) indicate that measures to curb violence in the ghetto schools have included the assignment of extra security guards, scotter patrol surveillances, and police, as well as the introduction of photographic ID cards for students. Meanwhile, educators and newsmen alike are reluctant to indicate that most of the assailants are black and the victims are overwhelmingly white educators.

According to Alsop (1967) black militants have taken the initiative to gain control of the schools and have resorted to violence as a tactic that, according to Stone (1969), has been condoned by such organizations as the Ford Foundation and the American Civil Liberties Union under the guise of liberal reform. Moseley (1972) describes the violence in the ghetto schools and the tactics of black militants:

> To march into a public school with a small group of de-
> termined militants and to arrogate to oneself the authority
> to keep it open or to shut it down, to use its students for
> one's own political purposes, to stand in the schoolhouse
> door and bar entrance to others, to seize the principal and
> hold him prisoner, to boycott the institution, to vandalize

> its property, occasionally even to burn it to the ground—
> all these are illegal actions. But they have been common-
> place, even daily occurrences for years [p. 560].

He points out that these tactics go unpunished, largely because public officials are afraid they will lose popularity among the black community. I would extend this line of thinking and claim that those in power in education and in other institutions will permit such illegal acts to go unpunished as long as doing so does not endanger their vested interests or positions; they will refuse to speak out and thus in effect condone such practices. By default, by lack of public statements or policies which confront the militants, those in power will permit others to be harassed and assaulted so long as they retain that power—and continue to draw their weekly salaries. What they do is merely deplore such actions in private conversation; but by their silence in public they cooperate with those who resort to terror tactics.

Ornstein (1972*b*) points out that most student violence has racial overtones.

> Many white teachers now find their black students, espe-
> cially the secondary school students, overtly antagonistic
> toward them. Years of white prejudice have collided with
> current black militancy within the larger society, and the
> schools reflect an intensification of this racial antagonism
> because of the nature of the superior role of the teacher
> and the tendency of youth to have a low frustration tol-
> erance and to resort to physical aggression and violence as
> a means to alleviate frustration.
>
> The teachers have increasingly become victims of student
> assaults, which many supervisors and administrators are
> reluctant to report, since it may be construed as a blot on
> their records. . . . Furthermore, many colleagues and
> supervisors do not support the victimized teacher, even
> during the immediate crises, since the staff members are
> sometimes divided along racial and political lines as well
> as demoralized and desiring to avoid additional problems
> themselves [p. 56].

Even worse, if the principal wishes to take stern action, he often risks a confrontation with the community—especially if the student is black and the community is organized by black militants. If this is what education is all about today, if violence and terror are accepted as means of reform or accepted through default of action by the public, then the school plunges into even lower depths—and with it goes society.

6. Community control will enhance the teaching of black pride and culture

Several recent studies (Roth 1970; Ward and Braun 1972; Zirkel 1971; Zirkel and Moses 1971) indicate that black students are expressing positive self-concepts (not self-concepts that are higher than those held by whites), a welcomed reversal of the findings of studies made prior to the 1960s and the black-pride movement that blacks reported significantly lower self-concepts than did whites. It is likely, however, that this change corresponds not with community control, as its advocates claim, but with the general black-pride movement.

With community control, the school board can obtain textbooks that minority groups can identify with. In fact, there is a growing, perhaps overflooded, market of books aimed at black children and youth of all age levels. Some whites may feel that anything addressed to blacks automatically rejects and condemns whites; however, this is not necessarily so. But the children's coloring books circulated by black militants, reported by the *Chicago Sun-Times* (July 25, 1972) as "showing children how to kill police" (p. 6), demonstrate that black pride can become excessive. To use a milder example, there are many books about blacks who are champions in sports, great poets and artists, and avowed advocates of black pride and power. How would blacks react to books that have related titles about whites who are champions in sports, great poets and artists, and avowed advocates of white power? The point is, an integrated reading approach, enabling us to judge people on their merits, achievements, and ideas and not on their color, is certainly a better approach if we are to achieve a pluralistic and integrated society. A multi-ethnic America can enhance black pride, de-escalate black and white racism, and find blacks and whites working together. Most important, it is dangerous to stress super heroes in a racial or ethnic vein. True, groups wish to learn about their heroes, but there is a point where this leads to racialism and ethnocentrism.

Granted we need a reinterpretation of black literature and history, and granted black students should recognize their heritage—Nat Turner, Frederick Douglass, W. E. B. Du Bois, Marcus Garvey, and contemporaries such as Malcolm X, Stokely Carmichael, Nathan Hare—rather than seek self-realization through Negro heroes "acceptable" to whites. But Glazer (1969b) and Sowell (1973) raise an important issue: many black militants are taking control of the schools and teaching not always black pride and culture but sometimes race hatred and a false view of history and reality. Their doing so poses a real threat, they feel, and we must hope that the good sense of the majority of black parents and black teachers will prevail. In the same vein, Record (1973a, 1973b) and Rustin (1969) claim that the black studies programs at schools and universities emphasize a militant philosophy and an antiwhite sentiment. We might hope that a more objective view would become the norm rather than the exception.

Although it is important for any racial or ethnic group to learn the heritage and heroes of its culture, it is questionable whether knowing oneself depends on learning to hate another group. Even Fantini (1970) and Smith (1972), who represent a liberal and black militant viewpoint, point out that a reinterpretation of black history and literature can turn into black propaganda.

Black Americans have a heritage and experience, long and distinct, that needs to be told. The question is, what is the correct reinterpretation of black history and culture? Which black persons or groups are qualified to determine the appropriate curriculum content? Which black persons or groups can decide whether a reinterpretation is objective or nonobjective, is true or false? Is it only the group in power who can make these decisions? (This question is discussed in chapter 6.) Does this group represent the larger black community? Who are the "authentic" blacks? (According to Sowell [1973], black authenticity is often linked to the degree of militancy.)

As there is danger in black pride turning into black power, white ethnic models of "cultural pluralism" are being influenced by the black phenomenon. As Levine and Herman (1972) point out, "all kinds of groups are claiming the right to be different, unique, particular, and special" (p. 3). Ethnic groups are demanding acceptance on their own terms, not the majority's terms. Not only are they seeking pride, they are beginning to demand power. And where does all this lead us?

The "melting pot" seems to be boiling over, and there is need to put out the fire before it is too late. As a nation we do not have the assurance of coexistence among racial and ethnic groups if each develops a strong pride that turns into demands for power. If anything, political and economic trends have polarized this nation, and ethnic power struggles can only intensify the polarization process.

7. Community control will lead to reform and innovation

The quest for community control originated with many liberal reformers and with the dissatisfied groups such as the poor and minorities which the reformers helped organize in the early 1960s. In general, these reformers are convinced that society is in deep trouble and that the poor and minority groups, and especially blacks, must be aroused and organized to action. In education, the reformers are convinced that the schools are status quo–oriented and unable to meet the needs of poor and minority groups. Since the professionals have failed to provide quality education, reform and innovation must come from the community. Feeling the need for change, and influenced by the rhetoric of the "oppressed," some of these reformers have sacrificed social scientific principles and rationality in decision making for reform and innovation based on political ideology. According to Kristol (1970), the ideas and procedures of most of these reformers are based on one or several of the following: (1) lack of empirical evidence, (2) faulty assumptions, (3) ideological commitments, and (4) vested interests. Furthermore, many of these reformers become radicalized as their reform ideas catch on and gain acceptance.

This radicalization process is reflected in the change of thinking of many of the original architects of the community action programs, such as Richard Cloward, Frances Fox Piven, and S. M. Miller. In the early 1960s, these sociologists were advocating the reform of society by the mobilization and organization of poor and minority groups; by the end of the decade and into the 1970s they were outlining methods for disrupting and bringing down the "decadent" system. A similar radicalization process is exemplified by the advocates of community-controlled schools (who are related to the above community action philosophers). In the mid-1960s, educators such as Mario Fantini, Marilyn Gittell, and Nat Hentoff were urging a "relevant" curriculum, greater community participation in the schools, and support for community-controlled experiments in the black communities of New York City. After a few years these educators became more radicalized and began to attack teachers and administrators as defenders of the Establishment; they linked reform and innovation to the dismantling of the school system and the redistribution of power to a few activists. As the liberal reformers gained in stature and influence in that city, both in community action programs and community control of the schools, they became more extremist and aroused the poor, who were often black, in other cities as well.

Whether the black-power movement developed independently of the liberal movement or each was influenced by the other is a moot question. Regardless of the exact direction of influence, the civil rights movement became more militant at the same time the liberals became more radical. Black militants also rejected the system and demanded "Power to the People." "Reform" became a euphemism for power. The idea was to bring down the system and re-create it on black terms; often, due process was to be denied to white educators (Banks 1972b; Moseley 1972) and even to moderate black parents (Shanker 1969, 1972b).

"Have-not" groups have good reason to be frustrated and alienated in a period of history when there is considerable prosperity and conspicuous consumption. The community organizers, community control advocates, and black militants were often the same persons by the late 1960s. Black activists had dislodged most of the liberals from these community movements and seized control and leadership within the poor communities of the cities, because most of the poor were black. Most of these activists were not and are still not interested in reform in the traditional sense; they utilize disruptive and conflict tactics as means to their ends, making it nearly impossible for the target institutions to operate, much less to think of legitimate reform and innovation. The professionals are put on the defensive, and squabbles erupt among local community interest groups; usually, energies are spent on maintaining or on obtaining power—not on helping the clients.

As Billings (1972) and Sizemore (1972) state, the objective is not reform but political power, with race and ideology serving as the means of unifying for action. Clark (1972a) contends that community-controlled school boards do not seem interested in reforming the educational process or in helping the students; they struggle for political power, jobs, and control of the purse strings, and they often resort to conflict and violence to gain these benefits. The *New York Times* (April 20, 1972) reports that fighting over money and power prevails in many of the communities and local school districts, thus overshadowing the real educational needs of the students. Finally, Feldman (1969) and Sizer (1968) point out that reform and innovation are unlikely under community control; community control connotes passing the buck and finding scapegoats; it shifts responsibility for the deterioration of the schools from political and school officials to local groups who lack the knowledge and finances to implement genuine reform.

8. Community control means decentralizing the bureaucracy and adjusting educational programs to local needs

Parents have a legitimate complaint about the remoteness of a centralized bureaucracy. Breaking down the system into smaller components will enhance local parental and community participation and bring about a viable partnership between citizens and professionals who are interested in education. But there is need to retain central authority so as to avoid take-over of the schools by militants or extremists. The goal is to make the school system more adaptive, not to surrender authority to a group of lay people who lack the knowledge and expertise to run a school system, nor to permit representatives of one or a few political groups to use the schools for their own selfish interests. In short, community control of these schools, black or white, is far more conducive to extremist and totalitarian take-over than a large, central system. Every pressure group claims it is for the general welfare of the community or school, but each has its own version of how to promote the welfare of others.

If decentralization serves as the first stage for community control, then local bureaucracies are created. Instead of having one bureaucracy and trying to streamline the central system so it can run more efficiently, we have a number of smaller bureaucracies. To some degree this can be compared to the creation of local community agencies by the Office of Economic Opportunity (OEO). Commenting on the network of local agencies, Nicolau (1968) contends that the central system of OEO lost control over and coordination of the local agencies and was overwhelmed by its own complexities and new bureaucracies. Relating this experience to the schools, Thelen (1967) points out that providing autonomy to each decentralized unit causes the units to become out of step with one another and conflict of interests to develop—eventually confusing and possibly wrecking the central school system. He also points out that duplication and extra costs add to the bureaucratic problem.

Similarly, the Council of Supervisory Associations (1968) in New York City points out that a decentralized plan that negates central authority and establishes independent, autonomous school boards creates duplication, financial waste, and confusion and disrupts the entire school system. On the other hand, a decentralized school system without local school boards increases flexibility in terms of specified activities for individual schools and communities and also avoids conflict and confrontation.

Featherstone (1969) contends that community control leads to conflict between blacks and whites but does not necessarily mean a change in teaching or learning. Existing school systems can be decentralized so the interests of ghetto residents are served through community participation. Grant (1971) and Kristol (1968) point out that although it is difficult to decentralize and yet integrate, once the variable of community control is introduced into the schools, the practical possibility of integration is further reduced. This is verified by events in New York City and Detroit, where black militants have implemented community control as a method of enhancing black separatism and white segregationists have adopted it as a method of restricting integration.

Retention of authority and power at the central level is recommended for still another reason: it permits the coordination of system analysis and the cooperation of the various social systems at the city and metropolitan levels. By the establishment of autonomous local school boards the school system is splintered and the various local boards cannot easily "mesh" with other social systems that operate on broader levels. As Etzioni (1969) maintains, with micro (community) control there cannot be macro (system-wide) reform. The political and economic social systems rarely respond to pressure by one decentralized unit but more readily respond to a larger system such as the centralized school system. While social change can be and sometimes is accomplished by action groups operating at the local level, broad and extensive reform is usually based on action by central sources at the city, metropolitan, state, or preferably national level. Whatever progress is made locally, or at the subsystem level, usually depends on the moral and intellectual sustenance of the larger social system. The central school system serves this necessary function, but to do so it needs to retain its power and authority.

It would be interesting to ask what the parents really want: administrative decentralization and community control, or administrative decentralization and community participation; political confrontation, or education for their children. I believe that a valid survey of the black silent majority would reveal a conclusion different from that reached by the intuition and logic of the advocates of community control. And, as has been repeated in this discussion of community control, in most instances the militants are merely serving their self-interests, their political and economic gain, and not the interests of the parents or students.

Once there is surrender to the advocates of community control—to the loudly voiced demands of a few extremists who rarely represent the majority of the community—the school system or any other institution under attack is bound to be burdened with greater problems. By surrendering, the institution is in effect sanctioning future conflict and confrontation, recognizing and giving credence to a political enemy that seeks to bring down the system as it is presently structured. The more power and authority that is surrendered to the militant advocates of community control, the greater the political liability to the system and the greater the chances of chaos and confrontation. To add a sad note, the officials of other social institutions may often sympathize with the officials of the social system under attack, but they will rarely speak out in public. The extremist and terroristic tactics of black militants will often prevail over the black moderates, as they did in most of New York City and Detroit, because the activists take the initiative to claim they "represent" the black community. With increased arrogance and precision, engendered by their past successes, they may engulf the entire social system under attack, thereby increasing racial polarization as the polarization has increased in New York City (Glazer and Moynihan 1970) and Detroit (Grant 1971).

9. Community control promotes equality of opportunity

Community control advocates reject the change instruments brought about by middle-class and American reform tradition. Intellectual rigor, standardized tests, merit promotions, civil service examinations and supervisory examinations graded equally for all groups are rejected as instruments of the system and as a means of excluding the community—especially blacks—from the system. Many advocates of community control see standards of excellence and professionalism as biased mechanisms that exclude them from the mainstream and reduce equality—not only in education but in other fields as well.

Thus we enter into an interpretation of equality: Do we promote equal opportunity for all groups or do we promote equal results for all groups and thereby bring about quotas and reverse discrimination for certain groups? Do we choose people for admissions into graduate and professional schools (such as law and medicine) and for employment on the basis of merit and ability or on the basis of race and color? Do we maintain standards of excellence for purposes of integrity, justice, and general prosperity in society, or do we lower standards in education, professional schooling, and private industry for purposes of group equality and thus possibly create a basis for the decline of American productivity?

Liberal reformers, racial minorities, and especially blacks refuse to recognize that there are group differences; for example, that some ethnic and racial groups are relatively higher achievers or perhaps better basketball players than other groups. Hook (1972) and Kurtz (1972) point out that the claim that some individuals are more intelligent than others is not "racist"; a racist is a person who refuses to recognize individual differences (for instance, that some blacks may be more or less intelligent or more or less muscular than some whites), who denies the normal policy and potential of individuals because they are members of a specific race, or who commits a hostile act out of racial motives.

Ironically, it is the affirmative-action advocates, the liberal-black community, who seem to be practicing racism; they are advocating a policy of reverse racism through group quotas and body counts, whereby individuals are discriminated against and denied advancement on merit. Hence, the normal policy and potential of the white individual is now to be limited because of his skin color; less-qualified individuals who are members of a minority are to have preferential treatment in the selection process for graduate schools and employment because they are not white.

One who believes in equality treats another person not as a member of a group but as an individual; he recognizes that individuals have different qualifications and competencies. A belief in equality depends not on the notion that all groups are equal but on the premise that all groups should be treated equally. One who believes in equality realizes that all people are not born with equal abilities and capacities to learn, but that all individuals are entitled to equal protection of the laws and equal right to fulfill their unique potentialities. As Hook (1972) claims, our democratic commitment depends on providing equal opportunity for all individuals to permit them to develop to their fullest; it means that there is recognition and appreciation of individual differences and levels of achievement; and it does not depend on the misguided notion that all groups are the same or equal. Similarly, Glazer (1969a) cites several important studies and prominent social scientists (i.e., Ruth Benedict, Margaret Mead, and David Riesman) showing that there are distinct differences to the degree in which different racial and ethnic groups achieve educationally, even when socio-economic class is considered. "To speak of the differences between groups is to raise incredibly difficult problems" (p. 187). There are even differences in thinking patterns and abilities among ethnic groups. According to the classic study by Lesser, Fifer, and Clark (1965), each ethnic group (Blacks, Chinese, Jews, and Puerto Ricans) demonstrates different processes of thinking regardless of class position. Socio-economic class does make a difference in the level at which a specific pattern or ability is manifested, but not in the pattern and ability. Race and ethnicity not only influence the pattern but also the level of abilities.

In the early 1960s the approach to equal opportunity was to seek out qualified applicants from racial groups, give them preferential treatment if their qualifications were roughly the same as those of other applicants, provide special tutoring and apprenticeships for "qualifiable" applicants, and bring the tests closer to job reality. As mentioned in chapter 1, quotas have replaced the process of competition in the choice of teachers, supervisors, and administrators in many city school systems, such as Chicago, Detroit, and New York, to create a racial balance among teachers and administrators that approximates the racial balance of the student population. Two examples, one on the east coast and one on the west coast, are indicative of what is happening across the nation. Writes Shanker (1972a):

> In New York City, Community School Board 1 has
> adopted a policy of staff hiring by which the ethnic com-
> position of the staff will come to be the same as that of
> the students in the district. Community Board 3 has an-
> nounced that "by September, 1975, at least one-third of

the teachers within each school will be from the minority/
majority groups through a program of recruitment and
selection that will ensure this." These two groups have
publicly announced a policy which others are practicing
quietly. (So far, [the] Chancellor . . . has remained silent,
and only two of the five members of the Board of Education have publicly opposed the imposition of hiring
quotas.) [p. 5]

In San Francisco the Board of Education, following the affirmative-
action guidelines of the U.S. Department of Health, Education, and Welfare,
attempted in March 1971 to demote 125 administrators, all of whom were
white, to make room for minorities. A lawsuit followed, and the school board
ended up demoting no one. However, the superintendent of schools, Steven
P. Morena, proposed a new reverse discrimination plan, which is described by
Rabb (1972):

No more than 20 percent of Other Whites will be hired
for or promoted to administrative positions in the first
year, no more than 10 percent in the second year, and no
Other Whites at all in the ensuing years until ethnic and
racial proportions among administrators equal the respective proportions in the school population [p. 43].

The outcome of the lawsuit was that Judge Samuel B. Conti ruled against the
San Francisco school board's plan because it was based on quotas. Superintendent Morena pointed out, however, in an interview that he was continuing
his program of appointing minorities to administrative positions to increase
the minority count, without setting any quotas (*San Francisco Chronicle*,
November 2, 1972). The subject of quotas is so grave that it deserves extended consideration.

The Return of Racial Quotas

Competition for jobs on the basis of ability is being eliminated not only in the
schools but also in most of the job markets. This sweeping change is being
brought about mainly by Executive Orders No. 4 and 11246, which were signed
by President Johnson to eliminate discrimination in hiring, but which were revised and issued by the Department of Labor, and which now force institutions
to give preferential treatment to minorities in hiring and promotion practices
and require that goals and timetables be filed annually by each employer. The
Orders cover public schools, universities, civil service (policemen, firemen, post
office workers, etc.), the armed forces, construction and trade industries,
unions, private corporations and businesses employing more than 50 people,
and *all* organizations that have contracts with government or are regulated by
one of the governmental agencies—in total, affecting about 95 percent of the
employment market.

According to the U.S. Commission on Civil Rights (1970) report, the federal government is the largest employer in the country and another third of the nation's labor force is employed by companies that are government contractors. These two powers, the power to employ directly and the power to force federal contractors to abide by the rules of the government, alone affect more than 75 percent of the job force. Title VII of the Civil Rights Act of 1964 reaches almost all the rest of the employers; the title asserts that no person may be discriminated against on the grounds of race, color, or national origin. The meaning of nondiscrimination, however, has been transformed into affirmative-action compliance and reverse discrimination. Almost every school district, hospital, local government agency, bank—almost every institution we can think of—receives some federal assistance and/or is covered by this regulation. The list of organizations covered by Title VII is endless, and these employers also must follow federal guidelines. Furthermore, quite independent of any executive order that stresses preferential treatment of minorities, and quite independent of Title VII of the Civil Rights Act, the federal government has enormous powers vested in insured and guaranteed loan programs, such as home mortgages, student scholarships and stipends, institutional contributions to social security, and those of the Veterans Administration. And finally, the government has tremendous power in such agencies as the ICC, EPC, FCC, CAB, SEC, and FTC, which regulate railroads, ship building and operating, securities, marketing, communications, and many other industries. All of the businesses in these regulated industries, according to Glazer (1971), feel obligated to give preferential treatment to minorities. Preferential treatment is also required by all businesses with more than 50 employees, enforced by governmental agencies in Washington and on a regional basis. The obligation to give preference to minorities is felt more intensely by all businesses and institutions with more than 100 employees, because they must file annual reports with the Equal Employment Opportunity Commission (EEOC), detailing the number of minorities in all job categories, from laborers to administrators.

According to the federal guidelines, the goal of equal opportunity is no longer equal equality for all groups but is, as the report by the U.S. Commission on Civil Rights (1970) states, that the number of members of minority groups found in employment, at every level, be equal to their proportion in the population. In other words, *equal opportunity* has become transformed into *actual employment* of minorities. These minorities include blacks, persons with Spanish surnames, Indians, Orientals, and women—but not Greeks, Poles, Italians, Irish and other ethnics, not Catholics or Jews. Thus the only eligibles for preferential treatment are racial minorities and women, supposedly because they have suffered the most discrimination and disadvantage because of sex and heredity. Needless to say, they are not the only ones who have been discriminated against in some way. Other groups, and certainly individuals in those other groups, have suffered disadvantages in school and society. To be sure, no one asks how we know that some black person did not come from a home more advantaged than that of some white person seeking the same job or trying to get into college. Remember, about 70 percent of the poor in this country are white. Thus Seabury (1972*a*) cites the frustrations of one poor white student.

> The ability to think in the abstract is hard for a person with my cultural background and economic background. My parents'. . . income barely exceeded the poverty level. My father is a Southern Baptist with a third-grade education. . . . I believe I am a victim. As a non-member of a minority group I feel that I . . . [am] discriminated against constantly. The same admissions standards are not applied because a certain percentage of minority students must be admitted in each class regardless of their qualifications. My test score, undergraduate record, and my family (poor white) deny me admittance to Harvard because I am white [p. 44].

The federal guidelines, according to Abrams (1972) and Seligman (1973), appear to be designed to scare employers away from any objective standards or test requirements which have a differential impact on minority groups. Moreover, the U.S. Supreme Court has ruled in *Griggs* v. *Duke Power* (1971) that tests can no longer be considered a reasonable job requirement; all arbitrary barriers to employment which demand certain skills, education levels, or test score results and have the effect of employing minorities in less than their proportion to the population are now considered illegal. The employer must now demonstrate conclusively that the skills are in fact needed for the job. If test scores are involved, he must now demonstrate that the tests are reliable and a valid predictor of job success. The fact that the employer has no discriminatory intention is irrelevant; it is only the effect that matters now.

The claim is that the tests are unfair and culturally biased because all groups do not obtain the same mean scores or pass the tests in the proportion that they represent of the general population. Ironically, the critics claim that blacks and other racial minorities are not getting an education as good as that of whites. When they apply to a college or go out into the job market, the blame for failure to qualify is no longer to be put on their schools and teachers but is now to be put on the tests. Suddenly, the words "unfair" and "biased" are used to alibi the inability of some groups to compete with others, ignoring educational abilities and differences in reading, mathematical, and aptitude scores even when educational levels are held constant. The claim is that standardized tests cannot be used, that we must either apply different standards to nonwhites who cannot compete with whites or eliminate standards altogether. (Some critics, according to Kurtz [1972], even contend that all testing should be eliminated and we should use lotteries to choose plumbers, teachers, lawyers, and physicians.)

Here it is important to note that females are considered as minorities in affirmative-action policies, but they have always been able to compete with males on standardized tests. The *Griggs* decision is not aimed at helping white women but is directed toward helping those racial minorities (except Orientals, who are high-achievers) who seem unable to compete on cognitive tests. All federal agencies involved in affirmative-action programs, such as the Office of Civil Rights (OCR), Equal Employment Opportunity Commission (EEOC), and Office of Federal Contract Compliance (OFCC), are rigorously enforcing this legal decision. This of course puts the employer on the defensive, and the easiest thing to do is just hire enough minorities to fill a quota.

According to Doppelt and Bennett (1967) of the Psychological Corporation, the cry that testing for job applicants is biased is a smoke screen to mask the political nuances. Granted, there are some technical limitations to tests, but there are many well-devised (reliable and valid) tests that measure "the individual's present capability of demonstrating his skills or knowledge for predicting job success" (p. 1). It is senseless to eliminate verbal and simple mathematical items on tests, or to exclude the tests altogether, when verbal communication and the ability to perform simple mathematical activities are important for a given job. The tests may be culturally oriented, but the job is embedded in a cultural milieu. The ability to "understand oral and perhaps written instructions" are not racially biased items (p. 2); they are "culturally laden" items which are likely to be criterion or job-related. The purpose of the test is to select people who will succeed on the job; outlawing such tests makes the selection process more subjective and political than without the tests. The politics of the charge, that tests are racially biased, is evidenced by the fact that it does not consider a large subgroup of the white majority who are educationally disadvantaged and do not perform well on many of these job tests. The authors conclude:

> Whenever the number of applicants exceeds the number of job openings, some applicants will be rejected. This is one of the hard facts of life. It is not surprising that those who are rejected sometimes attack the selection procedures on the grounds that these are invalid or unfair. Although testing is not free from defect or beyond criticism, appropriately chosen and properly administered ability tests are superior to most available alternatives.

> Some of the problems which stem from the testing of disadvantaged groups are of a technical nature and are not related to the issue of discrimination. Reduced reliability is often due to the fact that score distributions obtained from disadvantaged groups are compressed. The same compression (and reduced reliability) is also found when only highly capable individuals are being tested. These problems require technical study and, in some instances, may call for the use of different measures or the

> development of new and more appropriate tests. The
> basic issue is not necessarily one of discrimination against
> a particular subgroup [p. 5].

Society has the responsibility for providing jobs for people with
limited skills, but not at the expense of replacing qualified personnel with
unqualified personnel. Society has the responsibility of providing remedial
job instruction for disadvantaged populations, but this also should include
white disadvantaged populations. The rejection of such measurements that
register the consequences of educational deprivation is merely a political
move to kill off the messenger who brings the bad news, to deemphasize the
harsh fact that quotas will lead to a downhill trend in quality and abilities of
people employed in many jobs. New and artificial standards that mock excellence and replace it with mediocrity have little to do with equal opportunity.
The moral and ethical arguments are secondary; rather the political decision
to pay off militant blacks to curtail violent tactics seems to be the major factor. Indeed, the silent majority must now pay the consequences for being
silent.

The fact that a company or institution does not want to hire a member of a minority group because of his character or even because of previous
arrests cannot be deemed as an excuse for not hiring him. (Such an excuse
often is illegally used for not hiring a white person.) In *Gregory* v. *Litton
Systems* (1971) the federal district court in California ruled that an applicant
with a record of 14 arrests and no convictions could not be denied a job on
that basis alone. The plaintiff was black, and the plea of racial discrimination
was successfully used against the company. The court ruled that arrests
alone prove nothing about individual character and that, since a greater proportion of blacks are arrested, it is discriminatory to use this excuse for not
hiring them. Abrams (1972) points out that in the new interpretation of
Title VII, the federal government has gone a step further and has declared it
is now "unlawful to discharge or refuse to employ a minority group person
[notice that only minorities are mentioned and minorities in this case does not
include white women] because of a conviction record unless the particular circumstances of each case indicate that employment of that particular person for
a particular job is manifestly inconsistent with the safe and efficient operation
of that job." Although members of the EEOC admit that a bank robber should
be barred from employment in a bank, they argue that a person who is convicted of rape or murder "may be hired, since the act is not job-related" (p. 56).

Seligman (1973) points out that, although government officials
continue to profess that "you never have to hire an unqualified person," the
real point is that in all job sectors the pressure to file timetables and goals,
even though actual quotas may not be intended by the federal government,
turns the whole procedure of preferential treatment toward one of racial
quotas and reverse discrimination.

The advocates of preferential treatment of minorities refuse to admit that they have created hysteria in all job sectors, with the result that, rather than risk legal or financial problems with the government, almost all employers have overreacted and instituted quotas and reverse-discriminatory practices. Thus, Seligman (1973) also points out that major companies like IBM and Xerox have informed their executives that their futures depend on results in meeting affirmative-action goals. This type of hysteria is increasing as more and more large businesses are probed for alleged biases in recruitment and promotions (*Chicago Daily News*, September 18, 1973; *New York Times*, September 23, 1973). The threat of court action, compounded by possible loss of federal contracts, is sufficient to cause overreaction on the part of these industries and to negotiate a settlement with the EEOC. According to the *Chicago Tribune* (September 20, 1973) and the *New York Times* (September 23, 1973), a growing segment of the black civil rights groups openly use the term "quota system" and demand that it be implemented "to correspond with the size of the black population." Failure to adopt a quota system will lead to black boycott of goods, black demonstrations and picketing of the businesses, as well as lawsuits.

Similarly, Seabury (1972*a*) finds that quotas are widespread in colleges and universities, which he lists by name, and that such quotas represent "a stark remodeling of their criteria of professionalism and their standard of excellence" (p. 33). And, the president of Columbia University, William J. McGill, states that "the determination of superior ability and special excellence [is now viewed by] some officials as a mask for continuing discrimination" (*New York Times*, May 7, 1972, p. 12).

Preferential treatment is so common that many chairmen, deans, presidents, and professors who head search committees blatantly indicate (even in writing) to candidates and placement bureaus that they are interested in hiring only minorities and females, and especially minority females. Among the schools that have expressed such preferences in accordance with current affirmative-action policies are: City University of New York, Columbia University, Connecticut College, Indiana University, Lehigh University, New Mexico State University, Northwestern University, Sacramento State College, San Francisco State College, Stanford University, State University of New York at Albany, and the University of California, Berkeley.[4] These are but a few of the colleges and universities that give such preferential treatment. Many clearly state that their new hiring "goals" are based on recruiting minorities in proportion to the surrounding population. The prestigious institutions, where hiring and promotion standards tend to have been rigorous in the past, and the state and city-supported institutions and those receiving federal funds, are under the most pressure.

For example, the department head of a southwestern university responded to the inquiry of the placement officer at another university on May 27, 1971, by stating that although "four candidates seem qualified for [a] vacancy they cannot be considered" because he had been instructed to

make every effort to recruit "a qualified person from a minority group." He
pointed out that his recruiting policies had changed and he could no longer
"seek the best-qualified person available, regardless of race, color, or creed, as
[the university had] in the past." In other words, this department head is
forced to seek a "qualifiable" minority person, not the most qualified person.
Another chairman at a west coast state school wrote to placement bureaus
across the country on April 24, 1972 stating that the new goal of his school is
"to recruit and promote minority and women candidates until [their] proportion of [the] faculty is [the same as that of] the general population." A department chairman of an Eastern college compliments a person's "impressive"
research and states "I wish I could invite you to come for an interview," but
informs the candidate that affirmative action makes it impossible to do so.
He reassures the person that with his "excellent qualifications [he] will find
a position of [his] choice."[5]

In the same vein, the *Congressional Record* (May 22, 1973) points
out that letters are now even posted on bulletin boards and read:

> The Department of Philosophy at the University of
> ———— is seeking qualified women and minority candi-
> dates for all faculty positions at all levels . . .
>
> We desire to appoint a black or Chicano, preferably
> female . . .
>
> ———— State College is also an affirmative-action insti-
> tution with respect to both American minority groups
> and women. Our doctoral requirements for faculty will
> be waived for candidates who qualify under the affirma-
> tive-action criteria.

Letters between departments now read:

> —— —— College has a vacancy in its . . . Department. . . .
> We desire to appoint a black or Chicano, preferably
> female.
>
> I should very much appreciate it if you could indicate
> which of your 1972 candidates are either Negro or Mexi-
> can American [pp. 14–15] .

The list of these kinds of letters can comprise a textbook. While
women are often included in the affirmative-action categories, the above
letters keenly illustrate a distinction between minority and majority group
women. Preference is given to minority women, and the waiving of formal
qualifications is not geared to help white women, for these candidates usually
possess the necessary qualifications.

Now listing statements by highly influential people who determine
policy, Oscar E. Shabat, the chancellor of the City Colleges of Chicago (comprising seven units), has instructed the presidents of the various colleges that

race is to be the prime factor in hiring new faculty members as administrators. *Chicago Today* (March 8, 1972) further reports that at Kennedy-King College, whose faculty is already 37 percent black, Shabat has "told the president to hire 10 additional black teachers." The reader should note that the racial proportion of the staff at Kennedy-King already exceeds the general black population of the country, as well as that of the city of Chicago. (Here black demands are approaching community control.) Dr. Shabat also added that "when 52 systemwide contracts expire in July for teachers, many qualified whites will not be rehired and blacks will be sought to fill their jobs" (p. 10). In other words, whites, no matter how well qualified they are, will be replaced by blacks whose major qualification is the color of their skin.

At Columbia University, a memorandum written on January 20, 1972, by William T. deBary, executive vice-president for academic affairs and provost, to the deans, directors, and department heads, begins with a statement of the need (a) to demonstrate that hiring policies are in accord with the affirmative-action program of the Department of Health, Education, and Welfare, (b) to "make every effort to locate and consider women and minority groups" for openings, and (c) consequently, to state this need in all letters and communications sent to candidates and university placement bureaus. Each department is to keep a file for 18 months to provide a statistical base to serve as a record of what was done for hiring on the basis of race and sex, as mandated by HEW. Candidates are to be subdivided into five categories: black, Spanish-surnamed, Oriental, Caucasian, and other. The first two categories, it seems, are to receive preferential treatment. Further, although the memorandum urges that qualified people be sought for openings, they will not necessarily be the most qualified candidates, since race and sex are to be major considerations for hiring. Thus, even at Columbia University scholarship and excellence are being subverted under the guise of equality for all groups.

Although the practices instituted at Columbia are now common at other institutions of higher learning to meet HEW's requirements for body counts and quotas, ethnic categorization is carried to absurd and confusing extremes. For example, Seabury (1972*a*) points out that San Francisco State College now defines six racial groups to implement the affirmative-action program: (1) blacks, (2) Orientals, (3) other nonwhites, (4) persons of Mexican, Central, or South American ancestry (except those who have physical traits that resemble those of blacks, Orientals, and nonwhite races), (5) Indians, and (6) all other Caucasians or whites. As Seabury states, "All but the last category are eligible for discriminatory preference" (p. 43). Another of the institution's hiring policies is to make the college's nonacademic personnel ethnically mirror the population of the Bay Area.

According to a letter to the editor of the *New York Times* (January 6, 1972) by four professors at Cornell, the president of the university wrote to the deans, directors, and department heads setting forth a "new and innovative program to help achieve affirmative action"; this included the hiring of "unqualified or marginally qualified people." (In other words, under the guise of innovation, Cornell was to hire unqualified people.) One week after the letter appeared in the *Times*, the directive was clarified or changed— depending on one's interpretation—that the new hiring program applied only to nonacademic personnel. But it is hard to believe that the original directive was not related to the hiring of professors and administrators, since those who received it hire for such positions.

At the State University of New York (SUNY) at Albany, one of the 72 institutions of the system, six affirmative-action memorandums were issued between August 10 and December 3, 1971, by various vice-presidents. Department heads were asked to consider anticipated vacancies through termination of contracts over a five-year period and to determine "how many of these vacancies could feasibly be allocated to minority groups." The memorandums recommended the hiring of "qualifiable" people on the basis of race and sex and "temporary preferences . . . to members of minority groups." This hiring was to be on a three-to-one ratio for professors and a "one-to-one hiring of minorities affecting all of the administrative staff." In short, these six memorandums represented clear requests for quotas, violation of the Fourteenth Amendment, and disregard of individual merit. Furthermore, they virtually forced administrators to hire on the basis of race or let essential jobs go unfilled and advocated the debasement of academic standards by the hiring of "qualifiable" people.

The SUNY story was told by the *New York Times* (March 3, 1972) and subsequently by several upstate New York papers including the Albany papers. The director of SUNY's Office of Equal Employment Opportunity tried to ameliorate matters by explaining that "none of the memos or statements were issued as policy . . . they were suggested guidelines." With twisted logic, he argued that as policy the guidelines were illegal, but as suggestions there was nothing wrong with them. He failed to point out, however, that such guidelines, written by persons in higher echelons of the university, are usually followed—at least by people who wish to maintain their jobs. Sherman (1972) points out that on April 24, 1972, SUNY issued a new statement on affirmative action which showed some improvement. It supported "the selection of the best-qualified people," but in view of HEW's pressure it maintained that "a department with a black or female candidate still has a better chance of gaining a new position or retaining a vacant one." The new statement did not call for consideration of the nonretention of qualified whites, solely to support HEW's program, as did the first memorandum. The new statement represented a welcome concession but no guarantee that it would be followed. Sherman adds that it was a small triumph when one of the liberal assistant professors admitted that it would be unjust to terminate his contract "for the purpose of replacing him with a black person" (pp. 30–32). Indeed, a liberal educator had been educated to the realities of today's perverse "equality."

For the six-month period between January and June 1972, the *Chronicle of Higher Education* (a bimonthly newspaper on higher education which also lists job openings at colleges and universities) indicated that for more than 25 different positions a preference for minorities was expressed. There was a greater number of ads that included the term *affirmative-action employers,* often a euphemism for quota hiring; moreover, the June 5, 1972, issue[a] advertised an "active file of 111 minority candidates available for September 1972 employment" (p. 7). And, the *American Association of University Professors Bulletin* (March 1972) cites the "Harvard University Report on Academic Tenure" about the competition to find qualified blacks and that "Harvard and comparable institutions have been warned against 'raiding' black colleges in the South" (p. 66).

There are several court orders in the North and in the South, even in Alabama and Mississippi, which require that police, fire, and sanitation departments, as well as electrical, plumbing, construction, steel, iron, asbestos, and other labor unions, hire one black for every white or even a greater percentage of blacks than of whites until the ratio of blacks corresponds with their proportion of the population. The fact that blacks are not proportionately represented on the police force of a city may reflect the fact that, because of hostility to the police, many blacks, even if they are qualified, are reluctant to enter a career in the police department. As for blacks' inferior education and low test scores, these factors—although obvious and perhaps part of the explanation—cannot be mentioned or used as reasons for blacks' having had and continuing to have trouble passing civil service examinations.

The New York City plan gives a new twist to affirmative action. Former Mayor Lindsay initiated his own arbitrary executive order, requiring all contractors for the city to submit goals and timetables through 1977 along with their contract bids. At the same time, the city passed legislation that will give minority workers an average of 26 percent of the jobs in the construction industry by 1978. Contractors who violate the percentages or, more accurately, quotas are subject to loss of their contracts with the city. Similar executive orders are being implemented for all city jobs such as in the fire, police, and sanitation departments. What is questionable here is whether a city has the legal privilege to enact its own affirmative-action program that goes beyond the state and federal guidelines.

Revised Order No. 4, issued in April 1972, also rules that it is discriminatory to require of a new applicant qualifications any higher than those required of "the lowest-qualified incumbent." Rather than being permitted to upgrade the work force, educational, business, and other institutions are compelled by this regulation to lower the standards of performance. It opens the door to the hiring of someone who cannot meet current standards or qualifications because some incumbent was hired long ago either by some mistake or when standards were lower because of the scarcity of college-educated people, when there was a scarcity of people with advanced degrees, or when the institution was struggling for recognition. In effect, the government has applied Gresham's Law to the job sector; the result is bound to be a

---

[a] Note: Letter references a through g in this chapter connote postscript references. Postscript begins on p. 97.

downgrading of quality in the professions and in the work force. Furthermore, HEW now insists that an institution "may hold certain vacancies open until such time as qualified minorities are found and considered," although such positions may not be set aside to the exclusion of nonminorities. The question is, how long can an institution keep a position vacant? Is it not easier to hire someone who is unqualified, one who will meet the guidelines of the federal government, than to explain why someone could not be found? Does this posture not lead to the exclusion of nonminorities, and especially white males? In effect, the government requires that "qualifiable" minorities, not the most qualified persons, be hired and promoted to meet suggested goals and timetables. Revised Executive Order No. 11246, issued in October 1972, now mandates this to all federal contractors and employers.[b]

The absurdity of the quotas is evidenced by the orders issued to the National Guard in North Dakota. Federal government officials told the guard it had to recruit 20 blacks to balance its membership racially, although there are only 20 eligible blacks in the entire state. The general in command of the guard in North Dakota provided the following census breakdown. There are 2,496 blacks living in the state, and 2,346 are members of the armed forces. Active military personnel would seem unlikely candidates for the guard. This leaves 150 blacks: 60 are women, 40 are under 18 or over 45 years of age, and 30 are college students from other states with little interest in enlisting in the National Guard in North Dakota for six years. This leaves 20 eligible blacks, some of whom are physically unfit. Officials in Washington had studied the 1970 census to determine what proportion of blacks the state guard should have. They had come up with the figure of 20, although the general calculated the figure to be less than one person, as shown above. Said the *New York Times* (March 4, 1973), "this is further proof that Washington bureaucrats . . . know little if anything about life beyond the Potomac River" (p. 43).

As Rabb (1972) points out, the government has forced institutions to substitute quotas for achievement and competition. To argue that the minorities hired will be "qualified" is to evade the issue and fail to admit that "qualifiable" connotes something quite different from qualified. The inescapable assumption of this ascriptive approach, of what turns out to be a quota, is that minorities and especially blacks cannot compete, even with a competitive margin. "The proposers of such a quota system are calling, then, for a social welfare program, pure and simple, which indeed should not be considered performance-connected" (p. 43). And Seligman (1973) quotes a number of blacks who are growing uneasy about the idea of hiring less-qualified minority-group members. "It puts the 'less qualified' stamp on the minorities you do hire," many of whom are qualified (p. 168). There is the growing feeling among employees of those institutions and businesses that hire or promote blacks that capabilities did not enter into the hiring decisions. Questions concerning the qualifications of the person who was hired will occur to the white applicants who did not get the job, to the customers who deal with the black employee, to the student who is taught by the black professor, and, of course, to the black person himself. In effect, one aspect of reverse discrimination is that it makes both the white and the black persons involved feel that members of minority groups do not have the same abilities as whites and are not able to make it on their own.

Concerning quotas, Seabury (1972*b*) points out that, once they are established as an institutional practice, quotas are quite likely to be perpetuated for obvious reasons, that is, custom and pressure by the groups who benefit. For a complex society like our own, which depends on the skills of individuals composing it, the end result is mediocrity and a downward trend in our standard of living. We want tests that predict learning and show achievement levels and aptitude to perform jobs, yet such tests are being abandoned by schools, colleges, civil service, and private industry because of pressure from the black community and affirmative-action programs.

We want qualified students to go to college and universities, who can read, write, and calculate with a reasonable degree of proficiency; otherwise, there is a simple downward regression to the mean in standards and grading and the college diploma becomes meaningless for most graduates and highly suspect for minorities, including those who are able students. Yet most institutions of higher learning have adopted informal quotas for minorities, including many prestigious institutions such as Harvard, Princeton, Yale, and Michigan State. In Scholastic Aptitude Test (undergraduate) scores and Graduate Record Examination (graduate) scores for entering minorities, the great majority who are black are now often in the lowest 25 percentile on a national level, thus taking away a seat from an individual that would normally require a 90 or higher percentile range. Kilson (1973), the black economist, summarizes the whole situation at Harvard and other prestigious colleges as "irresponsible" (p. 32).

In line with this new policy, most colleges and universities are asking student applicants to voluntarily respond to a supplementary "civil rights questionnaire," where the applicant checks if he belongs to a minority group or is a Caucasian American. Here we can assume that a minority applicant gladly fills in the questionnaire—almost guaranteeing himself admission into a college or university. It is usually taken for granted that the individual who does not volunteer the information is white. Other admission forms now require the applicant to check an appropriate racial category, and many even require a photograph—a return to the pre-1954 Brown decision, only almost in reverse—to limit whites.

Admission into college and universities is seemingly guaranteed to minorities, despite academic qualifications. The U.S. Office of Education has established separate test norms for blacks, Spanish-speaking, and other designated minorities and another norm for the rest of the student population. Instead of outlawing tests for schools, which the Supreme Court did with tests for jobs, the USOE has devised a dual system whereby a black student who reads as well as other minority students of his age group is considered to be a "normal" or "average" reader. To put it in a different way, the black student who reads 3½ years behind his white counterpart at the twelfth grade (as purported by the Coleman report) is considered to be a "normal" or "average" reader. Although the USOE aims their action at the public schools and justifies their action on the basis of tests being unfair to minorities (notice they do not consider disadvantaged white populations or first generation students from Europe who have language problems), this approach now implies that universities will have no excuse not to admit minority students who have trouble reading, writing, or doing basic mathematics problems. Both the *New York Times* (September 9, 1973) and Shanker (1973*a*) point out that public schools across the country are acquiescing to this dual testing program, a program which will justify two racial learning standards because of fear of losing federal funds. At the present, one exception is District 19 in New York City, which refused to go along with the USOE and has been punished by the federal office and has had withheld its $964,000 in annual federal funds. The handwriting is on the wall for colleges and universities who refuse to honor these dual standards; they too can be threatened by loss of federal monies.[c]

We do want a qualified surgeon when we need an operation, yet there are now hard quotas in medical schools—seats reserved not for the most qualified applicants but for the most qualified minorities.[6] We want a skilled lawyer when we are in trouble, yet there are hard quotas for candidates applying to law school.[7] We want a plane serviced by skilled mechanics and flown by a skilled pilot when we travel by air, yet the airlines are under pressure and are hiring their share of minorities in all jobs at all levels and are upgrading minorities on the job. In universities we want high standards of scholarship and excellence, yet there quotas are pervasive and professorial positions are filled not with the most-qualified people but rather with "qualifiable" persons and some whose qualifications may be equal only to those of the lowest-qualified incumbent.

Despite all our legal, moral, and ethical talk about the need for affirmative action, it takes many years to educate and create qualified doctors, lawyers, professors, industrial executives, etc., of any color, and no increased federal pressure and no increased demand are going to increase the supply immediately unless we wish to lower standards. In effect, in the eyes and minds of many people, we are making "black" synonymous with "substandard." Within a few years people will really ask themselves and others, "How did the person get the job? Besides belonging to minority status, does he have any legitimate qualifications?" According to Seabury (1972*b*), "Our existence places us at the mercy of persons often invisible to us, who are certified for their qualifications." Although we may argue about how skills are elicited and measured, "we can hardly argue that certain people are more skilled and equal in given jobs than other people." But there are those among us who argue for equal results rather than equal opportunity for minorities and do injustice to the criterion of excellence. Those who accept this argument and its "spreading influence may well constitute the single greatest threat to the quality of our lives today" (p. 45).

Mayer (1973) contends that when students are admitted to colleges, medical schools, law schools, and engineering schools by open admissions or quotas, immense differences will soon begin to appear in a large number of difficult jobs.[d] And Ravitch (1973) maintains that social science has not found a way "to make those who are dumb, lazy, and unambitious win equal rewards in a fair competition with people who are smart, ambitious, and talented" (p. 88). But it seems that the government has found a way to do so, by abolishing fair competition and standardized tests for employment and by establishing separate test norms for minority and nonminority students. The government is ensuring equal employment and equal "success" for all groups and an egalitarian society through affirmative-action programs. But the goal is not the desire to promote equal opportunity but a political philosophy of equal results which, according to Ravitch, "requires not only efforts to upgrade those who are unequal below the median, but also active steps to level-down those who are unequal above the median" (p. 90).

In a society built in correspondence with this philosophy, almost anyone who displays talent or brillance and is white (white females are still discriminated against in favor of nonwhite females) is frozen in his position or sent to the end of the line to make room for a minority person. In effect, the white person is penalized for his abilities because of his color. In contrast to equal opportunity, which encourages competition and excellence, equal results discourages competition and ability and leads to reverse discrimination. Indeed, this is perhaps the only time in the history of a democratic society anywhere in the world when the majority has been discriminated against for the sake of the minority. It is perhaps the only time in history that a society has been told that reverse discrimination is an acceptable method of employment.

According to the Committee on Academic Nondiscrimination and Integrity (1972), these targets and goals—in effect, what has boiled down to quotas and reverse racism—are "defended as compensating for past injustices," yet we fail to recognize that "they only perpetuate injustice" (p. 4). Goodman (1972) points out that in a recent court case in Minnesota dealing with firemen, a dissenting judge argued that the plaintiffs seeking employment could not show how they were ever denied employment in favor of less-qualified whites. Furthermore, past racial discrimination against blacks did "not justify racial discrimination against white applicants" (p. 108).

The right to be free from discrimination is an individual right, as the Supreme Court has continually stated; it is not a right delegated to a broad mass or group, and it should not be abridged on the basis of a person's race. Justice for one group is utterly meaningless if it requires injustice toward another group. It is essential to outlaw all forms of discrimination, but not by promoting discrimination against other persons. The whole principle of reverse discrimination denies the basic American principle that an individual's advancement depends on his qualifications and not on his heredity.

"If quotas are justified for one group, why are they not justified for other groups?" ask white ethnics who have been discriminated against in the job sector. We can stretch our imagination and claim that quotas should be justified for registered Republicans at universities, since so few of them teach in institutions of higher learning, or for Poles, Greeks, and various Slavic groups as well as Catholics, since they also are underrepresented in universities. Since Jews are underrepresented in trade unions, banking, and insurance, why can't we have quotas for Jews in these fields? Since homosexuals are underrepresented in almost all phases of the economy, why shouldn't we have quotas for them, too? Since in proportion to the national population the number of blacks far exceeds that of whites in basketball, baseball, boxing, and parts of the entertainment industry, why shouldn't we use the principle of quotas now being applied against whites in other fields and thereby limit the number of blacks in sports and entertainment until whites catch up? If we can hire marginally qualified university professors because they are black, why can't we hire marginally qualified basketball players because they are white?

If illegal quotas are camouflaged and continued as goals and timetables in affirmative-action programs, what is to prevent any well-organized group form demanding its full share of quotas? Indeed, we already hear rumblings of "Irish Power," "Italian Power," "Polish Power," and the like. What is to prevent the majority from availing itself of precedents established by affirmative-action programs? Rather than continuing to polarize this country, rather than continuing to create bitterness and hostility among the majority groups who now feel discriminated against and argue that the government has overlooked their needs and concerns and favors only blacks, we need to implement a viable program of equal opportunity.

Such a program would consist of enforcing laws against discriminatory practices but would clearly safeguard against reverse discrimination. Quantitative measures must be used to establish some kind of criteria for standards, and there must be some tolerance for the fact that some groups achieve better in one area or do better in cognitive areas while others do better in psychomotor areas. The fact is, different people and different groups have different strengths, and it should not be taboo to admit that no two persons or groups are totally equal. Our policies should promote equal opportunity, with the person with the best qualifications receiving the appropriate job, not equal results, which fosters mediocrity and penalizes individuals for being talented if they belong to the wrong group.

If members of one group predominate in an area of employment, that fact is not adequate evidence of "discrimination" or "racism." Rather than proportional representation, we must consider the eligible manpower and qualifiable talent within the job market of a geographical area. For example, in 1972 there were only 1,500 black Ph.D.s in the country, not all of them in higher education. It is impossible for institutions of higher learning to have an adequate representation of blacks on their staffs without lowering scholastic requirements. The fact is that only 2 percent of the engineers are black. How can an engineering firm employ a proportional representation of blacks in the city of Chicago, which is nearly 35 percent black, or in Detroit, which is nearly 50 percent black? And yet, this is what the present affirmative action suggests.

In communities and states where the black population is less than the general population, the black community and affirmative-action officials are arguing that representation should correspond with the general population, whereas in places where it exceeds the general percentage they are arguing for job representation that corresponds with the local population. This tactic must be corrected, because this overall pattern of hiring and promotion is even more unfair to whites. Furthermore, overall the black population is younger than the white population. The U.S. Riot Commission Report (1968) indicates that 45 percent of the black population are under age 18, as compared with 35 percent of the white population. About one out of every six children under age five is black and one out of every six new babies is black. This means it is still more unfair to claim jobs in proportion to the local or general black population, since a greater percentage of blacks than of whites are young and are not looking for full-time employment.

It must also be pointed out that job applicants are at no time required to identify themselves by race, color, or nationality. No such records should be maintained by an employer or institution, yet a few bureaucrats in the federal government are breaking the government's own laws to implement affirmative action.[e] The government may have the right to enforce affirmative action, but it also must prevent abuses in such programs. Federal officials, although they seem overzealous in pressuring institutions to comply with their *illegal* quotas, do not appear to be as interested in stopping and correcting the abuses that stem from these quotas. In *Hughes* v. *Superior* (1950) it was stated that racial quotas and discrimination against an individual are unconstitutional, and this has been repeatedly upheld by the Supreme Court. Individuals who claim discrimination as well as reverse discrimination should be permitted speedy grievance machinery. Seemingly, only claims of the former type are acted upon with any haste, especially since the Office of Civil Rights, the Equal Employment Opportunity Commission, the Office of Federal Contract Compliance, and the Department of Health, Education, and Welfare are administered mainly by the liberal-black community. In addition, affirmative-action officers at the federal government level and within individual institutions are usually members of minorities. Affirmative-action officials should be interested not only in seeing that employers comply with government regulations but also in stopping abuses brought about by government pressure and in acting upon complaints by individuals who feel injustice has been done by the policy of reverse discrimination.

In the final analysis, reverse discrimination is unconstitutional, just as any form of discrimination is unconstitutional. We can expect the legal skirmishes concerning quotas at the lower courts to eventually reach the U.S.

Supreme Court. What is objectionable is not so much preferential hiring within reasonable discretion, but rigid quotas that leave little room for maneuver, and in the end are bound to be a denial of equal opportunity. Furthermore, a group of invisible bureaucrats who were never voted into office by the people and who are not accountable to the voters, should not have the right to make regulations that have the effect of laws.

It is essential that the reader understand that the Revised Executive Orders No. 4 and 11246, which have brought about affirmative action, have been decreed and interpreted by a few middle-ranking bureaucrats in the Department of Labor and its derivative organization HEW, and HEW's offshoot organizations such as the Office of Civil Rights and the Equal Employment Opportunity Commission. In particular, three bureaucrats are instrumental in devising affirmative-action policies: William J. Kilberg, principal negotiator of the Labor Department's Office of Federal Contract Compliance; J. Stanley Pottinger, former director of the Office of Civil Rights; and William H. Brown III, chairman of the Equal Employment Opportunities Commission. While the original Executive Orders have constitutional precedence, pursuant to the Civil Rights Act of 1964, it is questionable if the revisions are constitutional; moreover, it is doubtful if the Act was ever intended to authorize a few middle-ranking bureaucrats and their field representatives to exercise power of life and death over say General Motors, Columbia University, the International Brotherhood of Electrical Workers, or the entire civil service: city, state, and federal.

Both OCR and EEOC officials are using guidelines set forth in a document dealing with construction companies in Philadelphia—where there were specific problems of hiring minorities—and have transferred the guidelines from one specific situation to just about all industries and institutions across the country. This is incredible. They have taken a plan which was devised for a relatively uneducated pool of people and have proclaimed that the same percentage of minorities must be available in other fields such as the university, medical and legal professions, industry, skilled unions, civil service, etc.—and if they are not available, standards must be lowered to meet appropriate body counts, and tests for jobs and admission into professional schools cannot be applied because they tend to be used to maintain standards.

Advocates of affirmative action try to tell the critics that "affirmative-action goals are usually arrived at through collaboration between government and private parties, while quotas are imposed arbitrarily upon the employer." If what is going on between government and the various institutions is "collaboration," then what will happen when duress is used? The fact is, schools, universities, businesses, unions, etc., are being bullied into compliance under the threat of court suits and loss of federal contracts and federal funds.

The most fascinating aspect of affirmative action is that the concept of what are reasonable goals and timetables continuously changes, thus putting the investigated institution always on the defensive and at the mercy of the whims of the overzealous bureaucrats who search for evidence. According to Senator James Buckley (1973) of New York and Seabury (1972a), these field bureaucrats may reject goals and timetables at any time, giving the institution 30-day notice for swift rectification, even though no charges of discrimination have been filed. Innocence must be quickly proven, or acceptable means of rectification devised. The findings are not based on qualitative available manpower figures, but rather on quantitative figures with the assumption that if the number of minorities does not correspond with population figures, the specific institution has practiced past discrimination (*New York Times,* September 23, 1973). That there are a limited number of minorities in certain jobs does not necessarily reflect the institution's past discrimination, but more accurately reflects the pool of available qualified minorities. (Again, if in 1972 there were only 1,500 black Ph.D.s in the country, how can we reasonably expect all the universities to employ their share of blacks?)

The bureaucrats claim the right to search for evidence and investigate personnel files. In the past, institutions have denied the FBI and other governmental agencies access to these files. Liberals have always argued that this form of investigation approaches totalitarianism, but with millions of dollars at stake either in lawsuits or in the loss of federal monies, administrators are now literally afraid to say no. Employees, workers, and faculty members remain silent, and the fear of being denounced as a "racist" pervades. While the country remains in an uproar over the ransacking of Watergate, the people are silent about the ransacking of personnel files where job classifications are grouped according to racial and sexual counts. Under the guise of justice, we have permitted an illegal policy—a reverse South African policy—to suddenly erupt where individuals are either visually identified by race or voluntarily fill out policy forms of racial designation.

In no way do affirmative-action officials use the terms quotas or reverse discrimination; rather they rely on timetables and goals. Therefore, they argue that the critics are wrong in charging that affirmative action is a quota system or a form of racism. HEW bureaucrats know that they will lose their case if they use a quota system or the notion that we can rectify past injustices toward innocent victims by present injustices toward innocent victims (Seabury 1972a). Nevertheless, the thurst of affirmative action and the fears of administrators in schools, universities, private industry, the unions, and civil service are real (and in part illustrated by the above letters and policy statements). The thrust of goals and timetables have the effect, if not the purpose, of strict quotas and reverse discrimination (Buckley 1973).

The absurdity of this policy is self-evident; it is worse than absurd, it is designed to accomplish a vicious, inherently discriminatory policy toward the majority populace. It mocks everything that the civil rights movement has sought to accomplish in the past; it applies one set of rules for one group and another set of rules for another group, it is based on a standard of advancement based on heredity and color, and it discriminates against many people who have had no part in discriminating in the past. The whole policy penalizes individual excellence and is based on rewarding and producing mediocrity.[f]

When we reflect on this trend, we realize that justice is not found by some mathematical formula, but rather on some more humble process in which people correct their prejudices and consider the rights of others. As Frankel (1973) asserts, some of us may think this new policy is just, but "we can be fairly sure that what we have found will only have a temporary validity" (p. 61). In the meantime, the silent majority should seriously consider becoming a little more active and vocal in voicing their complaints to their congressmen. If the people were given a chance to vote on affirmative action, it is highly probable that what it affirms would be overwhelmingly defeated. And, if people had the guts to throw body count compliance questionnaires in the waste paper basket and file counter lawsuits and injunctions against interpretations of the Revised Executive Orders, the laws that were originally designed to protect individual rights and due process might be reapplied. If people claimed they were of minority status, and let the institution make their own interpretations, just think of what might happen to affirmative action.[g]

Surely there is a need to deal with a greater sense of reality. Who is supposed to share the blame for past injustices, or for that matter can we accurately determine who should be penalized? What is the minority pool of skills and talents? How can it be increased? What is the present trade-off between increasing minority employment and decreasing efficiency? Are all women included in affirmative action, or does it mainly apply to minority women? Where do the benefits of civil rights enforcement begin to fall off and lead to abuses toward the majority population? When do the arbitrary interpretations of a few unelected bureaucrats become a matter for the people to check?

Community Action and Federal Spending: Who Benefits?

The War on Poverty and its various social and community action programs, was launched in 1964 under an umbrella agency called the Office of Economic Opportunity (OEO). The OEO started with a $1.5 billion (1963 fiscal year) budget and dispensed funds rapidly without any real knowledge or evidence that what it was doing made sense or would work to improve the conditions of the target population, the poor. As Glazer (1972a) and Green (1972a) point out, the object was to spend the money for purposes for which the Congress had appropriated it, regardless of whether the programs were plausible or viable. Officials felt obligated to spend all the money appropriated, down to the last penny. It was the expense-account syndrome: "You know your boss won't increase your expense allotment unless you spend every bit of this year's budget."

It was only later that people in Washington began to question the results of these programs. Eventually, there was a realization that no one really knew what kind of social and community programs would solve the ills of the cities. Lekachman (1972) and Moynihan (1969, 1972b) contend that these programs were no better administered than they were drafted and coordinated. Strategies were eratic rather than consistent, irrational rather than rational, unorganized rather than organized. Too often the programs fell into the hands of local ideologists and timeservers. In the end, most of the programs were dismal failures; the beneficiaries were not the poor, who received few benefits from them, but rather the new class of consultants and social-community action bureaucrats who dispensed services and were rewarded with high salaries. To be sure, the pressure to continue and expand these programs persists today. Indeed, big money was and is still at stake—and the money does not go to the poor.

Charles L. Schultze (1972) former director of Johnson's Bureau of the Budget, analyzed the domestic spending and Great Society programs in the Brookings Institute report, *Setting National Priorities.* He and his colleagues pointed out that domestic spending climbed during the Vietnam War. Between 1960 and 1965 the annual rate of increase was 5.8 percent; between 1965 and 1970 it was 9.1 percent; and between 1970 and 1973 it was 10.3 percent. Thus in the ten years between 1963 and 1973 the money for these programs had jumped from $1.5 billion to $35.7 billion. This made little impression on the liberal-black demands. They simply demanded more—and more—and continued to damn Johnson and then Nixon for "cutting" programs. As Schumpeter (1950) maintains, the technique and atmosphere of the struggle for social legislation often discard the truth.

The figures given above show that the war in Southeast Asia did not interfere with social spending, as many liberals claim. We were spending for both guns and butter. We paid for the war not by reducing domestic spending but by increasing the national deficit—from a huge $15 billion in 1968 to $23 billion in 1971—and by another $23 billion in 1972, which in turn resulted in increased inflation at the expense of the middle class who were also being taxed for these programs. Nixon's deficits in 1971 and 1972 were more the result of social spending than of spending for guns; the cost of the war in Vietnam dropped as the war was deescalated, from $11 billion in 1971 to $6.8 billion in 1972. Of course, there is the possibility that money was siphoned off which could have gone to other forms of social expenditures such as for urban mass transportation, larger health benefits, and to implement antipollution policies.

Some of the domestic programs became unpopular with local and federal government officials. The reasons were manifold: there was growing evidence that agitators were being trained and encouraged; there was widespread misappropriation and mismanagement of funds; and the exchange of input for output seemed wasted. These problems are elaborated below.

The liberal reformers who initiated these programs were naïve in many ways. Many were caught up in the romanticism of crusading for "have nots" and some vague notions they picked up in college in the 1940s and

1950s. Perhaps because of their good will, they refused to recognize that the people they were helping to organize in the communities would eventually turn against them; rather, they held on to the liberal ideas of what is now a bygone era, the days of the early civil rights movement when blacks and whites could work together. As the programs became associated with the poor and blacks of the inner cities, black leaders were recruited to "represent" the community, and eventually many of the programs became a breeding and training ground for black activists. The tactics of Alinsky which some of the liberals espoused and promoted in the early 1960s easily shifted into the black militant tactics of the mid-1960s, since their strategies were similar. The riots of the mid-1960s and the increase of violent crimes in the cities coincide with this shift in community leadership from the white liberals to the black activists.

Numerous mayors voiced their concern about the agitation stirred by community-action programs, also that their power or political "machine" was being threatened. It should be pointed out here that most of the mayors of the cities were Democrats, that the Congress was predominantly Democratic, and so was Mr. Johnson. When the cities began to erupt and the mayors complained, the Congress and the President began to lose enthusiasm for the War on Poverty.

As black violence grew in the cities in the mid-1960s, according to Blumenthal (1967) and Glazer (1972b), the connection between these community programs and the violence grew in the minds of many congressmen. The explosions in the cities made many officials doubt the programs were operating as they were intended. They questioned the use of mimeograph machines to turn out activist literature, what the funds were buying (guns or butter), and whether taxes should be used to employ agitators who trained other agitators. Moynihan (1969) analyzed Castro's method of solving juvenile delinquency in Cuba by giving machine guns to delinquents, and compared this to "the telescopic sights and mimeograph machines of the community action programs" (p. 163).

One might argue, however, that the programs helped alleviate the frustration of blacks and even contain the riots. By this logic, the programs may have served as a "payoff," to sedate vocal and potentially violent militant groups. In effect, the programs employed blacks to solve the "black problem," or at least contain it, but the black leaders' "solution" was to organize the black community and promote dissonance to keep their temporary jobs. If there were no disruptions, no "black problem," there would be no need for such jobs.

Moynihan (1973) put it this way: "To terminate the programs would have been to declass a whole cadre of persons, many of whom for the first time in their lives, had something to lose." Power in the community and money was at stake; they had won their status in the throes "of real or threatened violence." Faced with the possibility of losing it, they encouraged disruptions and riots—thus the violence turned from spontaneous to induced violence, "a wholly different situation" (p. 23). Ironically, many of the liberals, according to J. Wilson (1973), approved of the violence, rationalizing it as a stimulus to desirable social change.

Any cause-and-effect relationship between community action and the growing violence in the streets of the cities is debatable. Nevertheless, the leadership of these programs had changed from white to black, and Mayor Hugh J. Adonizzio charged that these programs urged blacks to arm themselves against whites in Newark (*New York Times*, July 24, October 4, 1967). When the riots broke out in Detroit and New Haven, which had liberal and distinguished mayors—Jerome P. Cavanagh in Detroit and Richard C. Lee in New Haven—the officials in Washington began to ask what was the goal of these community programs.

When the rioting abated, the ploy of "self-victimization" began to emanate from the ghettoes. Central to this tactic was the argument that exploitation and suffering were due to white "racism," and any white who questioned either the philosophy and tactics of blacks or reason for the riots, or who raised questions about the behavior or family structure of blacks, was denounced as a "racist." The "victim" strategy was and still is seductive in many aspects of social life. Used in connection with rioting, it permitted blacks a right, or excuse, to riot that other groups are denied; it permitted the liberal-black community to denounce almost any critic—a black as a "Tom" or a white as a "racist"—who questioned black rioting or other black social deviancy. As Moynihan (1969, 1972b) points out, when the riots broke out, the subjects of community action and family structure became associated with these events. But as the rioting subsided, the ploy of "victimization" emerged, and it became less and less possible to discuss all the issues related to rioting.

The "victim" strategy permitted blacks to do no wrong; moreover, it gave the liberal-black militant new rhetoric with which to gain momentum and drive objective criticism and rational dialogue out of discussions. Black violence, or the threat to use it, became a political tactic to be employed against so-called sick society. It was condoned as a legitimate and healthy form of behavior, a response to the frustration of ghetto life and white "racism." In the meantime, a host of other factors were and still are generally ignored; they include the strategy of rioting and the threat to use violence so as to create jobs (Cohn 1970; Moynihan 1969), the fun of rioting and looting (Banfield 1970), and the large percentage of black families headed by females in which the children, lacking a male authority figure, grow up prone to resist civil authority and commit delinquent and criminal acts (Glazer 1969b; Hacker 1970).

As blacks gained control of the social and community programs, there was also a struggle among them for power and financial control of these programs. The internal fighting has since subsided, and the theme of black unity and brotherhood has evolved. Although blacks now have their "heads together" to fight "the man," the charges of scandal continue even at the time of this writing. A few cases will illustrate the point. In Los Angeles, the

Times (June 13, 1965) reported that black leaders were not fighting the War on Poverty but were fighting among themselves over who was going to run the war. The OEO Watts program started with a fight over who were to be the "generals" and who the "privates." In Syracuse, it was reported by the *Post-Standard* (November 9, 1967) that once blacks gained control of the OEO Crusade for Opportunity, the program began training "provocateurs" and the reading manuals for functional illiterates pointed out the necessity of using force. The local NAACP charged the materials and philosophy were "geared for rioting." In addition, there was the scandal of $7 million out of $8 million spent on salaries and consultant fees for the program. In New York City, the *Times* (July 3, 1968) reported that Marshall England, president of HARYOU in central Harlem, requested a federal investigation of where the money was being directed; in turn, his life was threatened and he was warned to "stay out of the HARYOU office or . . . be killed." The struggle over anti-poverty funds in Harlem was recently summed up by Kenneth Clark (1973), the black psychologist, in an interview for the *New York Times.* He pointed out that Adam Clayton Powell, the congressman from Harlem, told him: "Ah, Kenneth, stop being a child. If you come along with me, we can split a million bucks" (p. 64). In the end Clark quit HARYOU and Powell won, because Powell had the political power.

To bring the reader up to date, there is the case of Ted Gross, New York City youth service commissioner, who could not account for thousands of dollars in airplane tickets to various parts of the country, a long list of bills for plush restaurants, large consultant fees to other black activists and "grass roots" agencies, and the fact that some of the "experts" on his payroll were getting double salaries by working full time in other social and community agencies such as the Human Relations Office and the Youth Board Research Institute (*New York Times*, November 12, 1972).

Then we learn that in Chicago, Alderman Fred Hubbard embezzled $100,000 of funds in his charge that were earmarked to help minorities obtain employment; he was convicted and sentenced to four months in prison. There are the federal and city audits that revealed that Charles G. Hurst, former president of Malcolm X College, was charged with serious misuse of federal funds and improper spending estimated at $1.38 million,[8] and with nepotism in the hiring of personnel as well as tax evasion (*Chicago Daily News,* January 30, 1973; *Chicago Sun-Times,* January 11, 1973). A follow-up news story revealed that Governor Richard Ogilvie secretly arranged for $1 million funding for Hurst's Educational Foundation to start a child-care center, just a few days before the governor left office in January 1973.[9] Hurst, it was reported by the *Chicago Daily News* (January 9, 1973), "was one of the state's few prominent black leaders to work vigorously for Ogilvie" during the 1972 gubernatorial campaign (p. 1). It was learned that in still another political deal with Ogilvie while he was governor, Hurst obtained $2.4 million to furnish Malcolm X College with showcase glass and other decorating materials.[10] In the end Hurst resigned, but claimed he was the victim of white "racism"—of both the "racist" government and the "racist" press.

The list of scandals is endless. But we must realize that white officials too have been guilty of corruption in the use of public funds—and involving more money. The difference is, today, blacks tend to have a monopoly on representing other blacks because color is now considered the main qualification for understanding the black experience and representing the black community. The so-called qualified and representatives of blacks are often "ripping off" other blacks, just as they criticize whites for having done the same to them. Moreover, a larger percentage of blacks than of whites may be engaged in such venality, perhaps because it is a new policy for so many to be involved in the management of public funds. As the Reverend Ralph Abernathy asserts, "Every black leader I see is trying to get rich himself and they are so full of trickery" (p. 1). Nevertheless, when blacks are charged with misuse or misappropriation of funds, we hear from them the standard cry of "racism," as voiced by Hurst. Indeed, race and "racism" have very little to do with this "rip off." The crux of the matter is the position and power to do it.

Elections to choose representatives for community programs made the concept of "maximum feasible participation" seem absurd, because they gave organized militants the opportunity to gain control of these programs. In 1967 the voting turnout was only 2.7 percent in Philadelphia, 0.7 percent in Los Angeles, 2.4 percent in Boston, 4.2 percent in Cleveland, and 5.0 percent in Kansas City, Missouri (*Wall Street Journal*, August 25, 1967). But by 1972 the turnout had increased to the point where the *New York Times* (July 30, 1972) was able to run a major news article pointing out that blacks were taking part in community program elections. There was a record turnout throughout New York City to elect board members of antipoverty programs. However, we learn that the biggest turnout in the 26-community area was for the election in the Williamsburg section of Brooklyn, which attracted twice as many people as the previous year and set a record in the city: 7 percent of the eligible voters. Black leaders spoke about the new sophistication of the voters, yet it is safe to assume that the voters, who had to elect 241 out of 750 candidates (as many as 50 candidates in one community), had little idea who most of the candidates were, or what philosophies and goals they espoused.

In school board elections in New York City and Detroit, where there is community control of the school systems, the concept of "maximum feasible participation" was replaced with the concept of "participatory democracy." Yet it is questionable whether the parents or community really participated. According to the *New York Times* (August 15, 1971), the election turnout for the first school board election in New York City was only 15 percent, and in some black areas (including Ocean Hill–Brownsville) it was as low as 5 percent. And this was only one year after the heat and emotion of the ten-week strike by Ocean Hill teachers. In several districts, white majorities were chosen to govern schools that were overwhelmingly black and Puerto

Rican. Most of the people who voted were members of organized groups affiliated with political clubs, antipoverty agencies, and churches. When the votes were counted, Shanker (1971) points out, the "parents and minority groups found themselves with less power in the school than ever before. Obviously, the advocates of community control had grossly exaggerated the size of the demand for participatory democracy" (p. 11).

The second school election was in 1973, when the *New York Times* (May 6, 1973) reported that the turnout of eligible voters was 10 percent, even though there was widespread campaigning, including widespread media coverage. Again, most of the people who voted were not parents, but instead represented organized groups. Indeed, Walter Degnan (1970), the head of New York City's Council of Supervisory Associations, seems to be accurate in this summary of the situation, at least of that in New York City: "The average citizen has neither the time nor inclination to engage in 'participatory democracy' on a permanent basis. . . . Community control is not being demanded by the average parent, whose attendance at school meetings averages about 1 percent" (p. 93).

In Detroit, the voting turnout for the first regional election was substantially higher than that in New York City, but largely white and conservative; thus only three blacks were elected to the 13-member central school board and blacks won a voting majority on only two out of the eight regional schools boards, even though a majority of the students were black in six out of the eight regions and the population of Detroit is close to 50 percent black (*Detroit Free Press*, November 7, 1970).

That federal spending on community programs has benefited small, organized groups more than it has the community as a whole is illustrated, for the New York City and Detroit schools, by recent events in both school systems. Black militants have managed to intimidate parents so that they are fearful of going to local school board meetings and have harassed and threatened school board members. There are even charges of assaults on board members and vandalism of property. This has resulted in a large number of resignations and the appointment (not the election) of additional blacks to local school boards. For example, in the first year alone, 32 out of 279 elected community school board members resigned in New York City. In Detroit in a two-year period between 1970 and 1972, 50 percent of the elected regional board members resigned in three out of the eight regions. In both cities, resignations have been from predominantly black school boards. These trends have changed the philosophical and ideological tone of many local boards, which have become organizations for black militants.

Recently Congresswoman Green (1972a) pointed out that the educational-poverty industry, geared to solving the country's ills, had proliferated by ill-defined and wasted programs and was characterized by fraud and misappropriation of money. Having conducted hearings on the appropriation of federal grants and contracts, she declared that, between 1966 and 1971, 82 percent of the grants in the Department of Health, Education, and Welfare (HEW) and 90 percent of those in the U.S. Office of Education (USOE) were awarded on a noncompetitive basis; thus, she concluded, we are witnessing the rise of the educational-poverty industry, in which the federal government is able to grant hundreds of millions, even billions, of dollars "in deals that are close to arrangements between friends" (p. 83).

In this connection, Ornstein (1968) contends that "little time or energy is spent on validating the various assumptions, or anticipating the numerous variables that will affect a program." The educational-poverty programs are "hurriedly put together to get the money while it is still available," and the programs generally fail and end up chiefly "in ambiguous and dismal outcomes" (p. 253). Green (1972a) maintains that officials spend the entire federal allotment in order to request additional funds for the next fiscal year. The result is mass confusion and allocation of billions of dollars at the end of the fiscal year without clear understanding of the programs. Thus in the fiscal year ending June 30, 1971, the number of final decisions on federal grants and contracts reached a peak of 1,049 in one week in mid-June; the month before the highest number for one week was 192, and two weeks after the mid-June rush the number decreased to 227. The mid-June deluge occurs every year, and results in the same confusion and great number of rapid transactions and the eventual annual waste of billions of dollars.

Green (1972a, 1972b) cites about 20 examples of questionable procedures: in each instance hundreds of thousands and even millions of dollars were awarded for enterprises that generated no worthwhile information, goals and procedures that were vague, research designs that were inadequate or missing when it was necessary to include them, promises that were made and never filled although the contractors were paid in full, programs that were doomed to failure from the outset because of bizarre concepts and erratic planning, and people who were paid high salaries and consultant fees for doing no work. In most instances, the final reports were missing; the programs were not evaluated, and these missing reports were accepted as routine. In effect, there was no way to learn whether the objectives of the programs were achieved or what had been the overall value of these programs. Despite audit reports of missappropriated funds amounting sometimes up to $1 million per program, the same people or firms often were given contracts again. Indeed, it appeared that certain people were destined to be funded, regardless of their ethics or expertise. Thus, Green (1972b) points out, educators and community activists are

> . . . busily at work . . . reaping profit from the nation's legitimate interest in education and welfare . . . enriching themselves at public expense through sizeable consulting fees, often for work of which there is no record at all . . . taking money for work not done, for studies not performed, for analysis not prepared, for results not produced . . . using funds for research projects that have turned out to be esoteric, irrelevant, and often not even research [pp. 12–13].

> In instance after instance, firms have asked for, and re-
> ceived, fees in addition to overhead charges, on the pre-
> text that these fees were necessary to stimulate corporate
> stability and growth. . . . Over and over, a project would
> be escalated into a bigger activity than originally pro-
> posed or planned, with vast additional funds being allo-
> cated by OE through a non-competitive, non-reviewed
> amendment procedure rather than through the normal
> process of funding approval [pp. 22–23].

And the *New York Times* (January 27, 1973) described the government funding in education and social welfare as having "a reputation for
scatter-gun approaches, slipshod work, poor results or no results at all." A
lot of ideas, some constructive and some not, came from special-interest
groups and special friends of grant officials, "but the general public's priorities
were never determined," nor was there any real attempt to try to determine
these priorities. The *Times* suggested that the atmosphere was one of giving
away money without expecting any real benefits (p. 14).

Most of these funds went to liberal reformers who had friends in
Washington, as well as to blacks who claimed they spoke for the black community. Many of the people who wrote up and ran these programs seemed to
have little regard for integrity; for liberals, the main object appeared to be
change for the sake of change; for the militants who often ended up "representing" the black community, the major goal seemed to be conflict for the
sake of conflict. Both groups often had one major objective: to get substantial sums from the federal government, at the expense of the client or target
group, who gained very little from these programs, and at the expense of the
taxpayer, who paid for the programs.

The point is, the shoe salesman in Boston, the tailor in Cleveland,
the cab driver in Minneapolis, and the divorced housewife in Los Angeles pay
the money so that the new bureaucrats who administer these programs can
get rich. These blue-collar workers earn considerably less than do the "reform" educators, social workers, and community activists; nevertheless, federal policy has unwittingly taken money from those who earn small wages and
transferred it to liberal-black advocates because they are supposed to be
"saving" the cities. Rather than being of help to the poor, the redistribution
of income, from the blue-collar worker to the professional educator and
activist, has been at the expense of the poor—in the name of humanity and
decency.

Even the former commissioner of education, Sidney Marland (1972),
admits (but in a less incriminating way) that the funding of educational and
social programs is in need of improvement. "I must say that prudent program
management does not always result in the best immediate circumstances for
the children whom the programs are supposed to serve." He further maintains
that in the past the programs have either not been evaluated at all, or the program directors themselves have been permitted to carry out the evaluations.
He continues "I must assume they [the directors] possessed a natural and

healthy bias in favor of their own enterprises" (p. 88). Furthermore, it is easy to fill final reports or evaluations with overzealous judgments and distorted or even false data. Ornstein (1972*b*) adds, "Very few directors of a program will jeopardize their chances for additional funds and admit their present program is a failure." Even the "outside evaluators are often reluctant to state the truth, because of fear of being blackballed by the directors" (pp. 64–65). Marland (1972) assures the people, however, that his office, the Office of Education (OE), was in the process of improving the grant procedures. The public is asked to believe that changes were being made before he left the office.

Concealment of data and denial of facts, especially as they relate to student achievement and spending, also have become increasingly evident in the liberal-black community in Washington and in the universities across the country. For example, James Coleman was commissioned in 1964 by the Johnson administration to conduct a two-year, nationwide study on the lack of equal educational opportunity for minorities, in order to arm the administration with a public relations bludgeon to overcome opposition to spending in the Congress. It was the largest educational research enterprise ever conducted, its report consisting of more than 1,300 pages including 750 pages of sophisticated statistics, to find out what was considered to be obvious. Halfway through the study, Coleman stated in an interview that he assumed his survey would show vast differences in quality between the schools attended by blacks and those attended by whites. "You know yourself," he said to an interviewer, "that the difference is going to be striking."

He was wrong! Coleman was "staggered," in the words of one of his associates, to find the lack of difference. On the basis of the results of surveying more than 600,000 children, 60,000 teachers, and 4,000 schools across the country, Coleman and his colleagues (1966) found that the schools surveyed were similar in terms of input (facilities, class size, curriculum, etc.). The one variable that showed a consistent relationship to student achievement was family characteristics. It accounted for more variation in achievement than did any other variable; furthermore, black schools and white schools were found to be quite similar. Nothing could have more flatly contradicted the assumptions of the liberal-black community and the consultants to President Johnson—yet local, state, and federal governments had been pouring big money into compensatory programs for urban schools, and have since the Coleman report increased such spending.

Federal government officials first tried to bury the report. When they found this to be impossible, the officials tried to play down the findings. The OE issued a summary report that at best can be described as misleading. "Nationally," it concluded, "Negroes have fewer of some facilities that seem most related to academic achievement." That was true, but among the differences cited by OE to prove its own point was, for example, that blacks had less access to chemistry labs than did whites; the difference was that 98 percent of the white schools, as compared with 94 percent of the black schools, had chemistry labs. That was hardly the type of difference which could explain that blacks started about six months behind whites in reading in the first grade and ended up 3½ years behind in the twelfth grade.

Coleman and many liberals emphasized that, of all the school characteristics, integration did seem to make some difference in student achievement, while they deemphasized the major role played by family characteristics. They ignored the fact that the achievement scores of whites attending integrated schools were 0.4 less than the scores of whites attending nonintegrated schools and the fact that there was a strong tendency for achievement scores to decline among students from homes in which no father is present. The temper of the times would not permit Coleman to discuss these findings. Also, it must be remembered that when the report appeared, black militancy was on the rise. In some quarters, Coleman and the liberals were denounced for the interpretation, "Mix blacks with other blacks and you get stupidity."

By the mid-1960s, one research document after another, by such prestigious educators as Benjamin Bloom, Martin Deutsch, Irwin Katz, Henry Levin, and Herbert Walberg, pointed out the importance of family characteristics while avoiding discussion of family disorganization. Anyone who attempted to pursue the latter subject was abused, as was Moynihan (1965) when he reported on *The Negro Family*. Anyone who mentioned the genetic component and its effect on IQ and learning, or gave it as a possible reason for the failure of compensatory education, marched into a fierce cross fire. For example, Jensen (1969) was denounced as a "racist" and reproved and harrassed by both the professional and lay public. Even Herrnstein (1971) was severely condemned as one of "Hitler's propagandists" for touching lightly on the racial implications of IQ and suggesting that there was some evidence of a genetic factor in mental group differences even though environment seemed to be the most important factor.

Social scientists soon learned that it was impossible to have a frank discussion and hear all sides on the topic of race or on any related issue, such as some of the possible reasons for the failure of compensatory and social programs. Thus, the advocates of social programs curtailed such discussion of family disorganization and genetics and successfully demanded more money to solve the nation's social ills. They were able to do so even though research document after research document showed that compensatory education had failed. Despite evidence contrary to their wisdom, most of the liberal-black community continues to advocate more spending. To question their wisdom—and spending—means at best to be indifferent to blacks and at worst to be denounced as "racist."

Even Jencks (1972), who could hardly be thought of as having conservative, much less racist, views, was denounced at Harvard as a tool of the "capitalist" and white "racist" system. Jencks, formerly liberal editor of the *New Republic* and now a radical member of the New Left Institute for Policy Studies in Washington, concluded in his comprehensive analysis of *Inequality* that special programs and the quality of the school make no difference, and that family characteristics make the most important difference. Although

Jencks's research pointed out that 45 percent of IQ is determined by genes (35 percent less than Jensen's conclusions), 35 percent by environment, and 20 percent by the covariance factor, he de-emphasized these data and went on to urge a social policy that leads to equality of results, since equality of opportunity would not benefit most disadvantaged groups.

The advocates of compensatory education, like the advocates of other social and community programs connected with the War on Poverty and with the Great Society, admitted that they had no real answers to what programs would work but claimed that more money was needed. Even Gordon and Wilkerson (1966), who were two of the prime leaders and more conservative black educators in the field of compensatory education, argued for increased spending despite their own findings. After surveying thousands of compensatory programs in 108 different communities across the country, they concluded that the programs were primarily "based on sentiment rather than on fact" (p. 158). No one knew what worked under what conditions and no one had "yet found the right answers," yet they argued, "we cannot afford to wait for better answers" (p. 179). More money was needed, they claimed, to the delight of those who would receive the grants and jobs associated with running these programs.

The main argument presented by its advocates for the failure of compensatory education was that not enough money had been appropriated to make an impact. Without any evidence, it was hypothesized by such distinguished educators as Charles Benson and J. Mcv. Hunt that possibly an extra $1,500 per child was needed before any significant changes in learning would occur. Gordon and Jablonsky (1968), after reviewing the failure of compensatory education, increased the figure to $2,500 per student for a ten-month period each year exclusive of capital investment.[11] This would amount to $75 billion per year for 30.4 million disadvantaged children. They maintained that, in addition, $600 per child was needed for a summer program and that $15 to $30 per week was needed for jobs for disadvantaged youth from 12 to 17 years of age. The total bill would be $101 billion; at 1973 prices the cost would be about $127 billion, or more than half the total national budget for fiscal year 1973.[12] And these figures do not include all the other children—the majority—who are also entitled to be educated.

A year later the Westinghouse–Ohio University (1969) report was published. Again many members of the liberal-black community in Washington first tried to withhold the findings of the study from the public and then, when this failed, proceeded to play down the findings. The report evaluated the Head Start program, which was the best-known program based on the compensatory or enrichment strategy and one of the few programs still considered a success by many reformers. The report concluded from the sample of children in 104 Head Start centers that there were no significant differences in learning between children in the Head Start program and those in a matched control group and that the program failed either to help disadvantaged learners catch up with their middle-class counterparts or to alleviate any of their cognitive deficiencies.

Coleman (1973) actually defends those governmental officials and their consultants who tried to mislead the public and withhold data. He does so on the grounds that social and humanitarian values must be considered in research and that these values are important factors for purposes of determining policy. He states:

> Dissemination of results is also influenced by the values
> of the client. . . . Deliberations over results of policy
> research often center on the strategy for passing legisla-
> tion. The transmission of results back into the real
> world of action must be consistent with political
> realities [p. 17].

In other words, Coleman implies that it is sometimes proper to bury the results of research if it impedes social legislation or, to take the matter one step further, if the results are sensitive.

According to Frost and Roland (1971), federal spending on schools grew nearly 900 percent between 1957 and 1967 and continued to increase into the 1970s, yet the increases failed to reduce educational failure in ghetto schools. Funding of other social and community programs aimed at solving the problem of poverty and at this and the other problems of the cities increased even more during this ten-year period. (Increases have continued up to 1973.)

Despite the spending, there have been few successful programs. The promising compensatory programs, as well as most of the other HEW, OEO, and OE programs such as teacher corps, child welfare, job corps, job assistance, and public housing, did not really succeed. By 1970, Robert H. Finch, then in charge of HEW, was telling Congress that the administration, under Mr. Nixon, had serious doubts about the effectiveness of these educational and social programs; and Finch was cautioning the Congress to go slow in funding such programs, partly because his department did not know how to spend the money wisely. The same year, President Nixon was speaking about holding the line on the spending of HEW, OEO, and OE funds in order to counteract inflation. Still the liberal-black community insisted on more money and that the war in Vietnam was no excuse for curtailing funds; they claimed that our priorities were warped.

Hence there was growing realization that no one really knew what educational and community programs would solve the nation's ills. This realization, in the face of established government organizations, growing financial scandals and community agitation, and increased deficit spending and subsequent inflation—coupled with a growing conservative mood in the country—eventually caused Nixon to cut some of these programs in his second term. Lekachman (1972) points out that people began to take a hard look at these programs and to compare the promises with the results. By the early 1970s some of the liberals, in their humble admission of the lack of benefits of many of these programs, had joined with conservatives.

The conservative tradition emphasized the inflexibility of human behavior, the persistence of class and racial differences, and the modesty of results reasonably to be expected from government efforts to ameliorate social conditions. By the time Nixon was ready to announce the program cuts in 1973, many of the liberal economists and even some of the sociologists of the New Frontier and Great Society were in agreement with the president. Many of these reformers were in exile, in such havens as the Brookings Institute in Washington and the Kennedy Institute at Harvard. They had discovered the limitations of most of the programs and reluctantly agreed with the conservative judgment that spending money did not seem to solve the poverty problem.

The Brookings study by Schultze and his associates (1972) is a confession, topic by topic, of liberal regrets. According to the authors, no person alive can say what program in schools and communities has been successful. Compensatory education, racial integration, community control, and the rest did not prove to be successful in helping poor or minority children. The housing experts admitted that urban renewal and public housing were disasters, turning old slums into new slums vexed by corrupt real estate agents, salesmen, and construction firms; the housing program had also caused more friction, between whites and blacks and between citizens and local government, than had been expected. Job training did not seem to help clients acquire skills or obtain and hold jobs. The welfare system was plagued by a growing number of recipients, many of whom were ineligible. Community action caused agitation and polarization in one city after another. Chapter by chapter, we learned about the failure of one program after another, some of which cost the taxpayers billions of dollars.

In January 1972 the Rand Corporation published a report by Averch and others (1972) about schools and other related programs in the educational-poverty industry. The analysis suggested that, with respect to school financing, we were already spending too much for what we were getting in return. The data indicated that nearly 70 percent of the operating expenses of schools were for salaries, and that any increase in spending on education would mainly go to teachers and administrators, not to the target group.[13] In the early stages of school and related compensatory programs, input increments had a high marginal return, but returns gradually diminished until they no longer equalled input and, finally, to the point where further input was wasted, since it brought virtually no output results. The study concluded that in many kinds of spending on education and poverty we had reached a "flat area": less output, or even worse, no output resulted from additional input. By the same token, neither did trying hard have any discernible effect. Yet, because of their interest in profit and group ideology, some people were still demanding more. As Moynihan (1972a) suggests, no matter how hard the government tried to produce more output, it could not, so the original prophecy about the indifference of the government or system became self-fulfilling and the posture of demanding more was never endangered.

Boulding (1971) presented the same thesis about education in a report to the American Educational Research Association, noting that extra input in school programs was not yielding more output. The point of maximum return had been passed long ago, and the possibility of increasing school productivity was highly questionable. Private industry operating in the same manner as did the school industry would have long since closed down because of the losses.

Drucker (1973a) makes the same point for all social programs: as a result of research evidence, no one really believed that government programs designed to cure the nation's ills were effective. Spending more money on these programs did not produce more results. There was little in the record to substantiate the bright beliefs of the early 1960s and the wisdom of the War on Poverty. All the bright hopes of Camelot failed to materialize. In a rejoinder to a critic, Drucker (1973b) went on to attack the people with vested interests in these programs, and the naïve people who had nothing but faith to support their claims that these programs could work. He further criticized those who argued that these programs failed because not enough money was spent. He claimed this was a red herring. There was no evidence that additional money would improve the outcome, but there was a strong indication that the money already spent had produced no appreciable results.

Here the reader might argue that the results have not been that dismal, but then he must remember that the promises made about the social programs were not modest but mammoth. When the programs began to fail, their advocates claimed they had underestimated the problem and asked for more money, which resulted, in almost every instance, in escalating costs for social programs with picayune results. Drucker (1973b) feels the only protection against this danger is to implement programs on a modest basis, to test them before expanding them, to define goals and priorities, to effectively coordinate activities, and to postpone making promises until the results are in. Indeed, more rhetoric is not going to improve the quality or results of these programs, but some hard work and ethical practices, as well as admission of some basic facts, might help.

Another factor to consider is that these programs were affected by the law of bureaucracy: organizations once formed try to maintain their existence and extend their influence over the external environment. Individuals and interested groups that gain from these organizations also try to maintain their position and extend their profit and power. Organizations are always changing; they either grow or decline. The idea is for the organization (human or social) to arrest the entropic process, that is, the universal process that leads to decline or death. The opposite of entropy is growth, and the most common type of growth is multiplication—a change in quantity rather than quality. Animal and plant species grow by multiplication; the social-community organizations, as well as the educational-poverty grant bureaucracies, attempted to add more programs of essentially the same types. The idea was to maintain some continuous inflow of energy, new money, new programs, so the various bureaucratic systems could grow and the various jobs created by this system of dispensing services could continue.

Moynihan (1972*b*) and Wattenberg and Scammon (1973) point out that blacks continued to put pressure on the government, exploiting white guilt feelings, attacking anything that might lead to a lessening sense of obligation, and denying the recent and significant progress made by blacks (except those whose families were headed by a woman) in almost all social and economic aspects of society.

Using 1970 census figures, Wattenberg and Scammon (1973) state that the percentage of black families earning about $10,000 has increased from 13 percent in 1961 to 30 percent in 1971; these figures are in 1971 dollars, meaning the effects of inflation have been taken into account. In addition, these figures do not take into consideration that half the number of blacks live in the South, and the median income for all groups living in the South in 1971 was $8,000. When they are adjusted accordingly, it can be seen that more than half (52 percent) of the black families in the United States are now economically members of the middle class, a fact confirmed within very close proximity by such black scholars as Hamilton (1970), Rustin (1973), and Sowell (1973).

The ratio of black family income to white family income was 53 percent in 1961 and 63 percent in 1971. Granted 63 percent is still low, but this gap cannot ignore recent progress in the last decade, nor the black-white differences in educational levels and family structure. For example, more than 30 percent of black families are headed by women compared to 9 percent of white families. If we omit these black families from our assessment, black and white income is more likely to approach parity, 73 percent on a nationwide basis and 88 percent outside the South. If we also match educational levels, Banfield (1970) points out, there is no difference between black and white income.

Referring to the 1971 census figures, the median income of black husband-wife families living outside the South where the head of the family is under 35 years old is 96 percent of that of a comparable white family. If we consider families where both spouses work, the income of the black family is 104 percent of that of its white counterpart; and for such families with the head of the family under 25 years old, the black income is 113 percent of the white income. These discrepancies favor blacks by about $1,000 annually when the earnings of 1972 college graduates are compared. These trends, compounded by new affirmative-action programs throughout the job sector, where goals and timetables are changing into quotas and reverse discrimination, should result in larger discrepancies between the incomes of young blacks and those of young whites. In fact, these income figures are already dated, because of the vast increase in black preferential job placements since the census was taken. The new and better jobs in unions and apprenticeships in skilled trades are going to blacks (Wattenberg and Scammon 1973), and the same trend is apparent in civil service (Glazer 1971), private business and industry (Seligman 1973), and in schools and universities (Seabury 1972*a*; Shanker 1972*a*).[14]

Along with higher incomes and better jobs, the number of years of schooling completed by blacks between the ages of 25 and 29 years has jumped from 8.6 years in 1950, to 10.8 in 1960, to 12.2 in 1970. In 1965, 10 percent of blacks between the ages of 18 and 24 were enrolled in college compared to 18 percent of whites. In only six years, the gap had decreased considerably. As many as 18 percent of this black population were enrolled in college, compared to 27 percent of the comparable white population. The most recent figures released by the U.S. Bureau of Labor Statistics (1973) show that, in 1972, 47.6 percent of the black high school graduates went to college, compared to 49.4 of white graduates. These figures are fascinating when we consider that the reading scores for black students in the twelfth grade are 3½ years below those of white students at the same grade level, and that the scholastic achievement test scores of blacks are nearly one standard deviation lower than those of their white counterparts entering college. The fact that the recent college-bound figures for blacks and whites are similar while there is such a wide discrepancy in reading and achievement scores connotes reverse discrimination (which the liberal-black community denies) and the transformation of equal opportunity to equal results (which the liberal-black community advocates). We might argue that the percentages of black and white high school graduates are misleading, since there is a larger proportion of high school dropouts among blacks than whites. This point is true but mainly invalidated, since quotas now informally guarantee a minimum number of positions in most colleges and universities to minority freshman students (Kilson 1973; *New York Times*, May 20, 1973). Although these trends may be considered surprising and good, we should at least be able to discuss these trends as well as their implications without excessive rhetoric.

By the most important standards (income and education), blacks have made impressive gains in the period between 1963 to 1973, and these gains should increase as quotas become a hardened fact in American life. These socio-economic trends are supported by and elaborated in a feature report by the *New York Times* (August 26, 1973), the first of a series of ten articles about improved conditions in black America. These facts are denied by most civil rights leaders in order to maintain the pressure for increased preferential treatment for minorities; moreover, many of these recent facts are unknown to most of the public. Yet it can be concluded that blacks under 35 are the ones who can look to a brighter future; the old generation of unskilled blacks, trapped by past discrimination, will not get the same breaks. As the older generation dies off, the whole pattern of black socio-economic life will improve. Where there are two-spouse families, blacks soon will probably surpass their white counterparts, given the recent census figures and the increasing quotas.

Yet these figures and trends alone do not tell the whole story. The illegitimacy rate among blacks in 1968 was 86.6 per 1,000 unmarried black women between the ages of 15 and 44 years, and 13.2 among the same white population (U.S. Brueau of Census 1971*a*). Another point is that the fertility rate among nonwhites (90 percent of whom are black) is 133.9 births per 1,000 women between the ages of 15 and 44, compared to 91.4 births for a similar white group, or a 1.46 black to white ratio (U.S. Riot Commission 1968). Still another point is that 30.1 percent of all black families were headed by a female in 1971, compared to 9.4 percent of white families (U.S. Bureau of the Census 1971*b*). Probing this last figure in more depth, we note a serious change in the structure of the black family. In 1950, 17.6 percent of black families were headed by females compared to 8.5 percent of white families. In 1960, the percent was 22.4 for blacks and 8.9 for whites. In 1970, it was 26.8 for blacks and 9.1 for whites. In 1971, it was 30.1 for blacks and 9.4 for whites. In other words, the number of black families headed by females increased 12.5 percent in 20 years to almost one-third.

Moynihan (1972*b*) shows that in gross terms the number of black families headed by males below the poverty level declined 49.4 percent between 1959 and 1968, while the number of black families headed by females below the poverty line increased 23.6 percent in the same time period. In fact, as many as 60 percent of the black families headed by women are poor. Similar trends are apparent when white families headed by men are compared with those headed by women, leading one to conclude that family structure, and not race, is probably the most important variable associated with poverty. Similarly, Wattenberg and Scammon (1973) show that the percentage of blacks living in poverty has declined from 48 percent in 1959 to 29 percent in 1971, even though the number of black families headed by women has increased during the same period. In the face of widening family differences between blacks and whites, one would expect a widening discrepancy of income between blacks and whites; however, the opposite is true, illustrating advances in the civil rights movement and education, as well as the growing reverse discrimination and preferential treatment for the black population.

In 1970, Andrew Brimmer, the black scholar who was then governor of the Federal Reserve System, said in a speech at Tuskegee Institute:

> During the 1960s, Negroes as a group *did* make significant economic progress. This can be seen in terms of higher employment and occupational upgrading as well as in lower unemployment and a narrowing of the income gap between Negroes and whites.

> However, beneath these overall improvements, another—and disturbing—trend is also evident: Within the Negro community, there appears to be a deepening schism between the able and the less able, between the well-prepared and those with few skills.

> This deepening schism can be traced in a number of ways, including the substantial rise in the proportion of Negroes employed in professional and technical jobs—while the

proportion in low-skilled occupations also edges upward; in the sizable decline in unemployment—while the share of Negroes among the long-term unemployed rises; in the persistence of inequality in income distribution within the black community—while a trend toward greater equality is evident among white families; above all in the dramatic deterioration in the position of Negro families headed by females.

In my judgment, this deepening schism within the black community should interest us as much as the real progress that has been made by Negroes as a group.

More recently, Michael J. Flax (1972) of the Urban Institute, using rates of change for nonwhites of various social variables for the 1960–1968 period, calculated when the levels for nonwhites might reach 1968 levels for whites. He concluded that within the 1970s, blacks would reach 1968 levels in almost all the categories. At the bottom of the scale were three variables related to family structure: percent of illegitimate births, percent of children living with two parents, and percent of female-headed families. For these three categories, the table entry reads, "Probably never."

When the liberal-black spokesmen start drawing comparisons between black and white groups, they usually overlook family characteristics: illegitimacy, fertility rates, and head of household. Rather they claim white "oppression" and "racism" are the causes for all the ills of blacks. If family differences are mentioned, there is a scholarly attempt to claim that one-parent families function better than two-parent families and that blacks compensate for their illegitimacy rates by absorbing most out-of-wedlock children into extended families rather than putting these children up for adoption. There is the concurrent claim that the weakness of the black family is a white "racist" myth and a tactic advanced by many whites to keep down blacks. When increasing welfare figures are mentioned, the liberal-black answer is that it is a good thing and shows the new recipients, who were eligible all the time, have at last been made aware of their rights. When recent statewide surveys showed that there are 50,000 ineligible persons on welfare in Illinois at an annual cost to the state of more than $50 million, these figures are more than doubled in New York State, rather than seeing this for the waste and fraud that it is, many liberals and blacks branded the surveys as evidence of white backlash.

These are the facts that are often denied, or rarely discussed by many liberals and blacks, and to bring them up means to risk the race relations name-calling game. This racial ploy is used to intimidate potential critics, while most of the liberal-black community continues to claim the black situation is worsening. These "reform" spokesmen refuse to see that, while it is worsening for one group of black families, it is rapidly improving for the majority of them, and it would be improving faster for all blacks if there was not such a schism within the black group. Thus has accumulated a literature of denial having as its general theme the claim that there is nothing wrong

with the structure of less able black families and that, if there is a problem, it
lies with the "racist" nature of white society.

While data of black advancement is denied by many who presumably know otherwise, the black man in the street is perfectly aware of the
gains made. For example, a Gallup poll taken in 1972 (*Time,* December 25, 1972) revealed that, whereas whites on a whole felt their opportunities had lessened in recent years, blacks said their situation was becoming
better and expected it to become still better. In fact, of the 31 subgroups
interviewed in the poll, only blacks had a positive view of their opportunities.
Most of the liberal-black community knows what has happened; so does the
man on the street. Both groups will acknowledge it in private and even anony-
mously; however, in public, they will continue the strategy of denial. As
Wattenberg and Scammon (1973) claim, this is a mistaken strategy; the
liberal-black community "who refuse to claim credit for the successes they
have earned only lend themselves to the purposes of those who declare the
bankruptcy of liberalism altogether as a political strategy" (p. 43).

Part of the liberal-black strategy is also to demonstrate and organize
against the dismantling of the service programs and their derivative social-
community organizations which the government has created to help the poor.
In reality, these programs do not help the poor, as evidenced by the worsening conditions of less able families; however, they do provide lucrative salaries
to the black bureaucrats who dispense the services. In short, many blacks
have employed several tactics to successfully maintain control over these programs and to extend their power through the multiplication of such programs.
These tactics include: shouting down opponents, presenting themselves as the
underdog, appealing to the American conscience to wipe out racism and poverty, using the threat of disruption, and claiming that they are the only ones
qualified to run the programs.

Senator Abraham Ribicoff, the former Secretary of HEW, indicated
in 1972 that there were some 170 antipoverty programs sponsored by federal
money at an annual cost of $35 billion. He noted that if one-third of the
money was directed at the poor, there would no longer be any poverty in the
nation (unless, of course, the poverty level was revised upward). Thirty-five
billion dollars is a lot of money, much more than most readers can conceive.
Most of it never went to the poor, but to the people who ran the poverty programs. The success of many blacks resulted from the fact that they demanded
and were given the jobs that went with providing services to the black poor,
just as they are now demanding the jobs that go with educating black students.
Thus there now exists great pressure to maintain these subsidies, not in the interest of the poor, but in the interest of the new middle-class bureaucrats who
administer the services. If we could consider only the interest of the poor, we
could eliminate most of these social-community programs and simply allot a
minimum amount of money to the less fortunate of America; however, the
black establishment wants the poor to be fed while those around them are
nourished, even "enriched."

The whole question of personal profit versus social betterment needs to be reexamined, as does the cost-effectiveness of government-funded social-community programs. According to Green (1972b), two central concepts evolve: "[1] inefficiency, confusion, waste, breakdown, and corruption . . . of the federal bureaucracy . . . and [2] private technocratic bureaucracy." What is needed is to assess the prices we are paying and the results we are getting. How richly are we to subsidize "individuals for their expertise" (and, if this author may add, for qualifications that are based on race)? How are we to identify the "parasites when they surface and how might we control their growth" (p. 25)?

Thus long before the 1972 Nixon landslide victory, there was growing evidence that the Johnson method, according to the *New York Times* (February 4, 1973, sec. 4), of "throwing money at problems" was not working and that people were becoming impatient with the War on Poverty and Great Society programs (p. 1). Having obtained a large mandate from the people, having noted the conservative mood of the country, Nixon was able to defer, reduce, or rescind funds for various social programs over the angry cries and demands of certain pressure groups and idealistic persons who claimed that more, not less, money was needed. According to the *Times* (January 30, February 4, 1973), Nixon listed over 100 social programs that were reduced or ended, including the community action, model cities, urban renewal, subsidized housing, and job corps programs.

President Nixon, in his 1973 budget message to Congress, stated that it was his intention to propose spending authority for both new programs and those programs enacted in previous years which were still being funded, with the intention of reducing the inflationary nature of deficit spending. Thus for the fiscal years 1973 and 1974, the federal budgets were proposed with zero deficits at full employment and programmed deficits of $24.8 billion and $12.7, respectively, given the high probability that the nation would not be at full employment before the end of fiscal year 1974. This is the interpretation one should place on the federal budget, as reported in the *U.S. Budget in Brief* (1973). The aim was to reduce the rate of increase of the budget such that, without taxes, the budget outlays and receipts would be equal if full employment and budget outlays increased in percentage terms no more rapidly than gross national product (GNP). With this background data, Nixon proposed a budget with expenditures of $250 billion in fiscal year 1973, an increase of $18 billion from the previous year, and $269 billion for fiscal year 1974, an increase of $19 billion. Despite the rhetoric, these outlays were the largest ever proposed in our history, a fact the critics conveniently overlook, and came when we were trying to combat inflation and keep the lid on increasing taxes.

At one level, the budget was a triumph of managerial efficiency, cutting or totally eliminating the funds for popular programs that, even according to the *New York Times* (February 4, 1973) had proven to be impractical, obsolete, riddled with mismanagement, self-defeating, and unsuccessful.

Nixon pointed out these programs had not worked, and in his budget message he claimed that these programs were "poorly conceived and hastily put together." At another level, however, the budget with its cuts in social welfare programs was proclaimed by liberals and blacks to be directed against the nation's poor.

It did not matter that these programs did not work; various interest groups (and a few other naïve individuals who are seemingly influenced by catchy slogans) were shocked and angered. They ignored the fact that Nixon had increased spending for Head Start, food stamps, civil rights legislation, loans to minority businessmen, implementation of new laws against discrimination, social security benefits, welfare payments, and unemployment insurance. They also ignored the fact that revenue sharing was actually geared to making up indirectly many of the cuts in direct federal spending for community action programs.

The new efforts to shift responsibility to local government might be perhaps considered "counterrevolutionary" if the cities were supposed to finance the programs. According to Banfield (1973), the 1974 budget proposes to give states and cities more federal aid than they received in previous years. The new revenue sharing may represent "a facing of the fact, obvious in the Johnson administration but not faced by it, that federal programs have become too many and too complex to be administered from Washington" (p. 34). Granted, it might take city governments one or two years to make appropriate adjustments, but in the meantime many of the community action programs can still be financed under specific grants. Some community action programs are threatened, true, but this is probably for the good, claims Glazer (1973), since they did not solve the problems of poverty and often encouraged antisocial behavior.

The fact is, it is difficult to determine exactly how the residents of poor communities benefited from most of the old programs. This does not really seem to be the major concern of most of the liberal-black community, especially the militants. They have managed to mobilize public opinion against program cutbacks by creating false impressions and demanding "reform." And as the rhetoric for "reform" continues, it is often those with the loudest voices, rather than those with the most compelling needs, who are heard. Despite the loudness and the shouting of demands, perhaps with revenue sharing some of the silent poor groups (which local governments are often more aware of than is the federal government) may finally get some money for community plans.

Conclusion

In the early 1960s, the liberals successfully advanced the War on Poverty and various social programs. Subsequently, local antipoverty and community groups entered into the political arena to advance their own special interests. Most of these groups were connected with the civil rights movement; but as the white liberals faded from the picture, the groups became more militant, more assured, and less willing to compromise and to work within the democratic process. In the mid-1960s, community control exploded in the New York City schools and the theoretical idea spread across the nation with full impact in Detroit. Again liberals espoused this new "wisdom"; and as black militants entered this movement, white teachers and administrators became the new casualties.

Both community action and community control are linked to the black power movement. Traditional democratic methods envisioned by early liberals in the War on Poverty and in the school arena were rejected by black militants because, they claimed, such methods had failed in the past. They argued that blacks had to organize themselves and exert their own power. Rather than work within the system, black militants regarded it as illegitimate so long as whites were involved in educating or providing services to blacks. One black caucus after another asserted that integration was no longer viable to the black community and that whites were no longer wanted in black schools and communities. Conflict and confrontation—boycotting, demonstrations, picketing, physical assault, and violence—became the main weapons of those advocating community control and community action programs. These programs survived with Nixon, but barely, and some people are finally beginning to admit that many social programs did not do what was promised, just as we are discovering that "participatory democracy" in the schools is neither participatory nor democracy.

Postscript

a. Despite the surplus of available candidates, the 1973 issues of the *Chronicle* bulge with more than 200 "position available" notices per issue. The norm is now to include the words "equal opportunity employer" and/or "affirmative-action employer." Minorities are specified to apply. Prior to 1970 this would connote a color-blind, nondiscriminatory practice; today, it means a color-consciousness, discriminatory practice in reverse. In one issue after another (e.g., June 4, October 1, October 15, November 5, November 12, 1973), the *Chronicle* reports that university professors across the country are unionizing to protect their jobs, and authors link this trend with affirmative-action policies and the overall employment trends. Qualified individuals without tenure find their jobs in jeopardy, and themselves unable to find employment elsewhere in their fields, in order to make room for individuals defined by the government as minority-group members.

   Perhaps one of the most enlightening issues of the *Chronicle* is the October 23, 1973 issue, where it is reported that black professors accuse middle-class white women as being aggressive and deflecting attention away from correcting racism. There are countercharges by white women that so few blacks have the formal credentials for faculty appointments, and those that are qualified (and even qualifiable) are immediately hired and able to command higher salaries than their white male or female counterparts because of supply and demand. In this connection (although not mentioned in the above controversy), some racial minorities are considered more "minority" than others; that is, preference is given to some minority groups in comparison to others also defined by the government for special consideration. The difference usually coincides with local political power and the minority background of local compliance officers.

b. In its Sunday Midwest employment section, the *Chicago Tribune* (December 2, 1972) reports a similar dispute taking place between blacks and white women in the business and industrial job sector. Racial minorities blame the women's movement for taking away their jobs, and white women are claiming that they lose out in the job market "because the hiring of minorities make companies look good." Both sides contend that the other group will profit more from affirmative action.

In the meantime, the 1973 winter issue of *Business and Society Review* indicates that minorities and women are being advanced to desirable jobs in corporations on a quota system, not on merit. Corporation executives sense backlash and low morale and warn against declining production. Jules Cohn, author of the *Review* article, maintains that unrealistic affirmative-action plans will add to employee frustration. The plans must be based on realistic manpower needs and available labor markets. Those who are not members of protected groups should have access to grievance procedures and promotions should be based on merit.

c. There is now new evidence of imposed racism attached to federal funding. School districts across the country which are in the process of applying for the Emergency School Assistance Act (ESAA) are required for the granting of funds to create an advisory committee composed of teachers, community or civic representatives, and parents. The creation of such a committee is not unusual, as Albert Shanker points out in the *New York Times* (November 25, 1973), but they are different in that they call for racial quotas with respect to committee membership and specifically to teacher representation. "Minority" representation is defined in accordance with HEW's own definition.

Rather than work at racial harmony, the U.S. Office of Education (an agency within HEW) is surveying 30,000 fourth and fifth grade students in 183 schools in 95 school districts receiving ESAA funds. The first question of the new "Elementary School Questionnaire" asks if the respondent is "Black" ... "White" ... or "Brown." Among the questions that follow are "How do you think your parents feel about Black and White students going to the school together?" "How do you think your teacher feels about Black and White students going to the same school together?" "Do you think Black students in this school cause more trouble than other kinds of students?" "Do you think White teachers in this school are unfair to students who are not White?" (Each of these questions are repeated with black-white, brown-white, and black-brown combinations.)

The USOE defends this questionnaire and also claims that if parents object, their children may be excused from answering the questions. This is a dishonest reply, since the students were surveyed in late 1973 with the accompanying directive that they answer them immediately. Moreover, HEW's action in stripping District 19 in New York of almost 1 million dollars for refusal to cooperate in its testing program, combined with the federal government's mandates on affirmative action which are tied to federal monies, makes the schools afraid to resist because of the possibility of losing much-needed funds.

d. In November 1973, the U.S. Supreme Court agreed to consider the *De Funis* case; this should have far reaching implications for college admission quotas. With a near "A" average and a *magna cum laude* graduate of the University of Washington, Du Funis applied to the School of Law in September 1971. He was rejected, but he discovered that 38 other applicants, all racial minorities with worse grades and lower Law School Admission Test (LSAT) scores were accepted. The University's rationale was that preferential treatment was being given to minority groups. The Washington Superior Court ruled in favor of De Funis, and he was admitted into law school. The University appealed to the State Supreme Court which reversed the decision, ruling that the law school had the right to consider race as a special factor in admitting minority students and acknowledging that more qualified white applicants would be displaced. In an angry dissent, James B. Wilson asserted: "Racial bigotry, prejudice, and intolerance will never be ended by exalting the political rights of one group or class over another . . . . The circle of inequality cannot be broken by shifting the inequities from one man to his neighbor." And if this author may add, the kind of reverse discrimination being urged by social reformers unjustly penalizes innocent individuals who bear no responsibility for historical wrongdoing. Furthermore, while most minorities are "disadvantaged," many are not, nor are all whites "advantaged." Power politics prevents us from making this distinction. If white women can claim victimization, why can't they claim it on standardized tests and college admissions? Why can't other groups who have suffered from discrimination claim the right of preferential treatment? Why can't white ethnics who speak in a foreign language at home claim that tests are biased against them? The perils of contagion are manifest. *The Chicago Daily News* (November 26, 1973) reports that the Polish American Committee claim discrimination in educational and employment opportunities and are filing charges with the EEOC.

    By lowering our college admission standards, we are bound to have a regression of standards downward to the mean. And as Martin Kilson asserts in the November 1973 issue of *Change* magazine and Thomas Sowell points out in *Black Education,* there is a double standard in grading blacks and whites in institutions of higher learning. This double standard predominates in *all* levels and areas of higher education, just as it predominates in nearly all sectors of the job market. Students quickly perceive the benefits of this new grading system, and it is bound to affect their self-esteem, not to mention the impact it has on students who graduate without favoritism. Thus, graduation does not guarantee equality of academic outcomes and professional competence. Those who benefit from the less rigorous testing scale often must compete on professional licensing examinations with those who were not favored. The NAACP, combined with black militant pressure and the politics of the courts, have either eliminated or watered down licensing standards and objective tests in city schools across the country. The *Griggs* court decision abolished job related examinations for blacks in all sectors of the economy.

At the present, a law suit has been filed by black law-school graduates which challenges the Michigan bar examination. In 1971, 71 percent of the white candidates and 17 percent of the black candidates passed the examination. The plaintiffs claim that the test is "culturally biased" against blacks. Similarly, the National Bar Association, composed of black lawyers, has called for the abolition of the bar examination in all states for the same reason.

The claim of cultural bias has become a successful ploy to eliminate standardized and competitive examinations in school and work. It is difficult to understand what is culturally biased about solving mathematical problems, reasoning in the abstract, writing a simple sentence in formal English, or being tested on subject matter that is related to one's professional specialty. In lieu of test scores for some racial minorities, college admission officers and job personnel officers now rely on a vague and more subjective criteria: personal qualities, such as "motivation," "maturity," and "potential."

e. A new federal regulation now requires that all federal, state, and city employees be coded by ethnic and racial origin for purposes of "research" and for "affecting decisions concerning personnel with respect to . . . recruitment, assignment, and promotion." The EEOC admits that its definition of "White," "Black," "Spanish surnamed," "Asian American," "American Indian," and "Other" are inconsistent with anthropoligical data, but it contends that the definitions and coded classifications are "now . . . necessary and appropriate." The Third Reich (and more recently South Africa) also claimed that it was compelled to implement governmental classifications of people according to its own definition of ethnic and racial origin.

f. A balance must be struck between groups who claim preferential treatment and the entitlements of individuals who belong to groups in our society who are not favored, nor permitted special privileges, nor provided with legal counsel and support of civil rights organizations and federal compliance agencies; these individuals are entitled to their rights and opportunities, too. While group interests today supersede individual rights, the concept of group rights is antithetical to the Constitution. If the nation is to prosper, individual merit, measured as objectively as possible, must be re-implemented. The past clearly shows that discrimination does not work, nor does it result in social harmony. A double standard in society, especially where the majority must suffer, cannot work for long and can lead to political upheaval.

g. There are no easy solutions to this problem. While efforts should be made to recruit and promote *qualified* people from diversified backgrounds, we must recognize that it is impossible to bestow instant competency on anybody. While special efforts should be made to identify qualified individuals of minority status, and other programs are needed to assist potentially qualifiable minorities to become qualified, essential prerequisites and criteria for diplomas and jobs cannot be dropped for an extended time without social repercussions and a decline in economic growth. Being unable to test for competency and ability because of the ploy of "cultural bias" is at best well meaningful and illogical, but in reality, highly political. Indeed, the present use of numerical goals vs. body counts is not the main issue; neither policy should be permitted to mask the growing danger of a *de facto* system of quotas or incompetency. Individuals need to write to their Congressmen in Washington stating their position in their own words; they need to place ads in newspapers to mobilize grass roots action campaigns; and organized groups need to bring the issue to the attention of the voting public, to seek a referendum, and to find out where candidates for office stand on the issue of reverse discrimination. While expanding educational and economic opportunities for individuals of *all* groups is a long-range goal, thus diminishing the intense competition for scarce existing opportunities, a short range goal includes a workable coalitional strategy that is multi-ethnic and bi-sexual.

In 1960, John Gardner, in his classic book on *Excellence,* raised the question whether a society can strive for equality and excellence. No society yet had solved it. The book, although widely read, did not have a major impact: Gardner had raised the question ten years too early. Today, it has become a crucial issue, with equality transforming into equal results imposed by goals or quotas (call it what you want, depending on your own politics). Indeed, there is tension between the ideal of equality and that of maintaining excellence. Slacken standards, and we are bound to get poorer quality. Limit one's definition of excellence to intellectual areas, and we limit the ideal of equality. But the more we eliminate or even diminish the importance of intellect, the greater the danger of decline and of stretching the tension wire that snaps society altogether.

Notes

1. A shocking example of the potential effect of this patronage system was the arrest of two school guards and another school aide during a 1973 robbery attempt; it was found that all three had criminal records and that one of them was a murderer out on parole. All three were hired by Community District 3; no screening device or civil service check was used, as was customary during the pre–community control period.

2. According to the Research Division of the National Education Association (NEA), teachers with negative views on accountability outnumber those with positive views by 11 to 1. Both the NEA and the American Federation of Teachers (AFT) have expressed reservations about accountability programs. The NEA view is that teachers must decide "matters that relate directly to teaching . . . and by what standards teachers shall be prepared, . . . retained, dismissed, certified, and given tenure" (NEA, 1970, p. 3). The NEA views the growing demands of accountability advocates as impinging on teachers' professionalism. David Selden (1972), the president of the AFT, strongly voices that "accountability offers ready teacher scapegoats to amateur and professional school-haters" and accountability advocates are approaching the idea "with all the insight of an irate viewer 'fixing' a television set: Give it a kick and see what happens" (p. 50).

3. According to Tyler (1970), changes can be largely due to chance variations and guessing because the test scores are based on a very small
   number of items. Klein (1971) indicates that changes in pre- and
   post-test scores may illustrate regression effects, where the lowest
   original scorers make the greatest gains and the higher original
   scorers make the least. And, to add another, similar dimension, raw
   scores on tests are translated into grade equivalents. According to
   Stake (1971), a range of three to eight items is sufficient to account
   for an improvement in one grade level placement, say from 5.0 to
   6.0, in most of the popular batteries now used in the schools. In
   other words, by chance variation, guessing, and regression effects
   (and without instruction), it is easy for low-scoring disadvantaged
   students to improve their scores on post-tests.

   Furthermore, accountability schemes require special performance
   tests that have not yet been developed. Typical achievement tests—
   called *norm-referenced* tests—provide relatively reliable and valid information regarding where the student stands in his test performance
   in relation to a large norm group. But such tests do not include a
   sufficient number of questions covering the material on which he
   was working to find out whether a student has mastered specific
   skills and concepts during the year or to hold someone accountable.
   Criterion-referenced tests can be constructed for the competencies
   to be learned, and thus we can include a much larger sample of appropriate questions. The trouble is, most of these types of tests are in
   the beginning stages of development, and questions concerning reliability and validity are only now being discussed in the literature
   (Ornstein and Talmage 1973a, 1973b).

4. Almost every, if not all, college and university has an affirmative-action
   plan. These institutions are mentioned only because I managed to
   obtain xeroxed copies of such letters.

5. The truth is, this person was unable to find a job at a university. In the
   meantime, the *Chicago Sun-Times* (September 4, 1973) points out
   that a black male who has not yet completed his dissertation for
   sociology has already received job offers from ten different universities with salaries ranging up to $20,000. This is comparable to what
   the average full professor (after say 15 years of university experience)
   makes at the average institution of higher learning.

6. Shephard (1972) indicates that in 1971, 79 out of 101 medical schools
   reported that admission requirements were being lowered to admit
   additional racial minorities; more women also were admitted into
   medical schools. Yet I would conjecture that the requirements for
   white women were similar to those for white males.

7. The Committee on Academic Nondiscrimination and Integrity (1972)
   cites a recent study by the Association of American Law Schools,
   reporting that all but 2 of 50 law schools surveyed indicate preferential treatment toward racial minorities.

   As an example of a medical school's effort to reach this new
   "goal," the *Village Voice* (August 31, 1972) indicates that the University of Illinois Medical School has reserved 60 out of 300 places
   in its incoming class for minorities. A similar example, of a law
   school, is Stanford University, which virtually guaranteed admission
   in 1972 to any minority student whose grade-point average was not

below that of the lowest-scoring Anglo in the 1971 class and whose Law School Admission Test score was within 50 points of that of the weakest student in the previous entering class.

By the time this book is published, these statistics will be outdated, and we can expect quotas on a nationwide basis to have snowballed and to be apparent even to many college students attempting to gain admission to professional schools even though they may not be aware of the term *affirmative action* and what it affirms.

8. Malcolm X College received more federal funds than does any other two-year educational institution, about $10 million a year between 1970 and 1973.

9. This was one of the two largest day-care awards in the history of Chicago; the other was slightly in excess of $1 million but was to a center that served twice as many children as did Hurst's.

10. This was the first time the state of Illinois approved a special appropriation to equip a local school. Obviously, Hurst wielded a great deal of influence in the black community, especially among the militants. The large federal and state funding has political ramifications.

11. Frost and Roland (1971) and Glickstein (1969) also reviewed the failure of several different types of compensatory education. Like Gordon and Jablonsky, they maintained that more money was needed to solve the problems of the education of poor and minority groups.

12. The unified budget for fiscal year 1973 shows federal outlays of $249.8 billion. See *U.S. Budget in Brief* (1973).

13. During the 1970–71 school year the average salary of teachers was $9,210, and in 1973 it surpassed $10,000, with some teachers making as high as $20,000. In a HEW study, Simon and Grant (1972) assert more than 60 percent of teachers are women. If a teacher is a married woman, family income is likely to be in the top 5 to 20 percentile of income distribution. It may be said that increasing educational expenditures will actually increase inequality. The same analysis applies to the poverty and community action programs. Almost 80 percent of the budget in these programs goes to pay the salaries, in the range of $15,000 to $30,000, of the people who administer the programs, thus also increasing inequality between the poor and the middle-class groups.

14. The statements of the respective authors are based on statistical data, not commentary. The widest inequity is purported by Wattenberg and Scammon who show that blacks hold 12 percent of union jobs and 20 percent of apprenticeship slots in skilled trades, although they represent only 11 percent of the total population.

References

Abernathy, Ralph
1973 News article in the *Chicago Tribune*, July 26, pp. 1, 10.
Abrams, Elliot
1972 "The Quota Commission." *Commentary*, October, pp. 54–57. Reprinted from *Commentary*, by permission; Copyright © 1972 by the American Jewish Committee.

Alsop, Joseph
    1967 "Ghetto Education." *New Republic*, November 18, pp. 18–23.
American Association of University Professors Bulletin (AAUP)
    1972 "Harvard University Report on Academic Tenure." March, pp.
        62–68.
Averch, Harvey A., et al.
    1972 *How Effective Is Schooling? A Critical Review and Synthesis of Re-
        search Findings.* Santa Monica, Ca.: Rand Corporation.
Badillo, Herman
    1967 Quote in the *New York Times*, October 8, p. 14.
Banfield, Edward C.
    1970 *The Unheavenly City.* Boston: Little, Brown.
    1973 "Nixon, the Great Society, and The Future of Social Policy: A Sym-
        posium." *Commentary*, May, pp. 31–34.
Banks, James A.
    1972a "Imperatives in Ethnic Minority Education." *Phi Delta Kappan* 53:
        266–69.
    1972b "Racial Prejudice and the Black Self-Concept." In *Black Self-
        Concept*, ed. J. A. Banks and J. D. Grambs, pp. 5–35. New York:
        McGraw-Hill.
Bard, Bernard
    1972 "The Battle for School Jobs: New York's Newest Agony." *Phi
        Delta Kappan* 53:553–58.
Bereiter, Carl, and Siegfried Englemann
    1966 *Teaching Disadvantaged Children in Pre-School.* Englewood Cliffs,
        N.J.: Prentice-Hall.
Billings, Charles E.
    1972 "Community Control and the Quest for Power." *Phi Delta Kappan*
        53:277–78.
Blauner, Robert
    1969 "International Colonialism and Ghetto Revolt." *Social Problems*
        16:393–408.
Blumenthal, Richard
    1967 "Community Action: The Origins of a Government Program."
        Senior thesis, Harvard University.
Boulding, Kenneth
    1971 "The School Industry as a Possible Pathological Economy."
        Paper presented at the Annual AERA Conference, New York,
        February.
Boyd, William L.
    1972 "Community Status and Conflict in Suburban School Politics."
        Paper presented at the Annual AERA Conference, Chicago, April.
Boyd, William L., and David W. O'Shea
    1972 "Community Stature, Political Culture, and the Character of Subur-
        ban Politics." Paper presented at the Annual AERA Conference,
        Chicago, April.
Brimmer, Andrew
    1970 "The Deepening Schism." Paper presented at Tuskegee University,
        Nashville, Tenn., April. Reprinted in part with permission of the
        author.
Brown, H. Rap
    1969 *Die Nigger Die!* New York: Dial Press.
Buckley, James
    1973 Statement in *Congressional Record.* May 22, pp. 1–5.

Carmichael, Stokely, and Charles V. Hamilton
1967 *Black Power*. Vintage ed. New York: Random House.
Chicago Daily News
October 9, 1972.
January 9, 1973.
January 30, 1973.
September 18, 1973.
Chicago Sun-Times
July 25, 1972.
January 11, 1973.
September 4, 1973.
Chicago Today
March 8, 1972.
Chicago Tribune
September 28, 1972.
September 20, 1973.
Chronicle of Higher Education
1972 Bimonthly issues, January–June.
Clark, Kenneth B.
1965 *Dark Ghetto*. New York: Harper & Row.
1968 "Alternative Public School Systems." *Harvard Educational Review*
38:100–13.
1972*a* *New York Times*, May 8, pp. 1, 26.
1972*b* Quote in the *New York Times*, December 3, p. 7. © 1972 by the
New York Times Company. Reprinted by permission.
1973 Interview with Walter Goodman, *New York Times Magazine*,
March 18.
Cohn, Jules
1970 "Is Business Meeting the Challenge of Urban Affairs?" *Harvard Business Review* 48:203–209.
Coleman, James S.
1973 "ER News." *Educational Researcher* 2:16–17.
Coleman, James S., et al.
1966 *Equality of Educational Opportunity*. Washington, D.C.: U.S. Gov-
ernment Printing Office.
Committee on Academic Nondiscrimination and Integrity
1972 *Statement for Immediate Release,* June 9.
Congressional Record
May 22, 1973.
Council on Supervisory Associations of the Public Schools of New York City
1968 "Response to the Lindsay-Bundy Proposals." Interim Report No. 2.
New York, January.
Degnan, Walter
1970 Quote in M. D. Fantini et al. *Community Control and the Urban
School*, p. 93. New York: Praeger.
Detroit Free Press
November 7, 1970.
March 26, 1972.
Detroit News
March 14, 1972.
March 29, 1972.
Doppelt, Jerome E., and George K. Bennett
1967 "Testing Job Applicants from Disadvantaged Groups." From the
Test Service Bulletin, No. 57 of The Psychological Corporation.

Drucker, Peter F.
 1973*a* "Can the Businessmen Meet Our Social Needs?" *Saturday Review*,
       March 17, pp. 41–44.
 1973*b* "Rejoinders." *Saturday Review*, March 17, pp. 48, 53.
Etzioni, Amitai
 1969 "The Fallacy of Decentralization." *Nation*, August 25, pp. 145–47.
Fantini, Mario D.
 1968 "Discussion: Implementing Equal Educational Opportunity."
       Harvard Educational Review 38:160–75.
Fantini, Mario D., Marilyn Gittell, and Richard Magat
 1970 *Community Control and the Urban School*. New York: Praeger.
Featherstone, Joseph
 1969 "The Problem Is More Than Schools." *New Republic*, August 30,
       pp. 20–23.
Feldman, Sandra
 1969 *The Burden of Blame-Placing*. New York: United Federation of
       Teachers.
Flax, Michael J.
 1972 Quote in D. P. Moynihan, "The Schism in Black America." *Public
       Interest*, Spring, p. 13.
Frankel, Charles
 1973 "The New Egalitarianism and The Old." *Commentary*, September,
       pp. 54–61.
Frost, Joe L., and G. T. Rowland
 1971 *Compensatory Programming*. Dubuque, Iowa: Wm. C. Brown.
Gittell, Marilyn
 1970 "Urban School Politics: Professionalism vs. Reform." *Journal of
       Social Issues* 26:69–84.
Glazer, Nathan
 1969*a* "Ethnic Group and Education: Towards the Tolerance of Differ-
       ence." *Journal of Negro Education* 38:187–95.
 1969*b* "For White and Black, Community Control Is the Issue." *New
       York Times Magazine*, April 27, pp. 36–37 ff.
 1971 "A Breakdown in Civil Rights Enforcement?" *Public Interest*,
       Spring, pp. 106–15.
 1972*a* "The Great Society Was Never a Casualty of the War." *Saturday
       Review*, November 18, pp. 49–52.
 1972*b* "When the Melting Pot Doesn't Melt." *New York Times Magazine*,
       January 2, pp. 12–13 ff.
 1973 "Nixon, the Great Society, and the Future of Social Policy: A Sym-
       posium." *Commentary*, May, pp. 34–39.
Glazer, Nathan, and Daniel P. Moynihan
 1970 *Beyond the Melting Pot*. 2d ed. Cambridge, Mass.: Massachusetts
       Institute of Technology Press.
Glickstein, Howard A.
 1969 "Federal Educational Programs and Minority Groups." *Journal of
       Negro Education* 38:303–14.
Goodman, Walter
 1972 "The Return of a Quota System." *New York Times Magazine*,
       September 10, pp. 29, 103–108.
Gordon, Edmund W., and Adelaide Jablonsky
 1968 "Compensatory Education in the Equalization of Educational
       Opportunity." *Journal of Negro Education* 37:280–90.

Gordon, Edmund W., and Doxey A. Wilkerson
1966 *Compensatory Education for the Disadvantaged.* New York: College
     Entrance Examination Board.
Grant, William R.
1971 "Community Control vs. School Integration—the Case of Detroit."
     United Teacher Magazine, November 7, pp. 1–4.
Green, Edith
1972a "Education's Federal Grab Bag," *Phi Delta Kappan* 54:83–86.
1972b "The Educational Entrepreneur—A Portrait." *Public Interest* (Sum-
     mer, pp. 12–25. Copyright © by National Affairs Inc., 1972.
Grobman, Hulda
1972 "Accountability for What: The Unanswered Question." *Nation's
     Schools* 89:65–68.
Hacker, Andrew
1970 *The End of the American Era.* New York: Antheneum.
Hamilton, Charles V.
1968 "Race and Education: A Search for Legitimacy." *Harvard Educa-
     tional Review* 38:669–84.
1970 "The Silent Black Majority." *New York Times Magazine,* May 10,
     pp. 25–26 ff.
Herrnstein, Richard J.
1971 "IQ." *Atlantic,* September, pp. 43–64.
Hollingshead, August B.
1949 *Elmtown's Youth.* New York: Wiley.
Hook, Sidney
1972 "Democracy and Genetic Variation." *Humanist,* March–April, p. 7.
Jencks, Christopher, et al.
1972 *Inequality: A Reassessment of the Effect of Family Schooling in
     America.* New York: Basic Books.
Jensen, Arthur R.
1969 "How Much Can We Boost IQ and Scholastic Achievement?" *Har-
     vard Educational Review* 39:1–123.
Katz, Irwin
1964 "Review of Evidence Relating to Effects of Desegregation on the
     Performance of Negroes." *American Psychologist* 19:381–99.
1968 "Factors Influencing Negro Performance in the Desegregated School."
     In *Social Class, Race, and Psychological Development,* ed. M. Deutsch,
     I. Katz, and A. R. Jensen, pp. 254–89. New York: Holt.
1969 "A Critique of Personality Approaches on Negro Performance, with
     Research Suggestions." *Journal of Social Issues* 25:13–27.
Kilson, Martin
1973 "The Black Experience at Harvard." *New York Times Magazine,*
     September 2, pp. 13, 31 ff.
King, Martin L., Jr.
1967 *Where Do We Go From Here: Chaos or Community?* New York:
     Bantam.
Klein, Stephen P.
1971 "The Uses and Limitations of Standardized Tests in Meeting the De-
     mands for Accountability." *UCLA Evaluation Comment* 2:1–7.
Krathwohl, David R.
1972 "Going Public: Researchers and School Output Accountability to
     Society." Paper presented at the Annual AERA Conference, Chicago,
     April.

Kristol, Irving
1968 "Decentralization for What?" *Public Interest*, Spring, pp. 17–25.
1970 "Is the Urban Crisis Real?" *Commentary*, November, pp. 44–47.

Kurtz, Paul
1972 "The Principle of Equality and Some Dogmas of Environmentalism." *Humanist*, March–April, pp. 4–6.

Ladner, Joyce
1967 "What 'Black Power' Means to Negroes in Mississippi." *Trans-action* 5:7–15.

Lekachman, Robert
1972 "400,000,000,000 Plus." *Saturday Review*, November 18, pp. 44–49.

Lesser, Gerald S., Gordon Fifer, and Donald H. Clark
1965 "Mental Abilities of Children from Different Social-Class and Cultural Groups." *Monographs of The Society for Research in Child Development* 30: No. 4.

Lester, Julius
1968 *Look Out Whitey: Black Power's Gon' Get Your Mama.* New York: Dial Press.

Levine, Irving M., and Judith Herman
1972 "Search for Identity in Blue Collar America." *Civil Rights Digest*, Winter, pp. 1–6.

Los Angeles Times
June 13, 1965

Lyke, Robert F.
1970 "Political Issues in School Decentralization." In *The Politics of Education at Local, State, and Federal Levels*, ed. Mr. Kirst, pp. 111–32. Berkeley, Ca.: McCutchan.

Marland, Sidney P., Jr.
1972 "A Responsible Stewardship." *Phi Delta Kappan* 54:87–88.

Mayer, Martin
1969 *The Teachers' Strike*. New York: Harper & Row.
1973 "Higher Education for All?" *Commentary*, February, pp. 37–47.

McGill, William J.
1972 News article in the *New York Times*, May 7, p. 12.

Michigan Chronicle
February 5, 1972.

Moseley, Francis S.
1972 "The Urban Secondary School: Too Late for Mere Change." *Phi Delta Kappan* 53:559–64.

Moynihan, Daniel P.
1965 *The Negro Family*. Washington, D.C.: U.S. Government Printing Office.
1969 *Maximum Feasible Misunderstanding*. New York: Free Press.
1972a "Equalizing Education in Whose Benefit?" *Public Interest,* Fall, pp. 68–89.
1972b "The Schism in Black America." *Public Interest*, Spring, pp. 3–24.
1973 "A Country in Need of Praise." *Saturday Review World*, September 9, pp. 20–23.

National Education Association, National Council for the Accreditation of Teacher Education
1970 "The Meaning of Accountability: A Working Paper." Mimeographed, November.

New York Times
   July 24, 1967.
   October 4, 1967.
   February 21, 1968.
   July 3, 1968.
   July 23, 1970.
   August 15, 1971.
   January 6, 1972.
   March 3, 1972.
   March 26, 1972.
   April 20, 1972.
   May 7, 1972.
   July 30, 1972.
   September 24, 1972.
   October 1, 1972.
   November 5, 1972.
   November 12, 1972.
   January 27, 1973.
   January 30, 1973.
   February 4, 1973.
   March 4, 1973.
   April 29, 1973.
   May 6, 1973.
   May 20, 1973.
   August 26, 1973.
   September 9, 1973.
   September 23, 1973
   September 28, 1973.
Nicolau, George
   1968 Speech made to the National Association for Community Develop-
        ment, Atlanta, Ga., April 8.
Ornstein, Allan C.
   1968 "Anxieties and Forces Which Mitigate Against Ghetto School
        Teachers." *Journal of Secondary Education* 43:243–54.
   1972a "Hum, Don't Shout." *Nation's Schools* 89:45.
   1972b *Urban Education: Student Unrest, Teacher Behaviors, and Black
        Power.* Columbus, Ohio: Merrill.
   1974 *Administrative Organization of Metropolitan Schools.* Metuchen,
        N.J.: Scarecrow Press.
Ornstein, Allan C., and Harriet Talmage
   1973a "A Dissenting View on Accountability." *Urban Education* 8:133–51.
   1973b "The Rhetoric and the Realities of Accountability." *Today's Edu-
        cation: Journal of the National Education Association* 62:70–80.
O'Shea, David W.
   1972 "The Structure of Political Processes in Suburban School District
        Government" Paper presented at the Annual AERA Conference,
        Chicago, April.
Rabb, Earl
   1972 "Quotas by Another Name." *Commentary*, January, pp. 41–45.
        Reprinted from *Commentary*, by permission; Copyright © 1972 by
        The American Jewish Committee.
Ravitch, Diane
   1973 "The Limits of Schooling." *Commentary*, February, pp. 86–90.
        Reprinted from *Commentary*, by permission; Copyright © 1972 by
        The American Jewish Committee.

Record, Wilson
   1973*a* "More Than a Matter of Color: Black Studies and White Sociolo-
      gists." Paper presented at the annual meeting of the American Soci-
      ological Association, New York, August.
   1973*b* "Some Implications of the Black Studies Movement for Higher
      Education in the 1970s." Paper presented at the Annual AERA
      Conference, New Orleans, February.
Redford Record
   January 10, 1972.
Roth, Rodney W.
   1970 "How Negro Fifth Grade Students View Black Pride Concepts."
      Integrated Education 8:24–27.
Rustin, Bayard
   1973 "Debate: Nixon, the Great Society, and the Future of Social Policy."
      Commentary, May, pp. 51–53.
Rustin, Bayard, ed.
   1969 *Black Studies: Myths and Realities.* New York: A. Phillip Randolph
      Educational Fund.
San Francisco Chronicle
   November 2, 1972.
Saturday Review
   1973 "Blackboard Battlegrounds: A Question of Survival." February 19,
      p. 74.
Schultze, Charles L., et al.
   1972 *Setting National Priorities: The 1973 Budget.* Washington, D.C.:
      Brookings Institute.
Schumpeter, Joseph A.
   1950 *Capitalism, Socialism, and Democracy.* New York: Harper & Row.
Seabury, Paul
   1972*a* "HEW and the Universities." *Commentary,* February, pp. 33–44.
      Reprinted from *Commentary,* by permission; Copyright © 1972 by
      The American Jewish Committee.
   1972*b* "The Idea of Merit." *Commentary,* December, pp. 41–46. Re-
      printed from *Commentary,* by permission; Copyright © 1972 by
      The American Jewish Committee
Selden, David
   1972 "Productivity, Yes. Accountability, No." *Nation's Schools* 89:
      50–51, 56.
Seligman, Daniel
   1973 "How 'Equal Opportunity' Turned Into Employment Quotas."
      Fortune, March, pp. 160–68.
Shanker, Albert
   1969 "The Real Meaning of the New York City Teachers' Strike." *Phi
      Delta Kappan* 50:434–41.
   1970 "Violence in the Schools." *New York Times,* December 27, sec. 4,
      p. 4.
   1971 "Decentralization II: The New York Experience." *New York Times,*
      August 15, sec. 4, p. 11.
   1972*a* "A Quarrel with Quotas." *New York Times,* July 16, sec. 4, p. 5.
      © 1972 by The New York Times Company. Reprinted by permission.
   1972*b* "School Decentralization: A Troubled Picture Emerges." *New
      York Times,* May 14, sec. 4, p. 9.
   1973*a* "Nixon's Minimum Wage Veto: A Blow to Education." *New York
      Times,* September 9, sec. 4, p. 11.

1973*b* "Patronage Threatens the School Once Again." *New York Times*,
March 4, sec. 4, p. 7.

Shepherd, Jack
1972 "Black Lab Power." *Saturday Review*, August 5, pp. 32–35 ff.

Sherman, Malcolm
1972 "Letter to the Editor." *Commentary*, June, pp. 30–32.

Simon, Kenneth A., and W. V. Grant
1972 *Digest of Educational Statistics, 1971.* Washington, D.C.: U.S. Department of Health, Education, and Welfare–National Center for
Educational Statistics.

Sizemore, Barbara A.
1972 "Is There a Case for Separate Schools?" *Phi Delta Kappan* 53:
281–84.

Sizer, Theodore R.
1968 "Report Analysis: Reconnection for Learning." *Harvard Educational Review* 38:176–84.

Skinner, B. F.
1963 "Operant Behavior." *American Psychologist* 18:503–15.

Smith, Donald
1972 "The Black Revolution and Education." In *Black Self-Concept*, ed.
J. A. Banks and J. D. Grambs, pp. 37–54. New York: McGraw-Hill.

Sowell, Thomas
1973 *Black Education: Myths and Tragedies.* New York: McKay.

Stake, Robert E.
1971 "Testing Hazards in Performance Contracting." *Phi Delta Kappan*
52:583–88.

Stone, Adolph
1969 "A Criticism of the New York Civil Liberties Union Report on the
Ocean Hill–Brownsville School Controversy." In *The Politics of
Urban Education*, ed. M. Gittell and G. Hevesi, pp. 352–62. New
York: Praeger.

Summaries of Regional Board Meetings Minutes. Detroit: Office of School
Decentralization, Board of Education of the City of Detroit, January 1971–
June 1972.

Syracuse Post-Standard
November 9, 1967.

Thelen, Herbert A.
1967 "Urban School Systems." *Phi Delta Kappan* 48:327–28.

Time 1972 "Split Views on America," December 25.

Tyler, Ralph W.
1970 "Testing for Accountability." *Nation's Schools* 86:37–39.

U.S. Budget in Brief: Fiscal Year 1974. Washington, D.C.: U.S. Government
Printing Office, 1973.

U.S. Bureau of the Census
1971*a* *Current Population Reports.* Series P–23 No. 36, April.
1971*b* *Current Population Reports.* Series P–23 No. 39, December.

U.S. Bureau of Labor Statistics
1971 *Employment and Earnings.* Washington, D.C.: U.S. Government
Printing Office.
1973 *Employment and Earnings.* Washington, D.C.: U.S. Government
Printing Office.

U.S. Commission on Civil Rights
1967 *Racial Isolation in the Public Schools.* Washington, D.C.: U.S. Government Printing Office.

1970 *Federal Civil Rights Enforcement Effort*. Washington, D.C.: U.S. Government Printing Office.

U.S. Riot Commission
1968 *Report of the National Advisory Commission on Civil Disorders*. Washington, D.C.: U.S. Government Printing Office.

Village Voice
August 31, 1972.

Wall Street Journal
August 25, 1967.

Ward, Susan H., and John Braun
1972 "Self-Esteem and Racial Preference in Black Children." *American Journal of Orthopsychiatry* 42:644–47.

Warner, W. Lloyd, Robert J. Havighurst, and Martin Loeb
1944 *Who Shall Be Educated?* New York: Harper & Row.

Wattenberg, Ben J., and Richard M. Scammon
1973 "Black Progress and Liberal Rhetoric." *Commentary*, April, pp. 35–44. Reprinted from *Commentary*, by permission; Copyright © 1973 by the American Jewish Committee.

Westinghouse Learning Corporation and Ohio University
1969 *The Impact of Head Start*. Preliminary Draft: An Evaluation of the Effects of Head Start Experience on Children's Cognitive and Affective Development. Washington, D.C.: Office of Economic Opportunity.

Wilson, Alan B.
1963 "Social Stratification and Academic Achievement." In *Education in Depressed Areas*, ed. A. H. Passow, pp. 217–35. New York: Teachers College Press, Columbia University.
1968 "Social Class and Equal Educational Opportunity." *Harvard Educational Review* 38:77–99.
1971 "Sociological Perspectives on the Development of Academic Competence in Urban Areas." In *Urban Education in the 1970's*, ed. A. H. Passow, pp. 120–40. New York: Teachers College Press, Columbia University.

Wilson, James Q.
1973 Quote in D. P. Moynihan, "A Country in Need of Praise." *Saturday Review World,* September 9, p. 23.

Wingate, Livingston L.
1967 Quote in *Education for the Disadvantaged*, ed. H. L. Miller, pp. 219–20. New York: Free Press.

Young, Whitney M., Jr.
1969 "Minorities and Community Control of the Schools." *Journal of Negro Education* 38:285–90.

Zirkel, Perry A.
1971 "Self-Concept and the Disadvantage of Ethnic Group Membership and Mixture." *Review of Educational Research* 41:211–25.

Zirkel, Perry A., and E. Gnanaraj Moses
1971 "Self-Concept and Ethnic Group Membership Among Public School Students." *American Educational Research Journal* 8:253–66.

chapter 3

Research on Administrative-Community School Plans

There is very little current research related to administrative decentralization and community control; most of the statements about these two concepts are based on unsupported evidence. This chapter first examines current approaches to, and limitations on, research related to these areas, then examines future research possibilities.

Research on Administrative Decentralization and Community Control

In the middle and late 1960s the racial climate in the large city schools and the pace of change related to administrative decentralization and community control made it difficult for social scientists to conduct research on these twin trends. There was a growing resentment on the part of school officials toward the wholesale and often overgeneralized criticism of the schools by novice teachers (Herbert Kohl, Johnathan Kozol, James Herndon, and Henry Resnik), liberal educators (Mario D. Fantini, Marilyn Gittell, William Hazard, and Henry M. Levin), and black militants (Charles V. Hamilton, Rhody McCoy, Barbara A. Sizemore, and Preston R. Wilcox). The problem was aggravated by the general lack of communication between the research community and the practitioner, as well as by the growing militancy of many blacks, who were becoming suspicious of and often rejecting the social scientist solely because he was white. For all of these reasons, very little empirical data is available on administrative decentralization and community control. There is, however, a wealth of expository literature on these two trends which has been previously

113

explored by other authors in highly subjective ways that reflect each individual author's personal biases and political ideologies.

The research that evolved, then, is "quasi" or "soft" in nature, and consists primarily of descriptions and reports based on relatively unreliable and invalid data. Two types of quasi research resulted. The first described the pathologies of the school bureaucracy and boards of education on the basis of personal recollections, observations, anecdotal data, interviews, and, in some instances, nonstandardized measurements. The second type of quasi research were policy reports written for a specific school system whereby a list of recommendations or legislative statements were outlined for changing the system. The methods employed in this latter type of quasi research include observations in the schools; interviews with consultants, school personnel, and community residents; and various committees, commissions, task force meetings, public hearings, community forums, and write-in suggestions. These policy reports often received wide coverage in local newspapers, and the ones for New York City received national attention.

Quasi research describing the school system

With regard to the descriptions of the school bureaucracy and school boards, Gittell and Hollander (1968) studied six urban school systems (Baltimore City, Chicago, Detroit, New York, Philadelphia, and St. Louis). Because the tests used in the various school systems were not comparable, the portrayals were mainly confined to individual school systems. What emerged from these individual descriptions was that the school systems lacked flexibility and innovation; moreover, they seemed unable to adapt their administrative organizations and programs to the needs of their minority populations. External agencies such as the federal government and foundations were prime forces in encouraging innovation. Too often, however, the programs were abandoned when funds ran out. With no real empirical data but only subjective reference to recent trends, these researchers concluded that innovation could be achieved only as a result of strong community participation.

Crain (1968), while reporting on the politics of school desegregation, analyzed eight school systems (Baltimore City, Buffalo, Newark, Pittsburgh, San Francisco, St. Louis, Bay City (somewhere in New England), and Lawndale (somewhere in the West).[1] The school boards fell into three general categories: (1) political appointees (Buffalo and Newark), (2) professionals and businessmen who were of high economic status (Baltimore City, Pittsburgh, and St. Louis), and (3) a mixture of political appointees and elected business and civic leaders (Bay City, Lawndale, and San Francisco). All attempted to represent racial and religious groups but for the most part were not associated with the lower classes. The politically appointed school boards tended to be the most conservative. The high status elites tended to be the most reform-oriented, suggesting that school board members who are economically secure are least threatened by change or demands from minority groups. The school boards on which both political and nonpolitical members served tended to be the least cohesive and least able to implement change.

In attempting to characterize the typical school board, Crain asserted that few such boards had an articulated educational policy: board members simply reacted to satisfy various complainants.

> The typical school board . . . can be thought of as making school policy only in a firefighting fashion. If an issue comes up, it acts; otherwise, it does not. It may not take a position at all on some of the most fundamental issues of school policy, simply because those particular policies have not been made salient by community discussion.
>
> The typical school board avoids issues that are not important for no other reason than to save time for issues that are. . . . The board then appears to be defending the status quo. By the time [a group] begins to make noise, [it] can rightly claim the school board has been ignoring the problem, and the school board begins to discuss the issue with one strike against it [p. 125].

Lipham, Gregg, and Rossmiller (1967) found that school board members in school systems of all sizes tended to avoid the responsibilities of their positions and seldom resolved conflicts in open meetings. The public and the professional staff in small and large districts were not in agreement about what they expected the school board to do; moreover, school board members were no more in agreement than they. Boards of education generally lacked an articulated school policy and had difficulty in coping with change; they generally engaged in uncritical acceptance and unthinking mirroring.

Individual school systems were also described. Schrag (1967) pointed out that the Boston school administrators and central office, out of touch with the communities, were still operating on the premises of another age when enrollments were largely white and middle class and on the once glorious reputation derived from an educational history that went back to Horace Mann and the common school movement. The author emphasized the inbreeding of the school system (showing its Irish ethnicity), its rigidity and conservative nature, its administrative authoritarianism, and the conformity of its lower-echelon administrators at the expense of innovation. According to Schrag, from the very top to the bottom of the administrative hierarchy, the Boston system was characterized by traditional practices, covert racism, bureaucratization, administrative patronizing of teachers, and the hostility of teachers toward their clientele.

Gittell's (1967) description of the New York City school system emphasized the insulation of the administrative organization from the public and the monopolizing power of the school board members, general superintendent, and the middle-management staff at the central office. She claimed there was a tendency for decisions to be made by an inside core of top personnel who were divorced not only from politics but from the local communities as well. The major factor contributing to this condition was the rise of bureaucracy and professionalism.

Rogers (1969) also analyzed the New York City school system and concluded it was a "sick" bureaucracy, whose operations subverted the goals and whose status quo philosophy prevented any flexible accommodation to the rising demands of minority groups. Among the symptoms cited were overcentralization, headquarters control over and suspicion of field administrators, upward conformity of anxious subordinates, limited communication and coordination of departments, inbreeding and insulation based on the policies of the board examiners, promotion of supervisors with a minimum of daring, paternalistic supervision of teachers, pressure within departments and units to conform to codes and protect one another, compulsive following and enforcing of rules, increasing administrative insulation from the communities, and the tendency to make decisions in committees so as to make it difficult to pinpoint individual responsibility.

Joseph Pois (1964), a Chicago school board member, noted the frustration fellow board members felt in dealing with an overwhelming number of problems compounded by a lack of time and resources, unawareness of community needs and of what was happening in the individual schools, an inert central administration, and a great many petty administrative problems. Most frustrating of all was the distorted and inadequate flow of information upon which decision making had to be based. Pois wrote:

> Manifestly, a board should avail itself of the factual ma-
> terial and viewpoints emanating from the general super-
> intendent and his subordinates. Yet, if this is the
> exclusive source of systematic inquiry and analysis con-
> cerning the school system, the board's decision-making
> must inevitably be determined in large measure by the
> attitudes and concepts of the bureaucracy. . . . The
> Chicago Board, when it does seek to tap the informational,
> statistical, and research resources of the school system, is
> ordinarily expected to use its general superintendent as the
> point of contact. Although this may be justified on the
> basis of protocol or recognition of lines of responsibility
> in the administrative hierarchy, the end result is that the
> flow of information is subject to screening, selection, or
> restatement by the general superintendent. As organiza-
> tions expand in size it becomes less tenable to contend
> that the chief administrative or executive officer should
> be the sole conduit for the transmittal of data or analysis
> to the governing body. . . . [Even a subordinate duly
> authorized to deal directly] with a board . . . will be prone
> to proceed with considerable caution lest he incur the dis-
> pleasure of his superior [pp. 88–89].

Seven years later, Jack Witkowsky (1971) told of his experience as a Chicago school board member from 1968 to 1970. He too emphasized the feeling of frustration of being caught up in "petty details of day-to-day operation of the schools," and of wasting time dealing with irrelevant and inconsequential issues. He wrote that the school board's meetings "were designed to minimize . . . effectiveness." At a typical meeting, the board would hear more than 100 items on the superintendent's agenda, most of them trivial; "members had little time or energy left to discuss their own suggestions about critical issues facing the school system." The school board was remote from the community. Only twice a year did it permit the public "to discuss current problems during its regular meetings" (p. 91).

The large size and bureaucratic structure of the Chicago system were also pointed out. The teachers reported to the school principal, who reported to the district superintendent, who reported to the area superintendent, who reported to the deputy superintendent, who reported to the school superintendent. Each administrator above the principal had his own office and staff of experts. Buck-passing became the norm. When a community group demanded action, low-level administrators would "frequently pass the buck up on the line until it [reached] someone so remote that he [could not] be subjected to community pressure." The system's large size made it difficult for school board members "to get the simplest information about the school system. No one knew, for instance, how much money was being spent at each school" (p. 92).

Similarly Elliot Shapiro, one of the present 32 community superintendents in New York City, was interviewed by Hentoff (1966) when he was a school principal in one of Harlem's elementary schools. Shapiro spoke about the lack of communication within the New York school system:

> . . . all the way up the chain of command in the school
> system were people with a vested interest in keeping the
> truth away from the person on the next rung up. By the
> time anything came to the top, conditions were reported
> as being fine [p. 39].

Quasi research related to school policy reports

The policy reports fall into three categories: (1) those written by educational prestigious groups or panels; (2) those prepared by consulting management firms; and (3) those written by in-house committees. The 15 largest school systems and several of the medium-sized school systems each have recently issued at least one policy report, and in many instances, several reports, on some form of administrative-community organization. The most noted of these are: for Washington, D.C., the Passow report (1967); concerning New York City, the Mayor's Advisory Panel report (1967), commonly referred to as the Bundy report, and the in-house reports *Proposed Plan for a Community School District System in New York* (1969) and *District Boundary Lines Under the Community School District System* (1969); in Chicago, the Havighurst report (1964), Booz-Allen & Hamilton report (1967), and the Commission on Urban Education (1971), commonly called the Peterson Commission report; in Los Angeles, the in-house report entitled *Educational Renewal* (1971); in Philadelphia, the in-house report entitled *A Multiple Option Approach to School-Community Participation* (1970); and in Detroit, the in-house reports *Working Draft of Possible Guidelines . . .* (1970) and *Public Reaction Draft of Decentralization Guidelines* (1970).

With the exception of the Passow report, the above policy reports are well known because of the size and related visibility of the respective cities and school systems. In effect, we are dealing with the five largest cities and school systems of the nation which, because of their size and consequent influence, receive wide coverage in the national news and educational literature. On the other hand, the Passow report is influential because of the author's affiliation with Columbia University and his general influence on the academic community and the field of urban education; likewise, the report concerns the school system of the nation's capital, a city having the largest percentage of blacks of any major city.

Viewing the above policy reports in relation to the three categories, the Passow and Havighurst reports were written by outside, prestigious educational groups: Passow is affiliated with Columbia Unversity; Havighurst, with the University of Chicago. Both professors are considered to be part of the educational establishment. They formed task forces to produce their reports, relying on some graduate students to gather information and employing a number of university staff members as consultants. Questionnaires were administered to students, teachers, and community leaders. Passow and Havighurst were responsible for the end product. Both reports called for system reform and recommended school decentralization and integration. Both reports saw the advantages of strong community participation, but rejected total community control.

The recommendations of the Passow report (1967) for the Washington, D.C., public schools were that:

1. The school system be divided into eight areas, each serving approximately 20,000 students.
2. Each area be headed by a community superintendent, appointed by the central office and responsible to the deputy superintendent in charge of community school coordination.
3. Community boards of education be elected by the voters from each area, and these boards advise the community superintendent and set policy not in conflict with the rules of the central board.[2]
4. Schools be transformed into community schools, open 12 to 14 hours a day, six days a week, and all year.
5. The metropolitan area work toward comprehensive educational planning to reduce racial isolation.

The Passow report legitimized the need for decentralization in Washington, D.C., and, according to Fantini, Gittell, and Magat (1970), planted the seed for the Adams-Morgan Community School District, an experimental program based on the concept of strong community participation.

The Havighurst report (1964), which dealt with the Chicago public schools, favored:

1. Placing decision-making authority in curriculum and instruction as close as possible to the individual schools and increasing the authority of the school principals.
2. Creating three regions:
   X with three districts comprising high achievement and college preparatory high schools and their feeding schools;
   Y with seven districts comprising middle-level achievement and comprehensive schools; and
   Z with four districts comprising low achievement, inner-city schools.
3. The creation of six districts organized to promote integration and community development.

In effect, Havighurst was urging homogeneous grouping. Based on realistic achievement scores, this policy would have reinforced existing socio-economic and racial segregation, in marked contrast to Havighurst's avowed philosophy. He claimed that the grouping of students according to common educational characteristics would lead to the best possible curricula and school program. He realized that he would be criticized for promoting segregation, but argued that grouping the low-achieving students usually found in the inner cities would highlight their problem, making it possible to increase funding in these schools. (At the time, compensatory education was considered a viable idea and not subject to failure, as it is today.) It is possible to hypothesize that Havighurst recognized that Chicago was (and still is) the most segregated city in the North and perhaps in the entire country,[3] and that mass integration would not be implemented by the school board, at least not without a court order; therefore, only the six pilot districts organized to promote integration would be tolerated at that time by the white citizenry.

Two additional documents fall under the scope of the first category of policy reports; they were issued by prestigious panels, actually political groups, from outside the system. These are the Mayor's Advisory Panel report on the New York City school system (Bundy report) and the Commission on Urban Education report on the Chicago system (Peterson Commission report). Both panels issued statements in favor of integration but noted that the possibilities were remote and thus proceeded to issue their strongest recommendations in favor of administrative decentralization and community control. The concept of control was advocated as an essential ingredient for promoting participatory democracy at the local level. In this suggestion, both panels showed the strong influence of white liberal educators and black militants.

The Bundy report is perhaps the most important document in promoting the concept of community control. In it the Mayor's Advisory Panel suggested that:

1. New York City schools be decentralized into 30 to 60 school districts comprising between 12,000 and 40,000 students each.
2. Community school boards have control over curriculum, personnel, and finances.
3. The city board of education retain limited powers, namely over student transfers, contract union negotiations, and school integration policies.
4. Community school districts have authority over the elementary and secondary schools.
5. The citywide school board and state commissioner of education be responsible for maintaining standards.
6. The community school districts be governed by local school boards selected in part by the mayor.

The panel members overwhelmingly represented the liberal-minority community. Liberals serving on the panel included McGeorge Bundy, the head of the committee, who was president of Ford Foundation and former dean of faculty at Harvard, as well as advisor to Presidents Kennedy and Johnson; Francis Keppel, president of General Learning Corporation and former U.S. Commissioner of Education; Mitchell Svirdoff, the director of the city's Human Resources Administration, the agency that coordinated the antipoverty services, and close advisor to Mayor Lindsay; and Mario D. Fantini, staff director for the study, who has since become noted as an outspoken critic of existing school systems and one favoring community control. Two panel members were minority leaders: Bennetta Washington, director of Women's Job Corps and wife of the first black mayor of Washington, D.C.; and Antonia Pantoja, social work professor and leader in the Puerto Rican community. One panel member, Alfred Giardino, who was a member of the city's school board, did not fit the liberal-minority description. Needless to say, he was the only panel member who voiced a dissenting opinion. Consultants included David Rogers and Marilyn Gittell, both liberal educators noted for their anti-school system views, and a number of black militants such as Roy Innis, head of Harlem Core and later of national Core; David Spencer, one of the prominent educators in Harlem's I.S. 201; and several people connected with the Ocean Hill-Brownsville district, as well as various antipoverty agencies. According to La Noue (1972), "Ideology and politics seem to have shaped most of its community control-oriented recommendations" (p. 13). In this connection, the black community used the report to help advance its ideological and political demands centering around control of the schools, which eventually led to the Ocean Hill-Brownsville controversy between the black community and the predominantly white teacher's union and supervisory association, and the subsequent racial polarization of the city. The report was also a key document used by state legislatures in enacting into law the 1969 Decentralization Act.

The Commission on Urban Education (1971) recommended that:

1. Legislation be enacted to implement administrative decentralization and community control in designated urban areas of the state of Illinois, including the city of Chicago.
2. Local boards be elected by members of the respective communities.
3. Community control be ensured in the areas of curriculum, personnel, student policy, and financing.
4. Teachers and administrators be evaluated and held accountable to the community, and that criteria be established for transfers.
5. A position of educational ombudsman be established to serve as a liaison between the central board and the local boards.

In connection with the above recommendations for community control, the influences of such consultants as the liberal William R. Hazard, associate dean of education at Northwestern University, and black militants such as Barbara A. Sizemore, former director of Chicago's Woodlawn Experimental School District; Calvert Smith, director of black studies at the University of Cincinnati and former member of the Chicago Center for Inner-City Studies; and Rhody McCoy, former unit director of the Ocean Hill–Brownsville district, were apparent. However, the black community failed to use the report in its bargaining for greater control of the Chicago schools. To some degree, this failure indicates the lack of unity existing among Chicago black militants at that time and the fact that many blacks were "bought off" in varying degrees by Mayor Daley's "political machine" with school-related jobs and favors; these black educators are now part of the power structure of the Chicago school system. Almost all of the principal and superintendent vacancies in ghetto areas have been filled by blacks.

The Illinois General Assembly was influenced by the 1971 Peterson Commission report and established (Senate Bill 805) in February 1972 a Department of Urban Education within the state's Office of the Superintendent of Public Instruction. The bill mandated numerous functions of the new department, including the development of a three-year experimental program in local school governance with financial grants to eight participating school districts with an average daily attendance of 20,000 or more students. This community control experiment was vetoed by the state legislature in 1972 for an indefinite period.

As for the second category of policy reports, only one of the aforementioned reports was written by an outside consulting and management firm, that is the Booz-Allen & Hamilton report (1967). In 1966 the Chicago school system commissioned the firm to survey the public schools and provide a plan for decentralization. In May of the following year, the company made recommendations that the board of education:

1. Retain responsibility for setting policy and deliberating major issues;
2. Establish three standing committees (facilities, finance, and community relations) to identify key issues and present them to the central board of education;
3. Divide the system into three areas, each headed by an area asso- ciate superintendent and retain the 27 districts (approximately 9 districts within each area), each headed by a district super- intendent;
4. Continue to permit the district superintendents to have direction over the schools within their boundaries and permit the new area associate superintendents to have direction over the districts within their boundaries, the latter to be accountable to the dep- uty superintendent at the central office.

Coinciding with the interests and background of this consultant firm, management and administrative efficiency was stressed rather than com- munity input. The Chicago Board of Education adopted the plan; authority and accountability continued to be directed upward to the central office.

The third type of policy report is the in-house report prepared by a committee organized by the school superintendent and the board of educa- tion. In the course of their work, members of such a committee usually inter- viewed hundreds of teachers, school administrators, community leaders, and, in Detroit and Los Angeles, even students. They attended hundreds of com- mittee and commission meetings, public hearings, and community forums. They prepared and submitted a proposed plan, which was followed by addi- tional public meetings, as well as by the receipt of thousands of write-in state- ments. They modified the plan and then submitted their final report.

In 1969 the New York State Legislature enacted into law a school bill which empowered the New York City Board of Education to establish between 30 and 35 community districts, each with its own elected commu- nity board, and each with at least 20,000 students in average daily attendance. The local school boards were to control the elementary and junior high schools within their boundaries. They were to have extensive powers in areas con- cerning personnel, curriculum, student policy, and allocation of finances. The high schools and special schools were to remain under the jurisdiction of the central board of education, and the central board was also to be in charge of school integration plans.

In accordance with the 1969 decentralization law, the five-member New York City Board of Education issued in November 1969 a tentative re- port entitled, *Proposed Plan for a Community School District System in New York.* The report established 30 community districts. "More than 80 percent of the [people queried] stated in effect, 'We do not want any change,' while the bulk of the remainder spoke in terms of relatively minor changes" (p. 5). Consequently the school board implemented minimal boundary changes, consistent with the new decentralization law.

The most heated issue centered around the three demonstration districts. The school board's report reiterated that the School Decentralization Law did not permit "the retention of the districts as community districts because of the requirement that 'no community district shall contain less than 20,000 pupils in average daily attendance' " (p. 6). Because the average daily absentee rate in the city schools exceeded 10 percent, to meet the average daily minimum of 20,000, "the minimum register of the . . . schools in the district must generally be more than 22,000" (p. 6). No one of the three demonstration districts contained even half the number.[4] It was agreed that each demonstration district should remain together; however, there was a split opinion on whether they should be merged with nearby schools to meet the minimum prescribed number of students in average daily attendance or should continue to operate as separate administrative units. Three of the five school board members believed they did not have the power under the new educational law to continue the existing demonstration projects; two felt they did.

Public hearings followed throughout the city, and hundreds of written statements were analyzed. The boundary plans were finalized a month later in December 1969 in a report called the *District Boundary Lines Under the Community School District System.* Although there were some requests to continue the demonstration districts, for reasons outlined in the tentative plan, the majority of the school board members still maintained that the School Decentralization Law did not permit such action. Thus the 8 controversial schools of Ocean Hill–Brownsville were merged with 14 additional schools to form District 23 with a total register of more than 25,000 students.[5] The 5 schools within the I. S. 201 complex were merged with 19 additional schools to form District 5 with 24,000 students. And in downtown Manhattan, the 5 schools in the Two Bridges area were merged with 18 schools to form District 3 with 22,000 students. Each of the three new districts contained more than the minimum number of students in average daily attendance. A total of 30 districts were formed, with the borough of Richmond comprising one separate district. In February 1970 District 5 was split into two Districts (5 and 6) to form 31 districts; in 1973 a 32nd district was formed. In addition, the high schools were formed into a separate District, 78, and the special schools were formed into still another District, 75, both run by the citywide board of education.

In Los Angeles, an in-house Decentralization Task Force was established by the superintendent of schools in November 1970. The members were appointed during the aftermath of the New York City racial disruptions over community control. Influenced by the events in New York City, the task force, in its report *Educational Renewal* (1971), rejected the concept of community control on the basis that it could "polarize and intensify all latent racial and potential conflicts throughout the city" (p. 28). The report listed 26 recommendations which can be condensed into the following:

1. Increasing the school principal's authority in planning curriculum, ordering textbooks, determining elective courses, and converting unfilled teacher positions to dollar equivalents to employ additional personnel.

2. Organizing school-community advisory committees for each school. Members would include teachers, parents, and students in secondary schools, to be coordinated by the school principal.

3. Dividing the school system into 13 administrative areas, each headed by an area superintendent.

4. Establishing three experimental areas located in different (white, black, Mexican-American) sections of the school system. The policies envisioned in these three areas would correspond with increasing community participation (not community control), and with emphasis on innovation and experimentation.

5. Reorganizing the system of electing central school board members to correspond with the 11 electoral districts in Los Angeles.

The recommendations of the Decentralization Task Force (whose members were selected by the superintendent) reflect the philosophy of the system. There was greater opportunity for community participation, but with little opportunity for community control. The orientation was toward administrative decentralization and increasing the powers of the school principal. In March 1971, the Los Angeles Board of Education basically adopted the first recommendations, as well as the third with a modification that 12 administrative areas be formed. Recommendation four was approved, but the state legislature did not grant the necessary funds. The school board vetoed the fifth recommendation, pointing out the main idea was to concentrate on improving education, not to enhance politics in education. In June 1971, the essence of the second recommendation was adopted, and the board of education mandated the establishment of advisory councils for each school to serve as a resource to the principal, who would remain responsible for the decisions.

The Philadelphia in-house committee on administrative decentralization also was organized at the height of the New York City issue over community control. The committee met throughout 1969 and early 1970 and eventually submitted, in July 1970, the document, *A Multiple Option Approach to School Community Participation* (1970). The policy report rejected the concept of community control and emphasized that the central school board "retain [its] powers . . . essential to the efficient operation of the schools" (p. iii). Three options for administrative decentralization and community participation were recommended.

Option I: Informal Community Participation.

1. Many communities may wish to retain their present relations with the schools. With this in mind, school-parental groups generally remain the same, but the principal and present school associations evolve different patterns of informal community participation in school affairs.
2. The principal may arrange for community participation and consult the school association in the areas of curriculum, personnel, and finance. However, decision making remains with the principal who is subject to the policies and regulations of the district superintendent and central board.
3. For certain positions, such as those of vice-principal, department head, and team leader, the principal may make selections from a pool of eligibles determined by the central board.

Option II: Advisory Participation Through an Elected Committee.

1. School communities may choose to have a school advisory committee or designate the school association to advise the principal and make recommendations concerning curriculum, personnel, and finances.
2. The school advisory committee or school association serves in a consulting capacity. Decision making is still with the principal who is accountable to the district superintendent and central board.
3. The principal makes the final selection of the various leadership positions from a pool of eligibles determined by the central board. The school advisory committee or school association may recommend candidates for principal from a pool of eligibles, but the final selection is based on the approval of the district superintendent and central board.

Option III: Shared Authority and Responsibility.

1. School communities may choose to have a school board or designate the school association to share decision-making authority in the areas of curriculum, personnel, and finances.
2. If a school board is elected, it should consist of nine elected adult members of the school community. At the secondary level, the school board should also consist of two students, bringing the total membership to eleven.
3. If the school association is designated, it should determine the organization of its body.
4. The school board or school association, after hearing the recommendations of the principal, has the authority to modify them

in the following areas: (a) courses in addition to required ones, (b) books, and (c) instructional materials and media.
5. The school board or school association has the right to (a) select the principal, from a pool of eligibles, so long as he is approved by the district superintendent and the central board, and (b) testify before the central board or state legislature for purposes of obtaining funds.

In general, all three options reject the idea of community control but encourage a limited and safe degree of community participation. Under Options I and II, the principal retains his power and is accountable to the district superintendent and central board; only under the second option does the community have the right to advise the principal. Under Option III, the principal is, to a limited extent, influenced by the school board or school association. However, he is still accountable to the district superintendent and central board. In all three plans, the central board retains its authority and power, although the commission recommended that the central board be elected rather than appointed.

In 1970, Public Act 244 (revised to Public Act 48) legally decentralized the Detroit schools into eight regions, implemented on January 1, 1971. In accordance with these acts, the Detroit Board of Education and its Office of School Decentralization published two in-house reports. The first report was the *Working Draft of Possible Guidelines . . .* (1970), which was released in two parts, the first in April and the second in May 1970. About 100 issues involving decisions that could be made by the central school board, by the affected regional school board, or by the central and regional boards together were identified. For each issue, the choice of authorities to whom decision-making power could be delegated was defined according to the law. In a few instances, only one choice was legal; however, in most instances, the law permitted any of these three possibilities.

As a result of a series of in-house and public meetings, as well as questionnaires, the decentralization guidelines were revised, and in August 1970 the Detroit School Board issued the *Public Reaction Draft of Decentralization Guidelines* (1970). This draft represented the majority or plurality viewpoint on all issues. These *Guidelines* recommended that:

1. The school system be divided into eight regions, each containing between 24 and 56 schools, governed by an elected regional board of education, and headed by a regional superintendent.
2. The regional school boards be granted board powers over curriculum, instruction staff organizational patterns, and in-service training, and that these boards share power with the central school board in such matters as special education, student policy, testing and evaluation, employment and promotion of personnel, contracting special funds, and school-community relations.

3 The central school board be expanded from 7 to 13 members, 5 to be elected on a citywide basis and the other 8 to be the chairmen of the 8 regional school boards.

4. The final decision on all questions related to interpretation of policies which may arise between the central and regional school boards be decided by the central board.

In October 1970, the Detroit Board of Education made some minor revisions and issued the guidelines under which the system now operates.

In summarizing, it should be noted that the above two research approaches were based on soft data. First, the research on the school bureaucracies and school boards was, for the greater part, action or field oriented (natural and uncontrolled). The data were based on personal recollections, observations, anecdotes, interviews, and nonstandardized measurement instruments. While such data sources may be considered legitimate by some educators, they are thought to be of dubious value by many members of the research community, especially because there were few, if any, established procedures for verifying the reliability and validity of the personal data, the observers, and the measurement instruments; minimizing the value judgments of the investigators; confirming the data objectively; and turning micro-data (or data from a limited sample size or setting) into macro-data (or generalizations concerning larger settings or even the entire school system). The lack of proper safeguards made the final product susceptible to the personal biases, ideologies, and politics of the investigators. Except for suggesting hypotheses or perhaps encouraging overgeneralized judgments about some phenomena of school bureaucracies and boards, the research had little value and yielded few, if any, valid generalizations and conclusions.

Second, the policy reports were based on intuition and logic and were motivated largely by political and racial pressure. There was often an attempt to assess the attitudes of community residents and representatives of social-action, political, and business groups, a procedure which can be useful for finding out which recommendations are the most expedient. However, from a strict research viewpoint, such a procedure is highly unreliable because it tends to introduce personal biases and political ideologies in place of valid proof of the educational worth of administrative decentralization or community control. (For example, will these two concepts, if implemented, improve the education of the students, and which students, if any?) All of the policy reports assumed or implied the merits of decentralization, but varied in their assessment of community control. In every one of these reports, there was no evidence of research to support the recommended policies. Decisions seemed to be based on circulated and unchallenged "wisdom," linked to the urgency for educational change—and on the demands of liberal educators and especially the black community. Pressure and politics seemed to be the key factors, not education per se.

Present and Future Research on Administrative Decentralization and Community Control

In 1970, Mario Fantini, one of the major proponents of decentralization and community control, criticized those who urged caution because there was a lack of empirical evidence. He wrote:

> The first question [of the skeptic] usually is: What evidence is there that neighborhood control of urban schools improves student achievement? The answer is that if there is no evidence it is because there really are no community-controlled urban public schools. . . . However, what we do have ample evidence of is the massive failure that the standard, centrally controlled urban school has produced. It is ironic, therefore, that those in control of a failing system should ask others offering constructive, democratically oriented alternatives to demand results before there has been any chance for full implementation [p. 514].

That same year, Clark (1970) reviewed the books on decentralization, using this term interchangeably with community control, and concluded that:

> What a considerable portion of the literature on decentralization to date amounts to is special pleading for a particular solution. . . . Very little attempt is made to develop ideas coherent enough to warrant the term "theory," and the casual use of favorable examples seldom justifies the label of empirical research. Where knowledge is incomplete but problems immediate . . . one can still expect generalizing intellectuals and amateur politicians to come forth with solutions [p. 509].
>
> . . . decentralization . . . may ameliorate some pressing problems. Such efforts can serve as useful vehicles for social as well as social-scientific experimentation. But unless there is more systematic social-scientific analysis of these efforts than we have generally had to date, we may never understand their many consequences [p. 514].

These two statements clearly reflect the different positions of the liberal reformer and the social scientist (researcher). The former may seek change for the sake of change, often without regard for research evidence. In contrast, the social scientist often opposes mass change without evidence. According to Robinson (1972), "this confrontation is by no means new; in fact, its very existence may be deemed a necessary requirement for a vital society." But like so many other differences, today it appears much sharper, and it seems that "there is heightened respect for change per se, quite apart from any presumption . . . of improvement" (p. 587). In the same vein, Ornstein (1973) recently pointed out that there appears to be a decline in the value placed on research, and the claim is voiced by those who do not understand research (including many lay people and educators) that researchers are elitists. And Maeroff (1973) also has pointed out that " 'tradition' has become a dirty word" in many circles. It's very important "not to run a popularity contest in education and pick up the latest fads." Educational experimentation, although important, is "not something to be accepted naturally, the way you would accept polio vaccine," unless the results and implications are seriously considered and weighed with regard to what is good for the students (p. 473).

The central fallacy of liberal educators is that their ideas are usually based on "bandwagon wisdom," with little research evidence; in fact, they often help create this "wisdom." In general, these educators are unscientific and antiresearch; they often plunge into implementation without knowledge that what they are doing really works[6]; they use fashionable terms and clichés and expect others to accept their "wisdom" on faith. It is more fun for liberal reformers to think up new programs and ideas than to try to implement them; in fact, many of these educators run from their programs and ideas just before the roof caves in. In this connection, Smith's (1973) view that "schools cannot be indifferent to change and innovation but must at the same time operate within some rational organizational framework" seems worth repeating. Change and innovative ideas flourish for a period; then they wither away and "move on to new schemes of regeneration." The advocates of change need to temper their so-called imperative needs and ideas with reasonable expectations of success. While we should always reexamine our practices and be ready to change them when necessary, "change must be based on something more substantial than the slogans, ideological zealotry, and utopian sentimentality" that all too often reflect the desire for change (p. 443). In this vein, Bosco and Robin (1972) advocate change based on testable and proven data. They write:

> ... the "know-nothing" approach to education betrays itself through the proliferation of an endless stream of slogans and folklore which seem to function in lieu of substantiated knowledge. . . .
>
> The argument that innovations can occur without a scientific base does not negate the possibility that advances are effectively developed through the application of scientific study. While impressive technologies have been developed by trial and error, such development is slow and uncertain . . . [and] blinds us to its costs. . . . In the realm of education the errors are made with human beings, and the use of science to reduce the error factor . . . may be posed as a moral imperative [pp. 7–8].

Granted the pace of school reform does not lead one to be optimistic, but it is questionable whether the schools can solve all the problems of society. Certainly there is no empirical evidence that administrative decentralization or community control will solve the problems of the schools. Without quality research we base our claims at best on "bandwagon wisdom," at worst on political ideology. Such considerations do not seem to bother the liberal reformer or the black militant, however. Thus Clark (1970) claims that much of the data on administrative-community plans has been formulated in terms of a debate or a specific position (for or against) with little research to support the claims. He points out that many proponents of administrative decentralization and community control, "including some of Athenian stature, operate from a number of questionable assumptions" (p. 513). Similarly, La Noue (1972) contends that many of the conclusions about decentralization and community control, "either stated or implied, seem unjustified in terms of proper evidence" (p. 25).

The problem is further compounded by the fact that most of the issues involved in administrative decentralization and community control are not primarily educational. Once we enter into community control, the underlying nuances are more closely related to race and ideology, politics and economics. As pointed out in chapter 1, the gut questions are: Which ethnic or racial group controls the schools? Who gets hired or promoted to administrative posts with salaries ranging up to $30,000 or $40,000? Which teachers and principals are hired and fired? Or, as Billings (1972) asks, which group obtains power to run the nation's largest school systems? Ornstein (1973) wrote:

> Decentralization and especially community control have been advocated as though success were certain. Yet arguments for the concepts have been based mainly on dubious hypotheses, half truths, logic, and intuition rather than research evidence. The stakes are high, of course, especially for the proponents and for those who stand to gain (or lose) jobs. [Given] the usual discrepancies between rhetoric and reason, as well between promise and reality, most advocates of community control . . . would prefer to limit outside evaluation, or at least control it so that the "findings" are known before the report is written [p. 613].

Lack of research, lack of comparable data, and lack of concrete evidence tend to work in favor of those who advocate change. They can more easily end up controlling the new policies and programs and reaping important political and economic advantages. As Campbell (1972) suggests, "There is safety under the cloak of ignorance. . . . If the political and administrative system has committed itself in advance to the correctness and efficacy of its reforms, it cannot tolerate learning of failure" (pp. 188–89). And Caro (1971) has pointed out that a substantial portion of the claims of minority activists and administrators are linked to their own political ambitions and demands for extensive control of programs and policies. "It is difficult for [them] to see tangible benefits stemming from social research. . . . The would-be-indigenous spokesman from the poor has reason to be anxious if his claims are challenged by respected social scientists" (p. 99). These observations apply particularly to the new administrative and school board group, to the advocates of community control. The new power group is still visible, and possibly heated controversy accompanied the change. It has few buffers to ward off criticism or dissipate the energies of the critics, since the new political and administrative machinery has not yet matured.

Rossi (1972) says, "Research might find that the effects are negligible or nonexistent" (p. 227). In fact, if we set up controls for the possible Hawthorne effect, this probably would happen. New educational programs usually produce insignificant results or minimal changes because there are several other variables associated with school success over which the schools themselves have little control. (For example, there is a substantial body of research that shows that family characteristics make the major difference in student achievement.)[7]   As Guba (1969) suggests:

> Over and over, comparative studies of alternatives in edu-
> cation have ended in a finding of "no significant difference."
> . . . It is often observed that the educationalists are inca-
> pable of devising any approaches that are better than those
> things that they are already using. But, if this is so, we
> ought perhaps to applaud their remarkable consistency,
> since they do not devise alternatives that are any worse
> either [p. 31].

One might argue, then, that a new program need only to show no difference in student achievement to be considered legitimate. This is debatable. When advocating change, Guba and Rossi separately contend that the new program should demonstrate that it has a positive effect. But it is possible that the research will demonstrate a negative effect on student achievement, as in the case of New York's Ocean Hill–Brownsville District (and more recently the entire New York City and Detroit school systems).[8] Without research, Bosco and Robin (1972) contend, slogans and clichés "protect themselves from attack by their circularity or by their untestable nature" (p. 8). The argument that research or evaluation is unnecessary may or may not be true, but it is an argument used for maintaining ignorance and utilizing slogans and clichés. Ornstein (1973) points out that, without research, claims based on unsupported evidence can continue to be voiced, and testimonials from the advocates of change and ideology can always be found. So long as there is no adequate research related to decentralization and community control, the bite of the opponents' criticism is reduced. Moreover, opponents are put on the defensive, criticized for resisting change, and branded as pro-Establishment and status quo.

This, indeed, is exactly what happened in the Ocean Hill–Brownsville District according to Ravitch (1972). The advocates of community control claimed favorable changes: that "Ocean Hill had already achieved academic success"; innovative methods had "succeeded in raising the reading levels of many children in the districts in a remarkably short time"; by February 1, 1970, "every youngster in that school system [would] be classified as a reader" (p. 71). The opponents could only claim that there was no available statistical data, since "it [Ocean Hill-Brownsville] was the only district in the city which had not participated in the standardized citywide reading tests" (p. 72). The eventual comparison of reading scores showed the experiment to be a failure; nevertheless, the New York City school system was pressured into a citywide policy that provides for a strong measure of community control.

If a school system initiates an across-the-board change, such as community control, without evidence that this change will have positive effects on learning, such action is not only educationally unsound and irresponsible, but also suggests that education is not the real issue. As Bard (1972; concerning New York City), Aberbach and Walker (1971; concerning Detroit), and La Noue (1972; concerning both cities) suggest, the real issues of community control were political and economic, and the pressures behind the changes were racial and ideological. If the changes in the two cities of New York and Detroit prove to have a negative impact on the students, return to the former unitary school system will be difficult—actually, with the present racial situation, nearly impossible. Once a group gains power, it is unwilling to surrender it, despite the general harm it may perpetuate. Only in a school system where racial tension is minimal or nonexistent, as in the Clark County schools in Las Vegas, Nevada, can there be change from centralization to decentralization, then a return to centralization.

While blacks and whites draw farther apart in the cities and compete for political power and diminishing jobs, educators must work for depolarization on social issues such as education. Although this may sound impractical or utopian, there is no alternative. New bridges must be built between blacks and whites in order to promote quality education and equal educational opportunity for *all* children. If new understandings can be built, then research on decentralization and community control can proceed. But if the battle over community control continues, and if education continues to be discussed in terms of ideology, then little viable research on these twin concepts will be forthcoming.

As educators, we must seek political stances that permit legitimate research. We must advocate, according to Campbell (1972), "the importance of the problem rather than the importance of the results" (p. 219). To support our claims with evidence, we must be able to experiment and conduct evaluative research. We should advocate change that improves education and conduct research to support that change without the political excess that blinds us to the reality of results or the refusal to admit that a specific change has no effect, or even a negative effect, on student achievement. If, on the other hand, we are committed to change because of politics and economics, and not because of educational benefits that can be proved, then there is good reason for maintaining ignorance, preventing research, screening the research, or slanting the findings.

What kind of research in urban schools is feasible and potentially useful? The need is to implement pilot programs, with randomized and controlled comparisons. Not only ought we to conduct rigorous testing in the initial pilot program, but once it has been decided that reform is to be adopted as standardized practice throughout the system, we ought also to evaluate it in each of its stages. Data from such testing should tentatively validate or invalidate our hypotheses. The findings should be replicated in similar settings; however, it is misleading to take the results of one or even a few experiments as conclusive evidence. There are no typical cities, no typical communities, no typical decentralization plans, no typical community control plans.

Large samples should be used in identifying the multiple facets of administrative decentralization and community control. Recent research (Halinski and Feldt 1970) suggests that there should be at least 20 subjects for each variable being assessed. A single equation with five variables, therefore, requires at least 100 school districts; a model with ten variables requires 200. Without these appropriate sample sizes, unlimited generalizations should not be made.

To obtain a large sample, it may be advisable to perform a comparative cross-sectional analysis of several school systems. In such an analysis, considerable variability among the school systems should be expected; consistency of the parameters in the prediction equations will be a major concern (Hickrod 1971) and may also lead to false generalizations unless properly controlled.

Longitudinal studies for about five to ten years would supply a wealth of data, but are complicated by the fact that there are many kinds of change measurements. If because of politics and pressure we cannot wait that long to obtain longitudinal data, this type of study might be conducted in conjunction with the case study approach for one or more school systems, with tentative findings being disseminated every year. Regardless of the type of research, it would be advantageous to extend the logic and techniques of experimental (laboratory) research to action-oriented (field) research. Here the general aim is to conduct "true experiments" by considering threats to internal and external validity. When checking for internal validity, the investigator should ask: Did the independent variables (treatment or experimental variables, often represented by the symbol X) really produce a change in the dependent variable (criterion or predicted variable, often represented by the symbol Y), or what did account for the results? When checking for external validity, the investigator should ask: What relevance do the findings have beyond the confines of the experiment? To what extent can generalizations of the results be extended to other settings, other independent variables, other measures of effect?

The aim of the investigator is to eliminate as many as possible of the problems associated with internal and external validity through well-designed experiments that include, where possible, random control groups. Where randomized treatments are not possible, a critical use of experimental designs is still possible. Because education is a process involving a number of variables interacting simultaneously to form an effect, the investigator should also think of conducting experiments that include factorial designs and multi-variate analysis. Doing so would enable him to answer such questions as: What is the main effect of each of the independent variables that account for the results? What is the interaction effect, if any, of the independent variables on the results? Of course, it is essential that the investigator know which variables to control, for there is always the possibility that other variables (not controlled) may account for the experimental results.

A suggested experimental design might consist of six districts. Two districts would have complete control over curriculum, personnel, and the budget. Two districts would share authority with the central board, and two would serve as control groups to function under the traditional organization of the central board. The six districts could be matched by class and race. Three might be predominantly black (75 percent or more), categorized into three different income levels; and three might be predominantly white (75 percent or more), also categorized into the same three income levels. Ideally, the number of districts could be expanded to include three additional integrated districts (60 to 70 percent white, 40 to 30 percent black), also categorized into the same income levels. Other racial matches could be made in school systems having large numbers of Spanish-speaking families, Indians, or Orientals, or any white ethnic group that deemed it necessary to identify itself as a distinct group for cultural purposes.

Besides matching class and race, a number of dimensions of student performance could be measured and controlled in accordance with objectives. Characteristics of parents, teachers, administrators, schools, and the community could also be classified. Specifically what items are included will vary with the school systems, but each item would have to be quantified. After making adjustments for initial differences, one procedure would be to form a multiple regression analysis with the gains in student performance serving as the dependent variable or single criterion, and the other characteristics related to parents, teachers, administrators, schools, and community serving as independent variables or multiple predictors.

Future research in the area of school decentralization and community control might also focus on the survey questions listed in table 3.1. The first set of questions are specifically related to both concepts. Within-group differences, which may be as large as those between groups, should also be measured. The questions in table 3.1 are related to conflicting demands at different levels of intensity by various interest groups. To date, the issues related to decentralization and community control have not been satisfactorily resolved by the various interest groups. Indeed, there is continuing need for research to fill in the unresolved issues and unknown consequences of these two reorganizational models, to determine how to deal with the question of whether the students and society really benefit, and to clarify the roles of the various interest groups supporting administrative decentralization and community control in the school system. As of now we have no research evidence that either one improves education. A systematic response to the questions listed in table 3.1 is, of course, crucial for proponents of the various decentralization and community control schemes; otherwise, what we have are their unsupported assertions quoted as statements of fact.

Table 3.1

SURVEY QUESTIONS RELATED TO ADMINISTRATIVE
DECENTRALIZATION AND COMMUNITY CONTROL

Part I

School–Community Questions to Provide Background Information

School	*Community*
1. How does the school provide opportunity for the community to learn about the school?	1. How does the community provide opportunity for the school to learn about the community?
2. How do school personnel feel about the community? Why?	2. How does the community feel about school personnel? Why?
3. How does the school support the community?	3. How does the community support the school?
4. How does the school use community resources and leadership?	4. How does the community use school resources and leadership?
5. How does the school provide opportunity for the community to participate in the educational program?	5. How does the community provide opportunity for the school to participate in the community program?
6. What can be done to improve the situation?	6. What can be done to improve the situation?

Part II

Questions Related to Administrative Decentralization and Community Control

Administrative Decentralization	*Community Control*
1. Who are the advocates?	1. Who are the advocates?
2. What are the motivations of these people?	2. What are the motivations of these people?
3. How seriously does the public want to decentralize? (Is it wanted only by a small, well-organized group of educators or residents?)	3. How seriously does the public want community control? (Is it wanted only by a small, well-organized group of educators or residents?)

Table 3.1 (cont.)

Administrative Decentralization	*Community Control*
4. What are the various roles of the students, parents, community leaders, professional staff, etc.?	4. What are the various roles of the students, parents, community leaders, professional staff, etc.
5. Do students, parents, community residents, teachers, etc., have a greater voice under decentralization?	5. Do students, parents, community residents, teachers, etc., have a greater voice under community control?
6. What role problems develop among the various interest groups?	6. What role problems develop among the various interest groups?
7. How do various interest groups feel before and after decentralization is implemented? (What are the differences when race and class are controlled?)	7. How do the various interest groups feel before and after community control is implemented? (What are the differences when race and class are controlled?)
8. How do the various interest groups want to be represented? (What are the differences when race and class are controlled?)	8. How do the various interest groups want to be represented? (What are the differences when race and class are controlled?)
9. How do labor unions, political groups, and municipal and community agencies affect decentralization?	9. How do labor unions, political groups, and municipal and community agencies affect community control?
10. How does the current racial and job situation affect decentralization? (What impact has it had on the racial and ethnic distribution of teaching jobs and administrative positions?)	10. How does the current racial and job situation affect community control? (What impact has it had on the racial and ethnic distribution of teaching jobs and administrative positions?)
11. How does decentralization affect the student's learning?	11. How does community control affect the student's learning?
12. What decentralized unit size (in terms of geographical or metropolitan location, area size, number of students, and racial composition of schools) is most effective?	12. What type of community control (in terms of geographical or metropolitan location, area size, number of students, and racial composition) is most effective?
13. What administrative levels (central office, district or field office, individual schools) should be decentralized?	13. What administrative functions (curriculum, personnel, student policy, budget) should be controlled by whom?
14. When does large size lead to inflexibility?	14. When does community control lead to racial discrimination or political chaos?
15. When does small size lead to reduced range of educational services?	15. When does professional control lead to racial discrimination or status quo education?

Table 3.1 (cont.)

Administrative Decentralization	*Community Control*
16. What is the cost of decentralization?	16. What is the cost of community control?
17. What support (internal and external) does a decentralized unit require to function successfully?	17. What support (internal and external) does a community school board require to function successfully?
18. What changes in educational policy and approaches have decentralized units been able to implement that were not possible under the centralized administration?	18. What changes in educational policy and approaches have community school boards been able to implement that were not possible under the central school board?
19. How does decentralization affect school integration? (Can they be implemented together?)	19. How does community control affect school integration? (Can they be implemented together?)
20. What is the impact of school decentralization on metropolitan development and cooperation? (Can we decentralize and still promote metropolitan cooperation?)	20. What is the impact of community control on metropolitan development and cooperation? (Can we have community control and still promote metropolitan cooperation?)
21. What is the impact of school decentralization and federal reform? (Can they be implemented together?)	21. What is the impact of community control and federal reform? (Can they be implemented together?)
22. How can conflicts be reduced so basic educational issues take priority over power?	22. How can conflicts be reduced so basic education issues take priority over power?

Questions number 1 and 2 under decentralization are derived from La Noue (1972).

Research is expensive, but lack of research on decentralization and community control may be more expensive in the long run to students in particular and to society in general. Until the evidence is clear, we should proceed with caution. The point is, the so-called solutions—decentralization, community control, even community participation—are mainly slogans, rather than carefully worked out concepts and thoroughly understood consequences. We assume that the "community" voice is the most vocal and articulated, but we have yet to hear from the majority of silent parents who have their own aspirations for their children's lives and their own ideas about how the school should fulfill these. Once these plans are adopted on a systemwide basis, they are very difficult to change in many large school systems, especially where ideology and racial conflict are apparent. Writes La Noue (1972), "Given existing racial hostilities and other problems in our cities" decentralization and community control will not be easily reversed. If these changes fail, "the human social costs will be great" (p. 25). What we need, then, is research that will test the worth of unsupported statements and claims. We must test our hypotheses and use caution against coming to unwarranted conclusions. We need a partnership between practitioners and researchers, among the various interest groups, and especially between blacks and whites, if a breakthrough is to be made to a higher level of mutual understanding and quality education for children and youth. We also need to conduct honest research, and we have to recognize and be willing to speak out when personal interests and group ideology influence or coerce social scientists.

On a more general level, but one that is relevant to research on decentralization and community control, it is important to remember that research can produce knowledge which can eventually lead to change. While research does not guarantee change, it produces knowledge for helping to determine whether change is necessary or possible. Wynne (1970) writes:

> Research can produce knowledge. This knowledge can give the public tools to make new demands on schools. The tools can change the power relationship between schoolmen and communities.
>
> While the only important product of research is information, information is the major source of change in any society in which people are not killing each other on a large scale. . . . [N]othing important happens differently in a democracy unless some members of the society are told something they didn't realize before. Note that I did not say that the communication of "new" information automatically produces change, but that such communication is a precondition to change [p. 246].

The question of what information will effect that change is complex and related to political, economic, social, and scientific factors. Nevertheless, we should not underestimate the relationship between the research community and the federal government; the federal government possesses the experts, resources, money, and legal apparatus to implement reform and effect changes on a mass scale. In fact, almost all our major reform measures and changes in education (and other social services such as medicine, health care, employment practices, housing, and social and welfare services) have been derived from and implemented not by the local communities, but by the federal government.

In connection with reform and effective change, the research community has become increasingly aware that they must be relevant. Writes Popham (1971):

> Whereas a decade ago the bulk of investigations being reported in educational research journals and at professional meetings could be characterized, kindly, as somewhat esoteric, the current drive is for practical relevance.

> I am suggesting . . . that the mood among American edu-
> cational researchers has clearly changed. They now see a
> crucial national need to improve the schools which,
> though operated by dedicated school personnel, are far
> less effective than they should be [p. 3].

It has become evident that not only must researchers listen more closely to the problems and needs of school personnel in order to better understand what must be studied to improve education, but they must also communicate with policy makers in order to ensure application of their research results. Just as educational research must be restructured "to maximize the relationship between the basic researcher and practitioner and, consequently, minimize the gap between basic research and practice" (Farmer 1971, p. 3), so should the relationship be enlarged to include officials who are in a position to affect social policy.

It is also important to recognize that the black community feels it has been "surveyed and studied to death" and that little good has occurred as a result. According to blacks, too often the research has stressed negative or uncomplimentary findings. Social scientists often look for problems, emphasizing negative traits and behaviors. The black community claims that black-white differences are usually viewed in relation to the norms of the larger society with black differences considered as "problems" or "abnormalities." Studies are more likely to focus on the pathologies of blacks than on the people and institutions that have caused them. (Nonetheless, the responsibilities of the individual must also be recognized, otherwise society breaks down; moreover, not all individual problems can be blamed on society.) Not only have the contributions of black social scientists been scanty, but in the past white social scientists have been considered to be experts on black families and culture.

It should be pointed out, too, that research concerning the black community is often characterized by public visibility and emotionalism. The findings can be threatening to the black community, the practitioner working in the ghetto, or the power structure. While the social scientist must recognize his role and responsibilities, as well as the potential impact and possible dysfunctional outcomes of his research, the black community must recognize that the social scientist has the right to free inquiry so long as his research does not degenerate into systematic distortion or propaganda. Similarly, no one has the right to subject the social scientist to harassment or threaten him because his findings do not agree with popular rhetoric or political ideology.

The researcher must go where the current problems are, and he must be allowed to investigate all facets of society; otherwise, his work becomes irrelevant. He must not be denied access to the black community on the grounds of race, for he can do more good than harm for the black community, especially in helping to effect social change. As Deutsch (1969) claims, "Social scientists are best qualified to remove obstacles created by their own assumptions." In doing so, they can "bring into question . . . aspects of public policy which may rest on outmoded or invalid assumptions" (p. 9).

On the other hand, there is need for the social scientist to give serious consideration to the complaints of ghetto dwellers and to be more sensitive to their needs and concerns. At the same time, the black community has the right to know the overall purpose of a specific study without contaminating its validity and the right to decide whether or not to participate. The variable of investigator's race should be controlled: members of the black community should participate as researchers wherever possible, and they should be allowed to attach a rebuttal to the study report before—not after—it is released or published. Brown (1971) also points out the need for two types of research reports: one for the professionals and research community, and the other for the lay public and community, similar in intent and fact though different in language and technical approach. However, research controlled or censored by the black community for political or ideological reasons will be rejected by most social scientists as invalid.

Conclusion

It must be realized that most of the so-called experts, whether they are from Harvard University or the black community, are as flummoxed as the rest of us when it comes to solving the problems of school and society. To a large extent educational reformers draw on a shared vocabulary: social justice, racial equality, equal opportunity, and so on. The difficulties come, and the splits appear, when the vocabulary must be translated into action. One who is familiar with the literature grows weary of the leftward reformers who offer few constructive and realistic solutions. One begins to feel their imagination has outstripped reality.

What is even more disturbing is the increasing inability of all sides in the great debate about improving the schools to find a dialogue that can bridge the concerns of the various interest groups. Write Ornstein and Talmage (1973):

> What we need is a common language . . . which permits self-examination and openness on both sides of the philosophical, [racial, and ideological] dividing lines. We need to put away our political and economical motives, to talk to one another as concerned persons for the welfare of our students [or target population]. We need to advocate the importance of research, not rhetoric. We must provide a forum that permits us to fully understand issues . . . before advocating any idea as one certain cure-all [p. 80].

We need to put aside our self-interests and ideologies, to reduce the rhetoric and emotional exchanges, and finally, to depolarize. In short, we still need to learn how to communicate with one another. We also must learn to understand one another's feelings. Whites must understand that most blacks need no specific reason to dislike them, or not to permit whites to conduct research in the black community or work in their schools. The past alone is sufficient reason for dislike and for many blacks to advocate a "liberation" policy, to demand control of their own schools, as well as of political and economic institutions. Blacks also have reason to reject the data that show their conditions have improved, and to censor anything that puts them in a defensive position, because such data could undermine their demands and interests. Blacks must understand that most whites do not feel responsible for the past— for decisions they did not make—and the increasingly hostile tactics of many black militants elicit little sympathy or support from the white target population. Whites also have grievances, and many resent that black priorities must now come first—at their expense—in an era when jobs, housing, openings in college and professional school, and scholarships are scarce and when inflation and rising taxes victimize both low- and middle-income wage earners. They reject the concept of black power, because it connotes domination and reverse discrimination rather than equality. Indeed, it is time that we realize that we are all in this society together and we must learn how to live with one another and respect the interests and rights of individuals and groups—not tomorrow, but now!

Notes

1. The latter two school systems were given pseudonyms because the superintendents and several board members objected to the analysis of their respective school systems.

2. The report states, "If the local boards are given complete responsibility and authority, including power to allocate funds, the present system would split into six or eight nearly independent school districts." However, tokenism was rejected and it was recommended that "local boards be given considerable autonomy" (p. 10).

3. The 1970 census in Chicago confirms that "Chicago . . . is the most segregated city in the nation" (*Chicago Tribune*, November 5, 1972, sec. 1B, p. 1).

4. See Fantini, Gittell, and Magat (1970) and Ornstein (1972) for a discussion of the three demonstration districts: Ocean Hill–Brownsville, I.S. 201 complex, and Two Bridges District. The 1968 New York City ten-week teachers' strike centered around these three districts, especially Ocean Hill.

5. District 23 school board members were black moderates. They were denied access to the records of the Ocean Hill District. Threats and assaults were made on several of them, allegedly by black militant supporters of the experimental district; their offices and homes were ransacked.

6. For example, compensatory education cost us billions of dollars before we found out that it does not work. By late 1972 there were more than 250 performance contracts, although there was little evidence that

such contracts achieved what they purported to achieve. Across the country reformers now advocate the use of behavioral objectives and performance criteria. Institutions of higher learning often find they cannot get federal funds unless behavioral objectives and performance criteria are written into their teacher-training programs; yet there is very scanty evidence that these ideas work, improve teacher training, or can be successfully implemented.

7. See Coleman et al. (1966), Jencks et al. (1972), McPartland (1968), U.S. Commission on Civil Rights (1967), and Walberg (1969).

8. Granted many variables are related to student achievement (especially family characteristics), and granted conclusions should not be made from tentative findings, but the reading scores continue to reflect a downward direction in the two school systems that have implemented some form of community control. In response to this trend, some proponents of community control now tell us that quality education was not the real issue: it was power!

References

Aberback, Joel D., and Jack L. Walker
1971 "Citizens Desires, Policy Outcomes, and Community Control." Paper presented at the annual meeting of the American Political Science Association, Chicago, September.

Bard, Bernard
1971 "The Battle for School Jobs: New York's Newest Agony." *Phi Delta Kappan* 53:553–58.

Billings, Charles E.
1972 "Community Control of the School and the Quest for Power." *Phi Delta Kappan* 53:277–78.

Booz-Allen & Hamilton
1967 *Organized Survey: Board of Education—City of Chicago.* Chicago: the author, May.

Bosco, James, and Stanley Robin
1972 "Reconstruction in the Relation of Social Science and Education." Paper presented at the Annual AERA Conference, Chicago, April.

Brown, Roscoe C., Jr.
1971 "How to Make Educational Research Relevant to the Urban Community—The Researcher's View." Paper presented at the Annual AERA Conference, New York, February.

Campbell, Donald T.
1972 "Reforms as Experiments." In *Evaluating Action Programs*, ed. C. H. Weiss, pp. 187–223. Boston: Allyn & Bacon.

Caro, Francis G.
1971 "Issues in the Evaluation of Social Programs." *Review of Educational Research* 41:87–114.

Chicago Tribune
November 5, 1972.

Clark, Terry
1970 "On Decentralization." *Polity* 2:503–14.

Coleman, James S., et al.
1966 *Equality of Educational Opportunity.* Washington, D.C.: U.S. Government Printing Office.

Commission on Urban Education
    1971 *A Report to the General Assembly of Illinois.* Chicago: State of
        Illinois, February.
Crain, Robert L.
    1968 *The Politics of School Desegregation.* Chicago: Aldine.
Deutsch, Martin
    1969 "Organizational and Conceptual Barriers to Social Change." *Journal
        of Social Issues* 25:5–18.
District Boundary Lines Under the Community School District System
    1969 Special Committee on Decentralization (Committee of the Whole).
        New York: Board of Education of the City of New York, Decem-
        ber 22.
*Educational Renewal: A Decentralization Proposal for the Los Angeles Uni-
fied School District*
    1971 A Report by the Decentralization Task Force. Los Angeles: Los
        Angeles Unified School District, February 22.
Fantini, Mario D.
    1970 *The Reform of Urban Schools.* Washington, D.C.: National Educa-
        tion Association.
Fantini, Mario D., Marilyn Gittell, and Richard Magat
    1970 *Community Control and the Urban School.* New York:
        Praeger.
Farmer, James A., Jr.
    1971 "Indigenous Interactional Research." Paper presented at the Annual
        AERA Conference, New York, February.
Gittell, Marilyn
    1967 *Participants and Participation: A Study of School Policy in New
        York.* New York: Praeger.
Gittell, Marilyn, and T. E. Hollander
    1968 *Six Urban School Districts: A Comparative Study of Institutional
        Response.* New York: Praeger.
Guba, Egon G.
    1969 "The Failure of Educational Evaluation." *Educational Technology*
        9:29–38.
*Guidelines for Regional and Central Boards of Education of the School
District of the City of Detroit*
    1970 Adopted in accordance with Public Act No. 48 of 1970, State of
        Michigan. Detroit: Office of School Decentralization, Board of
        Education of the City of Detroit, October 26.
Halinski, Ronald S., and Leonard S. Feldt
    1970 "The Selection of Variables in Multiple Regression Analysis."
        Journal of Educational Measurement 7:151–57.
Havighurst, Robert J.
    1964 *The Public Schools of Chicago.* A Survey for the Board of Education
        of the City of Chicago. Chicago: Board of Education of the City of
        Chicago.
Hentoff, Nat
    1966 *Our Children Are Dying.* New York: Viking Press.
Hickrod, G. Alan
    1971 "Local Demand for Education: A Critique of School Finance and
        Economic Research Circa 1959–1969." *Review of Educational
        Research* 41:35–49.
Jencks, Christopher, et al.
    1972 *Inequality: A Reassessment of the Effect of Family and Schooling
        in America.* New York: Basic Books.

La Noue, George R.
  1972 "The Politics of School Decentralization Methodological Considerations." Paper presented at the Annual AERA Conference, Chicago, April.

Lipham, James M., Russell T. Gregg, and Richard A. Rossmiller
  1967 *The School Board as an Agency for Resolving Conflict.* Madison: University of Wisconsin.

Maeroff, Gene I.
  1973 "The Traditional School: Keep It Among the Alternatives." *Phi Delta Kappan* 54:473–75.

Mayor's Advisory Panel on Decentralization of the New York City Schools
  1967 *Reconnection for Learning: A Community School System for New York City.* New York: Ford Foundation–Praeger.

McPartland, James
  1968 *The Segregated Student in Desegregated Schools.* Final Report to the Center for the Study of School Organization. Baltimore, Md.: Johns Hopkins University, June.

A Multiple Option Approach to School–Community Participation
  1970 Report of the Commission on Decentralization and Community Participation. Philadelphia: Board of Education of the City of Philadelphia, July 22.

Ornstein, Allan C.
  1973 "Research on Decentralization." *Phi Delta Kappan* 54:610–14.

Ornstein, Allan C., and Harriet Talmage
  1973 "The Rhetoric and the Realities of Accountability." *Today's Education: Journal of The National Education Association.* 62:70–80.

Passow, A. H.
  1967 *Toward Creating a Model Urban School System.* A Study of the Washington, D.C., Public Schools. New York: Teachers College Press, Columbia University.

Pois, Joseph
  1964 *The School Board Crisis: A Chicago Case Study.* Chicago: Educational Methods. Reprinted by permission of the publisher.

Popham, W. James
  1971 Statement Presented to the Appropriations Committee, U.S. House of Representatives, Washington, D.C., March 10. Excerpted in *Educational Researcher* 2:3–4.

Proposed Plan for a Community School District in New York
  1969 New York: Board of Education of the City of New York, November 17.

Public Reaction Draft of School Decentralization Guidelines
  1970 Detroit: Office of School Decentralization, Board of Education of the City of Detroit, August.

Ravitch, Diane
  1972 "Community Control Revisited." *Commentary*, February, pp. 70–74.

Robinson, Donald W.
  1972 "Change for Its Own Sake." *Phi Delta Kappan* 53:587.

Rogers, David
  1969 *110 Livingston Street.* Vintage ed. New York: Random House.

Rossi, Peter H.
  1972 "Boobytraps and Pitfalls in the Evaluation of Social Action Programs." In *Evaluating Action Programs*, ed. C. H. Weiss, pp. 224–35. Boston: Allyn & Bacon.

Schrag, Peter
    1967 *Village School Downtown.* Boston: Beacon Press.
Smith, Mortimer
    1973 "CBE Views the Alternatives." *Phi Delta Kappan* 54:441–43.
U.S. Commission on Civil Rights
    1967 *Racial Isolation in the Public Schools.* Washington, D.C.: U.S. Government Printing Office.
Walberg, Herbert J.
    1969 *An Evaluation of an Urban-Suburban School Bussing Program: Student Achievement and Perception of Class Learning Environments.* Draft of Report to METCO. Roxbury, Mass.: METCO Education Program, July 1.
Witkowsky, Jack
    1971 "Education of a School Board Member." *Saturday Review*, September 20, pp. 90–92. Copyright 1971 by Saturday Review Co. First appeared in *Saturday Review* (1971). Used with permission.
Working Draft of Possible Guidelines for Implementation of Public Act 244
    1970 Detroit: Office of School Decentralization, Board of Education, City of Detroit, April and May. 2 vols.
Wynne, Edward
    1970 "Education Research: A Profession in Search of a Constituency." *Phi Delta Kappan* 52:245–47.

chapter 4

Social Science, Research, and the Black Community

Although all the sciences search for knowledge, they do not achieve it to the same degree of precision and exactitude. Certain sciences, because of their subject matter, are in a better position to control experimentally the variables with which they deal and to arrive at exact laws. As a group, the social sciences tend to be less accurate than the physical sciences. The oldest and most venerable of the social sciences is history, which is the record, as the historian Ranke said, of "what has actually happened." Other social sciences include such fields of study as political science, economics, geography, sociology, anthropology, psychology, and, some say, education. Social science is a selective process, the selection of factors being dependent in part upon the values and knowledge of the social scientist; it cannot be totally objective or totally valid in findings because of the complexity of human factors, which cannot all be measured, isolated in controlled experiments, or reduced to a single cause. Compounding the problem is the fact that the same findings can be interpreted in more than one way, also reflecting the social scientist's views and ways of looking at the world.

Since the late 1960s, coinciding with the rise of black power, there has been a growing trend to create a black perspective in social science research. This new perspective challenges traditional concepts of social science and research. This chapter attempts to analyze some of the implications of this trend, bearing in mind that this social scientist is also influenced by his own ways of looking at the world, and some of these ways may differ from those of the reader.

The White Researcher and the Black Community

The problem at hand is illustrated by the suspicion and distrust with which the black community regards the social scientists, who are usually white. Billingsley (1970) writes:

> . . . the reason black families have fared so much worse
> than white families in social science is that they are black
> and social science is white. . . . When black people have
> been the object of analysis by white social scientists . . .
> the relations between white and black people . . . [have]
> been at the center of their interest.

> . . . these social scientists have been victimized by their
> own Anglo-European history and culture. They have
> tended to view other cultures primarily as objects of
> assimilation [pp. 133–34].

Glazer (1969), on the other hand, reports on several prominent studies by sociologists, anthropologists, and psychologists and contends that:

> History and social research convince me there are deep
> and enduring educational differences between various
> ethnic groups, in their educational achievement and in
> the broader cultural characteristics in which these differ-
> ences are, I believe, rooted; that these differences cannot
> be simply associated with the immediate conditions under
> which these groups live, whether we define these condi-
> tions as being those of levels of poverty and exploitation,
> or prejudice and discrimination; and if we are to have a
> decent society, men must learn to live with some measure
> of group difference in educational achievement, [and] to
> tolerate them . . . [p. 187].

Glazer is concerned about our attitudes toward these differences: Do we believe that they are solely the consequence of the ill will and "racist" feelings of teachers, administrators, social scientists, and society in general? About the differences he writes:

> How elaborate are we to make the efforts to wipe them
> out, and how successful can we hope to be no matter
> how elaborate our efforts are? Are our measures to
> equalize to include the restriction of the opportunities
> of those groups that seem to find school achievement
> easy [p. 195].

The conflict of opinion between Billingsley and Glazer goes beyond the issue of social science research, but racial conflict, which can destroy our society, appears to be growing. We need to research educational differences within and between racial and ethnic groups, to investigate the multiple causes and solutions. The right of free inquiry should be supported, but will black community leaders still permit the social scientist (who is often white) to conduct research in the black community? And if there are continued differences, how will white society react to the differences? Will white society use these differences to rationalize discriminatory practices? And how will black society react? Will blacks explode in a storm of emotion and rhetoric?

Even though researchers may believe that their efforts contribute to the cause of poor and minority groups, black activists may react with hostility. Part of the problem is related to basic issues that strain the relations between practitioners and researchers. Recently Ornstein (1972) wrote:

> While the social scientist is concerned with research and knowledge for its own sake, the practitioner is concerned with service and the application of research and knowledge. The researcher usually is not concerned with practical problems because what is appropriate in one situation is often not applicable to other situations. On the other hand, most research is impractical for the practitioner who is working not with mean scores but with individual variability. The gap between the social scientist and practitioner is perhaps even wider in the black community, because the problems of the practitioner are more difficult, and he feels the research is less applicable to his situation. Furthermore, the practitioner in the ghetto is often concerned about covering up the inefficiencies and problems that he is confronted with; therefore, he views the social scientist as a possible threat who may uncover the truth or expose the present conditions of the school or social agency [pp. 132–33].

Caro (1971) notes other problems:

> Preoccupied with the immediate, tangible, dramatic, and personal, the minority activist is likely to be impatient with the evaluator's [researcher's] concern with the future, abstract concepts, orderly procedures, and impersonal forces. In contrast to the activist, who often seeks to generate open conflict, the evaluative researcher typically emphasizes cooperative approaches to problem solving. The evaluator [researcher] may also find himself in an awkward position in the power struggle between client spokesmen and professional administrators. If he entered the program at the invitation of a funding agency or a professional administrator, the evaluative researcher is likely to be mistrusted immediately by minority activists who see him as a potential spy [p. 99].

As these quotations suggest, part of the misunderstanding between practitioners and researchers is related to race differences, and this latter aspect of the problem seems to be worsening. In fact, the race relations problem has (1) forced many social scientists to abandon certain premises, (2) made it almost impossible for them to follow their research to where it leads them, and (3) compelled them to bury certain findings. Thus, there seems to be a limit to what social scientists can research or introduce into the literature about minorities. Few social scientists want to educate others, or disseminate findings that are critical of, or purport negative traits of, a minority group, when the price for doing so includes being subject to the race rhetoric of name-calling, being physically harassed or threatened, having one's files rifled, or risking one's professional career. In this connection, Moynihan (1968) contends that social scientists already are "sensitive as to what kinds of things they 'find out' about low-status groups . . . [and some] subjects are best left alone" (p. 30). He points out that the social scientist is secure when conducting research about "neutral" school characteristics and related student achievement, but in a precarious situation when conducting research on family characteristics. Armor (1972) is outraged and has gone so far as to accuse liberals of deliberate dishonesty, pointing out "there is danger that important research may be stopped when the desired results are not forthcoming" (p. 91). He contends that the current controversy over the effects of school desegregation and busing are prime examples. When he published his own findings on busing, after being warned not to publish them by many of his liberal colleagues at Harvard, and after having his records almost destroyed, he was publically condemned and pressured to such an extent that he left the university.

Wilson (1972) contends that within higher education one finds today "the harassment of unpopular views, the use of force to prevent certain persons from speaking . . . and the politicalization of the university to make it an arena for the exchange of manifestos rather than the forum for the discussion of ideas" (p. 50). To question the liberal-black dogma, to seriously discuss all sides of an issue related to race "is risky, if not impossible." Speakers who have attempted to do so "have been subjected to mental and social duress." He concludes that, while the radical-militant disruptions have subsided, and consequently the violence on campus has declined, most professors have acquiesced to this flirtation with authoritarian politics, and thus there is good reason to "doubt the legitimacy of . . . the principles of free discussion" (p. 51).

More and more speakers have come to the conclusion that making statements in public or in print that question or run counter to liberal-black dogma is no longer worth the personal costs involved. Increasingly, we are hearing only one point of view, while almost any view to the right of the center on college campuses is being chocked in public and driven into private discussions. Podhoretz (1973) also testifies to the hostility to free discussion on many college campuses, where it is impossible to hear "almost any idea which is critical of the liberal orthodoxy of the moment on any subject whatsoever" (p. 8). The result is an atmosphere no longer conducive to free inquiry and academic freedom. Several events and trends cannot be objectively examined, much less criticized. Thus Podhoretz concludes that independence of mind and critical spirit are fast waning on most college campuses, and we are entering a period where "inquisitorial agents of a dogmatic secular faith" prevent frank discussion on many topics (p. 8).

In particular, Scriven (1970), who is a colleague of Jensen's at Berkeley, described how Jensen was treated after publishing his article in the *Harvard Educational Review* on the importance of the genetic component in IQ. He was "savagely attacked for being a racist" in print and in speeches throughout the country; radical-militant groups on campus demanded his dismissal, and many of his colleagues signed a petition dismissing his views as essentially ignorant, "despite several and probably most of the signers never read the article" (p. 542). (It is also common knowledge that his life and family were repeatedly threatened; he often needed police protection, and he was often unable to speak at public meetings because of harassment and heckling.) His critics usually misquoted and distorted his views; their arguments were "ill-informed, illogical, and politically motivated." The uncivil treatment accorded to Jensen and the way the radical and militant Left succeeded in enlisting the support of thousands on campus and at public meetings illustrate the vulnerability of "free inquiry and academic freedom" at many universities (p. 543).

In the same vein, Herrnstein (1973) reported about his own difficulties and the abuse he has endured at Harvard and on other college campuses since publishing his article in the *Atlantic* which merely touched lightly on the genetic factor related to IQ, and which was based entirely from the study of whites and the syllogism was based on "ifs." His critics also misquoted and distorted his views, posting signs and handing out leaflets which denounced him as a racist and an elitist. Often the material was identical, even on different campuses, indicating the high degree of intercommunication among radical-militant student groups. Herrnstein was unable to speak in his own class and at several speaking engagements at other places, even though his discussion usually had nothing to do with the topic of race. Radicals often traveled more than one hundred miles to harass him. For example, when he was speaking in Iowa, they came from Chicago and Madison, Wisconsin. He canceled his speaking commitment at Princeton University only after he was told in writing by the administration that the institution could not guarantee his safety or protect his right to speak. Princeton's President Goheen then made a public statement, which was printed in the *Daily Princeton*, that "the administration can do nothing 'to guarantee a scholar's right to speak,' when the scholar withdraws from an invitation to lecture" (p. 59). Mr. Goheen chided Herrnstein for canceling his plans and a group of students called the "USA" for an ad they placed in the same newspaper protesting the university's failure to protect the author and his right to speak. At the same time, Mr. Goheen failed to mention the radical-militant groups, whose pressure forced Herrnstein to give up his plans, who admitted in the same paper that, had the author attempted to speak, they would have harassed him and prevented him from leaving until he answered certain questions to their liking. At several universities (including Harvard, Iowa, and Princeton) administrators "could not make too public a display of solidarity" about Herrnstein's right to speak, "although privately [he] often received unqualified support" (p. 60). One might conclude, then, as Podhoretz (1973), Record (1973*b*, 1973*c*), Scriven (1970), and Wilson (1972) have, that most professors and administrators are hesitant to publicly question the liberal-black orthodoxy; they surrender to the uncivil acts of a small minority or even to the possibility that these acts may occur. In doing so they help curtail free inquiry and free speech at most institutions of higher learning; moreover, they rarely take active steps to uphold academic freedom; they are usually afraid of being villified and badgered, of even losing popularity with members of the college community on whose esteem they substantially depend.

The harassment that Jensen and Herrnstein have experienced is not unusual; in fact, it represents a large and growing trend that is well known but rarely discussed in public. Indeed, it is becoming evident that thousands of less well-known professors and social scientists across the country have experienced similar kinds of harassment and threats by vigilante groups protesting their views on subjects dealing mainly with race relations. The facts seem clear: to exist on campus, to conduct research or hold classes, it is best to limit criticism of the liberal-black dogma, and to bury sensitive research or not mention sensitive data in class or at public meetings.[a]

And if we cannot explore both sides of a social policy or report research on an important topic at the university, a place that is supposed to be conducive to the free exchange of ideas, then where else can we expect to have a frank discussion? As Ornstein (1972) wrote:

> [We are] reaching the point where there is a lack of tolerance toward controversial findings [involving racial studies] and where the oppressed minority is becoming the oppressive minority. . . . Hypersensitivity to racial and ethnic differences (some real, some imaginary) can only impede frank discussion and legitimate reform—and transform the social scientists' tolerance to hostility [p. 135].

This, indeed, would be a serious problem, because the social scientist, by virtue of his expertise and affiliations, can still influence social and political legislation and introduce social reform.

Record's 1972 study of what is happening to white sociologists across the country is instructive. He noted that they are criticized and harassed by black militant students as being "biased," "irrelevant," and "racist." In some instances it was impossible for many of them to hold classes, and in other instances not only they but their families were threatened with physical assault. There are an estimated 750 white sociologists specializing in race relations in the United States. Record found that, of the 174 of these he contacted, 22 percent have abandoned their field of inquiry and another 31 percent have shifted their emphasis from blacks to other minorities. He (1972*b*) reported:

> All over the U.S., white social scientists who once prided themselves on being unprejudiced and basically sympathetic to the blacks they studied have found their motivation and competence challenged by militants who claim that only a black can understand the black experience. The antagonisms toward these white social scientists have also spread through the black ghettoes, making it difficult for them to continue their research [pp. 46–47].

The quotes from Record's study (1972*a*) which follow illustrate the feelings of these sociologists. One sociologist from the west coast, who was undaunted by being called a "nigger lover" in the 1950s, stated:

> It is too much of a hassel to try to be an impartial behavioral scientist when everything which is not praise is racist, and where the sole criterion for knowledge, understanding or credibility is the color of your skin [p. 5].

Another sociologist explained how he abandoned objectivity to appease blacks.

> I was very sympathetic with the blacks and made no bones about it. . . . I was bending over backwards and wasn't very agile or honest in doing so. I don't think I was ever really convincing. . . . Looking back, I am somewhat ashamed; however, I try to tell myself it was part of a grouping effort to relate to both blacks and white students in my course [p. 7].

Self-censorship was another problem. One sociologist from the Southwest stopped using the Rainwater-Yancey (both authors are highly liberal) collection on the famous Moynihan report. He stated that blacks refused to listen and merely denounced the report as

> . . . a "bunch of lies" and [said] that the critics of the Report weren't critical or militant enough. . . . I made a change and dropped the book. I don't think a one of the black students ever read the Report; they had only read *about* it—what militants *said* about it, but never the *Report* itself [p. 8].

According to Record (1973*b*), one sociologist from the Midwest, who recalled getting threatening calls from white bigots, was now worried about the black bigots: "It's getting pretty rough on me and my family, and I'm taking off for a year. Maybe things will be better when I return" (p. 3).

Another sociologist from the East spoke of his family's being threatened while he was constantly harassed, and concluded, "I am out of the race relations field because I literally was driven out. Period" (pp. 26–27). Still another sociologist from the west coast said, "that *if* I continued, I would be involved in one unending confrontation with the blacks. . . . I just couldn't cope. When the term ended (in 1970) I vowed that I would never offer another course or do another piece of research on blacks; and I haven't" (p. 27). Another sociologist from the Southwest asserted that he even lowered the standards in his race relations course; in fact, he abolished all term papers and tests. He explained, "Eliminating myself was the only response acceptable to them" (p. 28). One female sociologist found the pressure from blacks too much to handle in her minority group class and suspended the class "until such time as it can be conducted with some civility and the blacks can see me as something more than a mean white bitch" (p. 23). And another female sociologist, who had been active in the civil rights movement in the early and mid-1960s and who was jailed in Alabama, Mississippi, and Oakland for her participation, was dismissed by militant blacks as "irrelevant" and "racist." "Some of the black women activists," according to Record, "even charged that her principal motive was to attract black men." Although she would prefer to teach courses in race relations, she has decided to develop courses "on the sociology of women—white women" (p. 29).

Black militant pressure was even evident against black moderate sociologists who were connected with black studies programs. As many as 9 out of 40 blacks suspended classes or resigned from their directorships because their moderate views conflicted with those of militant students who usually had strong influence on faculty selection and curriculum organization. Record (1973*b*) points out that these black moderates denounced the black studies program as being political and ideological, not cultural, programs. They were pressured to lower their academic standards, limit their contacts with their white colleagues, and espouse the militant rhetoric. As one black sociologist who resigned said, "I was tired of being called 'Oreo,' 'Tom,' and 'white man's nigger' " (p. 29). Another black studies director claimed the black militants monitored all courses in the black studies program and demanded that certain faculty members be fired because of "failure to spout the current black party line . . . or being too tough in assignments and grades. . . . To make a long story short, I bucked them for a time, and then I finally said to hell with it" (p. 31).

Record's (1973*a*, 1973*b*, 1973*c*) survey results indicate that the overwhelming percentage of white social scientists agree on the following points:

1. University officials tend to be weak and are reluctant to support professors in a conflict with black militants; rather they concede to militant black demands in order to maintain peace on college campuses, even at the risk of stifling presumed objective (or nonideological) research and limiting academic freedom.

2. University officials are quietly making agreements with black student organizations to clear research proposals that deal with blacks.
3. Self-censorship is prevalent in social science classes because of coercive measures taken by black militants; and even though the tensions on college campuses have diminished, this censorship seems to have had a permanent effect on what is taught, even when militants are not enrolled in, or monitoring, the class.
4. It has become increasingly difficult to use a single grading system because a greater percentage of blacks than whites would fail, leading the professor to be denounced as a possible racist.
5. Black studies programs are often used as a base from which to organize and attack white social scientists.

Some readers may object to these charges because they are being made by white social scientists. Their very objections are an example of how the ploy of white racism can be inserted into the discussion while black bigotry is overlooked. Several black militant social scientists, such as Draper (1970), Edwards (1971), Hare (1972a, 1972b), Sizemore (1972), and Staples (1971), admit to these trends; but because of their own ideology, they claim these are justified and necessary. They see the need to promote such conflict, to wipe out so-called white racism in social science while developing a black perspective. Black moderates such as Clark (1969), Kilson (1971), Patterson (1971), Rustin (1969), Sowell (1973), and Vontress (1970) object to these trends, for the greater part agreeing with the above white social scientists and further pointing out that the black studies programs are usually propagandistic, antiwhite, lacking in intellectual content, and used by weak students to bolster their grade point average; that militant students frequently intimidate moderate students as well as professors who refuse to espouse the militant party line or who attempt to uphold academic standards; that these militant students are often given teaching and administrative positions in black studies and other programs as a "payoff" and in preference to moderate black students who are not considered to be "authentic" blacks and are denied these positions. Most of these black critics claim that black ideology polarizes society and promotes segregation, thus playing into the hands of white bigots. They also claim that the black perspective in social science is propagandistic, and that whites will only begin to respect black social scientists when the latter conduct color-blind, nonideological research.

The moderate view seems to have less and less influence in education today as the militant view increases in scope and influence within the larger society. Similar trends are apparent throughout the social, political, and economic institutions of the country. Because of the general unwillingness of most black moderates to speak up, their lack of organization, and the coercive measures used against them by militants, the militant view regarding schools, colleges, social and community agencies, welfare organizations, and local politics usually becomes recognized as that of the black community as a whole. In most instances, the black militants get what they want because public officials and administrators hesitate to take a strong position against those who claim to represent blacks (Clark 1969; Moseley 1972; Record 1973b; Sowell 1973). It is a good measure of white naïvete and reluctance to challenge black demands that officials are willing to take the militant voice as representing the voice of the silent majority of blacks (Riesman 1970; Shanker 1969; Sowell 1973). Thus when we speak about the black perspective, we are often, in effect, talking about the philosophy and demands of black militants. Increasingly, the word "black" among blacks on and off college campuses is coming to connote a political and ideological stance, not a cultural or racial group. More and more, black caucuses are being organized as a permanent part of professional conferences: within these caucuses white social scientists are often lumped together and condemned as "racists" and political strategy and demands are outlined. To be sure, social science as most people know it is either condemned or no longer discussed at these meetings.

Besides limiting social science research and academic freedom, particularly as they relate to race relations, part of the black strategy is to denounce social science data (past and present) that is anything less than complimentary to blacks. In this connection, many black social scientists reject conventional social science methods and concepts that relate to race relations as a product of "white racism." Most social scientists, including a number of black scholars, reject the notion that social science is a conservative white ideology. For them, social science has universal concepts and methods, plus durability, which apply equally to all groups.

Black militants refer to such authors as Malcolm X, not Martin Luther King; Eldridge Cleaver and LeRoi Jones, not Roy Wilkins and Bayard Rustin. Similarly, an increasing number of blacks in social science fields no longer consider the ideas of black scholars such as Andrew Brimmer, Kenneth Clark, Martin Kilson, and Benjamin Mays to be relevant or important, because these scholars are not sufficiently militant or their ideas are politically "impure." Black social science, or the black perspective in social science, in effect, seems to be developing into political ideology and propaganda. Furthermore, black scholars such as Blackwell (1973), Bonaparte (1973), and Sowell (1973) point out that most of the able black scholars do not want to be associated with this "race" social science, but are pressured by their black cohorts to contribute to the "struggle"; moreover, whites continue to perceive them in this role.

Equally important is the fact that many militants do not realize or are unwilling to concede that many of the ideas they claim as their own were developed by the same white social scientists whom they arbitrarily dismiss in classes, public discussions, professional meetings, and journals as "irrelevant" or "racist" because of the color of their skin. Many blacks who espouse the new black perspective are either ignorant of or refuse to admit the fact that the concepts and empirical findings they often cite to condemn white society were developed by white social scientists: Robert Blauner in sociology,

Thomas Pettigrew in psychology, Charles Valentine in anthropology, Marilyn Gittell in education, Gary T. Marx in political science, Herbert Aptheker in history, Karl Tauber in demography, and Samuel Bowles in economics. In addition, Record (1973a, 1973b) points out, a large number of social scientists feel that the blacks who espouse militancy, black studies, and a black perspective in social science are usually ignorant of or distort research concepts and methods (which are racially neutral) and the findings. They often were hired simply to meet black demands for black professors and fill quotas; their formal credentials are usually limited, and many tend to have little knowledge outside their immediate backgrounds and gut experiences. Once they exhaust the rhetoric, they often are repetitious.

Most of the sophisticated black students recognize this hustle but are unwilling to admit it in front of the white students. A few black professors voice concern in public, but the majority of them deny these facts, dismiss them with a knowing smile, or merely agree without caring. As Record (1973b) asserts, when one white social scientist asked a new black colleague if "he didn't feel squeamish about holding high rank and in effect being unqualified for his job . . . he said it didn't bother him one damn bit" (p. 22). In the meantime, blacks respond publicly to charges that many black professors are unqualified by labeling the charges "racist," by claiming that blacks, regardless of formal credentials, are qualified by virtue of their color, or by claiming that their qualifications are not second-rate but different.

The insistence of many blacks that only a black person is qualified to conduct research in the black community serves only political and ideological purposes. According to Ornstein (1973) and Record (1973c), the claim challenges two basic assumptions: that quality research and scholarship reside with those who have mastered knowledge in a given area and have acquired professional skills, and that research and scholarly methodology are functions of a person's education and abilities, and not of his race or racial beliefs. The claim that only blacks are capable of researching black culture because only blacks know the "truth" about other blacks also favors blacks in that it creates jobs for them regardless of formal qualifications. This strategy serves the same political, ideological, and economic ends as when it is claimed that only blacks can teach black students, or only blacks can dispense social services to other blacks or judge literary works, poetry, the films, and the art of other blacks.

The rationale behind the black strategy, where only blacks are equipped to evaluate or work with other blacks, is easy to understand but difficult to discuss frankly in public. Furthermore, the implication that only members of one racial or ethnic group have the ability to relate to their fellows (and get appropriate jobs) does not prevent blacks from studying whites, teaching or dispensing services to whites, or judging white writers or poets (often as "racists"), nor does it now bar blacks from obtaining high-paying positions in predominantly white institutions and communities.

We have reached the point where formal credentials, scholarship, and ability may no longer count as much as heredity. Race and color are being used as an asset for blacks to voice their demands and further their political, ideological, and economic needs, while heredity is now considered as a liability for whites. In addition, most private and public officials are hesitant to oppose these black demands, and the same officials are under pressure from affirmative-action orders to hire marginally qualified minorities in lieu of more qualified whites—to meet quotas. The fact that many blacks are unqualified by traditional standards to be social scientists is no longer crucial for institutions under governmental pressure to hire them, especially when that pressure is in the form of implied and/or actual threats of losing federal funds amounting to several millions of dollars.[1] Ironically, almost anyone who raises objections to this trend is denounced as a "racist."

While many blacks claim that only blacks know the "truth" about black culture, they fail to admit that blacks like white social scientists are not immune to being biased or selective in conducting research and reporting data. "Telling it like it is," or "telling the truth," can be just as difficult for blacks as it is for whites. All social science is value-laden, but the researcher must not intrude his own personal values into the objective world; indeed, he must control his own biases, at least minimize them, not generate them into the flow of research. As B. Brown (1969) points out, social scientists "are supposed to be impartial"; they are supposed to stress "absolute accuracy through perfect disinterestness or objectivity. Affiliation with some partial interest results in a loss of the scientific spirit" (p. 237). And White and Duker (1973) assert that social science research is based on a reasonably reliable, valid, and systematically gathering data process. It should be "independent of the views of those who collected the data." Objective data and research procedures "are not used to support, substantiate, or prove a point of view. Data do not have opinions" (p. 107).

It is doubtful if the black perspective, which is a product of black politics and ideology, can or intends to be nonbiased and objective. While the typical black response is that social science research principles do not apply to blacks, because social science is white-dominated, the great majority of social scientists, black and white (who are not expounding propaganda) feel that social science has universal principles that apply to all groups (not just one group) and that racial factors can be controlled. In addition, most white social scientists have not been propelled by politics or ideology which claims to know the "truth" about a racial group, nor as a group have they sought to systematically fit research to coincide with preconceived dogma. Some critics claim that social scientists are highly subjective and struggle to support political interest groups, but as a group the divergence is toward the Left and highly supportive of all minorities and especially blacks. If anything, as Armor (1972), Moynihan (1969), and Record (1972b) point out, most social scientists have a liberal stance and now bury their findings if the data purports negative traits of minorities.

The point is, the black perspective starts out with a strong political bias and emotional slant. Rarely does anyone deliberately judge research data for their conformity to preexisting opinions, but this is exactly what the black perspective amounts to. As Wilson (1973) points out, all research in social problems produces the intended effect—if the research is carried out to prove or to disprove a point. This is what it seems that many black social scientists intend to do. In fact, many black social scientists are under pressure to come up with favorable "findings" about blacks. As one black sociologist described research under black auspicies in an interview with Record (1973c), "I'm afraid there [is] too much pressure to come up with favorable results" (p. 22). To put the problem in different words: the way the social scientist perceives a problem, conducts research, and interprets data depends on his value system; but there is a disjunction between the social scientist who seeks knowledge and will report data that do not coincide with his original hunches and the social scientist who is working to advance a political ideology and censors data that oppose his views and even manipulates the data to coincide with his original biases. The disjunction comes from the fact that we are no longer dealing with values but with propaganda, a continuing struggle between social science and those who wish to expand their political beliefs and power. Indeed, there is nothing wrong with political tracts or ideology; however, we need to recognize that much of the research conducted by blacks about blacks will not conform to standards of objective evidence or objective interpretation. It will most likely be just what it is intended to be—mythology and dogma.

We must also recognize that an increasing number of black social scientists see research as a tool of the black power movement, a weapon to be used against white-dominated social science just as the overall black power movement is to be used as a force against white-dominated society. Black social science has only recently gotten under way, having developed as an off-shoot of black power. The black perspective in social science, then, is evidently a trend of large and political appetites. It is not so much exceptional as it is characteristic of the entire black power trend; it is part of a growing political and ideological force; it is the tip of a growing iceberg, an inevitable result of the attempt by blacks to mask social rhetoric under the guise of social science, to discover relationships that bolster their popular suppositions. The aim of black social science is to eradicate so-called black stereotypes and replace them with new information and judgments which advance the cause of blacks. Indeed, black social science is not intended to be objective; its methodology is slanted and needs to be so labeled.

The implications of this new social science are illustrated by the opposing views of two white social scientists, as reported by Record (1972a):

> If [social scientists] really wanted to help blacks, they
> would condemn the whites and make the black cause
> their own. That's what I intend to do. I'll use sources
> that serve these purposes and to hell with the others
> [p. 9].

And in another interview, Record (1973*b*) quoted another anonymous social scientist:

> It's pretty clear now that whites are being discouraged
> from doing further research on blacks. If this continues
> and if fewer whites enter the field, as is now the case,
> within a couple of decades research about any minority
> group will become the monopoly of that group, and we
> will run the high risk of getting only insider, self-serving
> interpretations [p. 19].

While both social scientists recognize that black social science is turning into black censorship and propaganda, the first one is condoning this practice and the other is condemning it. The former seems crippled by guilt feelings, the same type of feelings that have crippled many officials into acquiescing to black demands in order to maintain the illusion of peace. The latter is strong in his opposition to race demands and is against disarming the field of social science. His stand will not win him a popularity contest among most blacks, and he will often find himself alone in his public position because most of his colleagues, like most university officials, are weak and unwilling to take a public stand against any group that claims it represents blacks. They fear being denounced as "racists," possibly being subjected to individual harassment, threats, and violence, though large scale disruptions on college campuses have subsided at the present.

The Evolving Black Perspective in Social Science

Indeed, most social scientists find it difficult to publicly admit to the restriction of research on minority subjects and institutions. Analyzing and interpreting the strengths and weaknesses of one group should not be taboo. Not all good points or important strengths are favorable to one group, and not all the problems of one group can be attributed to the prejudices and discrimination of the other group. Until the early 1960s, the black spokesmen were in a defensive position; however, things are reversed now. The strategies of "victimization" and "racism" have emerged as successful ploys and have made reasonable discussion or comprehensive analysis of the research on cognitive learning patterns, family structure, and social behavior of blacks almost impossible. Liberal and black leaders interpret every such research effort as "racist," then usually attack the author and denounce the magazine that published the article (or the institution that funded the research) for perpetuating "racism" and claim that the problem it describes lies not with the black community but with the "sickness" of society. Thus almost every statement or research document that may be interpreted as damaging or even less than flattering to the cause of blacks is usually denounced and the author's motives questioned.

The black strategy is to keep up this pressure, to espouse the "victimized" status of blacks and the "racist" nature of society, as well as to prevent a frank discussion on all the issues related to race and race differences. Any attempt to discuss some of the glaring problems of blacks (and every group has problems) is usually cut short by the liberal-black community as a white "racist" attempt at self-exculpation, an evasion of the so-called continued responsibility for the black condition, a threat to reduce rising double standards in education, employment, and social policies which favor blacks.

Blacks have learned that maintaining their "victimized" and "oppressed" image provides them with many benefits not regularly accessible to other groups. To avoid the ephithet of "racism," the social scientist is required to view the differences between the IQ and reading scores of blacks and those of whites solely as an environmental factor; to view standardized tests as culturally biased and invalid for blacks but not for low-income white ethnic groups, and not to mention that Orientals, who have also experienced racial discrimination and have foreign language patterns, do extremely well as a group in formal test situations; to dismiss the failure of compensatory education as attributed to lack of funds and inadequate methods; to ignore student input and home factors and to attribute the learning problems of many students solely to the failures of teachers and schools; to view black female-headed families and high illegitimacy rate as a strength; to view birth control for those blacks who must rely on the taxpayer to support their children as racial "genocide"; to view ghetto life as intrinsically healthy, even to glorify it, attributing all its vices to white "racism"; to consider black pathologies as a healthy way of coping with white "racism" or to deny that these pathologies[2] exist at all; to reject abnormal behavior and social deviancy among many blacks because their definitions are based on another set of criteria or to excuse it as a reflection of the "sickness" of society; to denounce whites who dare to judge black drug, delinquency, violence, and personality disorders or to resort to the claim of black "racism"; to ignore growing black crime trends directed toward whites or to interpret these trends as reparations for the past and as a political tactic;[3] to consider riots in black ghettos as solely related to black frustration and white "colonialism." The political fact is that black people must be given priority, regardless of these problems and behaviors, because they are still considered to be "victimized" and "oppressed," when, in fact, it seems that they are now victimizing and oppressing whites who work in black schools and communities; and it is blacks as a group who are curtailing the rights and due process of the white individual through black power and affirmative action, and under the guise of historical justification and black reparations.

If today's social science literature can only stress the problems and pathologies of white racism, and put all or almost all of the blame on society for the behavior of the individual, then there are either many naïve or gutless sociologists, psychologists, economists, and educators. All groups (including whites) have problems; all individuals have problems; this is a fact of life. Some groups and some individuals have more problems than others. To think that the problems and characteristics among groups are evenly distributed and correspond to a bell-shaped curve is highly theoretical and ignores the real world. Granted white society has discriminated against blacks (and other minorities) for hundreds of years. But racism cannot explain away all the problems of a group or an individual. If we cannot talk about the problems and prospects of people in a civil way then we might as well put up a sign and list the topics that are to be censored.

      Not only does the black perspective make white social scientists reluctant to objectively criticize blacks in public (especially in their own classrooms), it also seeks to enhance the "victimized-oppressed" status of blacks. Part of the black perspective (as we have previously indicated),[4] is to deny that conditions of blacks have improved. Writes Moynihan (1972), "It is apparently become necessary to deny that the conditions of blacks have improved in any respect. . . . Blacks [continue] to keep up the pressure on whites, and to be intensely suspicious of everything that might lend to a lessening of obligation" (p. 17). He goes on to point out that this pressure is linked to the goal of gaining increased political power and additional jobs despite lack of formal qualifications. Similarly, Wattenberg and Scammon (1973) maintain that civil rights leaders and many liberal-black social scientists know that economic and social conditions for blacks are fast approaching parity with whites "and even acknowledge it in private; but they have elected as a matter of policy to mute any public acknowledgement or celebration of black accomplishments" (p. 43). To be sure, they have elected this strategy for purposes of keeping up political pressure on legislators while trying to favorably shape public opinion.

      Banfield (1970) points out the differences between the "Statistical Negro," that is the black when nonracial variables are controlled, and the "Census Negro," the person grouped to compare with whites. In most respects, the statistical black group is indistinguishable from its white counterpart. In other words, once such variables as education, age, occupation, and region are accounted for, there are almost no differences between whites and blacks. Banfield asserts that the black leader tends to magnify the importance of prejudice and pretend that it is still a glaring facet of American society, even that it is worsening. He writes, "To acknowledge that nonracial factors are more important than racial ones would cool the zeal of his supporters . . . and destroy his very reason for being." For the black leader, "there is everything to gain and nothing to lose by treating all problems as if they derived solely from the racial one" (pp. 85–86). In this connection, it is simplistic to name any one variable as the sole or major cause for a social situation or social condition. It is wrong to attribute the plight of blacks solely to race while ignoring other influences, such as education, income, and family structure, just as it is wrong to attribute IQ, criminal behavior, or mental illness solely to heredity. While most social scientists have progressively abandoned monistic (single-cause), determinist theories of social behavior, the black perspective seeks to introduce white "racism" as the major reason for the black plight. Research has shown the causes of social phenomena to be more complex. Any social event is both the result of a multiplicity of causes and itself a contributing cause to other social events. As Rose (1965) asserts, good social science recognizes "all the institutions of a society and its culture are interrelated over time" (p. 16).

The problem is further compounded. Wilson (1972) points out that when one has developed strong feelings about the plight of a group, "one is especially reluctant to continue a critical discussion of the merits of the case." People who feel strongly about racial injustice are likely "to be impatient with, and even actively hostile toward, those who wish to say that the injustice does not exist or the social problem is the fault, not of society, but [of] those who display the symptoms. Efforts will be made to silence such persons." Most people will not participate in such efforts, "but if they believe the doctrine being silenced is sufficiently odious, they will take no active steps to oppose the censorship" (p. 52).

As mentioned earlier in this chapter, part of the black strategy is to deny white social scientists and researchers access to the black community. This strategy not only coincides with that of denouncing white social scientists as "irrelevant" and "racist," but also conforms to that of using social science for black group purposes and self-serving interests. Because research is important in helping to decide social policy, if blacks can gain control of research in the black community, it can be used to promote their interests. As Wilson (1973) maintains, the loyalties and commitments of the researchers, the efforts of partisans to defend or advance a given position, to praise or criticize a problem in question, can easily influence the findings and interpretations of the research, as well as what is reported and what is excluded from the report.

The leaders of this black perspective in social science (Andrew Billingsley, Roscoe Brown, Nathan Hare, Robert Hill, Joyce Ladner, Barbara Sizemore, Madelon Stent, Chuck Stone, and many others) claim that such a perspective is necessary to attack black stereotypes which have been promulgated by white social scientists. In one swoop, they usually condemn most white social scientists because of their color and urge the need to replace them with black social scientists in the field of race relations. More and more, the claim is that only blacks know the "truth" about blacks. Even white radicals are held in suspect because they cannot "think black." While some of these white social scientists may be permitted to conduct research in a black community if a black coinvestigator is also involved in all phases of the research, this white person's major role is devoted mainly to the technical and statistical work related to the research.

In this connection, Shanahan (1973) points out that the issue is not the researcher's ability to conduct research in an impartial and unbiased manner. The issue is just the opposite, that political and social realities have persuaded portions of the black community to claim that only black social scientists are qualified to conduct research on blacks because they can be trusted to advance a position and disseminate data that will serve the ends of blacks. Sizemore (1972) extends this argument by oversimplifying research unfavorable to blacks as the work of white supremacists. She further claims that blacks must use research and social science as vehicles for developing black ideology. Ideology generates solidarity, and blacks must maintain solidarity and reject the alien, white social scientist. She also contends that research must be used as part of the struggle for "liberation" and to intensify a "we groupness," a strong black nationalistic movement which builds pride and power.

Billingsley (1972) literally calls for the overthrow of social scientists who are white, over forty, and study blacks. He would replace them with so-called more objective black social scientists. The fact that the latter group of researchers may end up promoting a political cause and be less interested in honest research is not mentioned, only that black social scientists must combine their gut experience with their technical experience to wipe out the misconceptions about blacks and show how "they are in a true sense colonial-type subjects [who] are victimized by a careless and malignant society" (p. xvii). Stone (1972) uses the same type of rhetoric, contending that, if blacks "are going to break the stranglehold of white colonialism," they must define new criteria and concepts of education and social science research. He maintains that the ideas of white experts on race relations must be overhauled and that blacks are "determined to 'do [their] own thing.' " Stone calls for a black-white "technical assistance partnership" (implying that blacks need white assistance for statistical and research procedures), so long as the ground rules are developed by blacks (pp. 5-6). The question is, is this really a partnership? Ladner (1973) has even entitled a book she has edited *The Death of White Sociology*. In this book, five general themes emerge:

1. Social science is "white," "conservative," and "racist."
2. Blacks must eliminate white social scientists who work in the area of race relations.
3. Sociology and related subjects dealing with blacks must be reconstructed on black terms.
4. A more "accurate" picture of black culture must be disseminated to counteract white "racism."
5. White "racism" is the underlying cause of the black problems.

A few years ago, Deutsch (1969) observed that suspicion of the white social scientists was so great that it was becoming increasingly difficult for them to conduct research in many black communities. Four years later Shanahan (1973) contended it was impossible for "the white researcher to even secure a sample from within the black community" (p. 5). Black parents were asserting their newfound power to refuse to allow their children to participate in white-directed research. She contended that this raised serious questions with which white social scientists would have to grapple. As a white social scientist, Lahnston (1973) tried to deal with the problem by taking a defensive position and claiming that white researchers had no business in the black community without black researchers. He advocated a team approach and accommodated blacks by claiming this partnership would make "the white researcher to more accurately interpret the results of the research efforts" (p. 3). He failed to point out, however, that as pressure and intimidation continued to develop, this so-called more "accurate" view would probably result in a one-sided picture which stressed "positive" findings, even at the expense of distorting data and excluding anything that might be viewed as detrimental to black politics and ideology.

Obradović (1972) has also pointed out that the white social scientist is under close scrutiny and in direct conflict with black leaders and most black community dwellers. While her research was conducted in three southern urban areas and it is common knowledge that most blacks in the South tend to be less militant than those in the North, yet she found among southern blacks a distinctly negative attitude toward the researcher: he elicited emotional responses "such as 'white man,' 'the man,' . . . 'outsider,' and 'exploiter' " (p. 6). Blacks expressed the belief that their needs and priorities had been ignored by traditional researchers; they felt exploited and saw the time, effort, and money used in research as serving primarily the researcher's publication and grant purposes.

Obradović states that the research community must accommodate itself to the needs of the black community and that there is need for black researchers to conduct research among blacks. Few people would dispute these statements; however, she also contends that the black community must have input on all phases of research, implying agreement with the respondents of the survey, who insist that blacks "monitor all research done in their communities and that research findings [first] be reported to the people from whom the data was collected" (p. 7). She even recommends that there be "community members on the student's dissertation committee" if he does research in the black community (p. 9). Here we need to recognize that monitoring implies censorship and that lay community members, black or white, often lack the formal education and other qualifications to help determine what is legitimate research. Obradović seems to anticipate this criticism, suggesting that when we study the black community we make allowances: the study "may not be readily amendable to a clean research design or be conductable under controlled conditions" (p. 10). Rather than suit the research community, continues Obradović, "we must suit the black community and even find ways of rewarding professors who do not publish tightly controlled research" (p. 10).

These suggestions are anti-intellectual and antiresearch; they imply that, because some black social scientists and professors are incapable of conducting valid research, they should be rewarded on the basis of their color, not their merit or research ability. This implication coincides with the fact that the emphasis at many universities has shifted from research and productivity to community service and social action. Obradović's proposals also lead to black censorship and black ideology, not to research. We should be honest and admit these facts if this is the route research in the black community is to take—under the guise of eliminating the so-called middle-class biases and bigotry of the white social scientist.

According to Williams (1973), blacks have concluded that the social scientist is antithetical to black purposes and "have therefore determined to keep that researcher, who is generally white, out of the Black community." This conclusion, she contends, is based on the assumption that white social scientists "are unaware of their own roles as perpetuators of institutional racism" (p. 2). Not only does she resort to race relations rhetoric in denouncing whites as "racists," but she also fails to point out that all social scientists— even black ones—are influenced by their biases and values. There are procedures for the researcher to follow to minimize the influence of his biases and values on his research; but if white social scientists seem unable to follow these procedures when conducting race relations research, why should blacks, who are promoting ideology, be better able to control their biases and values, or be more objective? Williams claims that academic freedom and scientific inquiry are not the issues for blacks, rather "the possible policy statements and political decisions that could erupt from the various research outcomes" (p. 6). Thus she contends that white social scientists should "begin to look more closely at the ethical and/or political implications of their areas of research interest, [or] they may find themselves permanently barred from the Black community" (pp. 6–7). In other words, the fact that the researcher is no longer permitted to pursue his research to its end without interference is of little concern to Williams. She and many other black leaders feel that, if the research is detrimental to the black community, it should be buried; if it provides data that enhance social policy for blacks, it should be disseminated. Thus, many black social scientists not only seek the "truth" as they define it, but also consider the social ends for which the knowledge is being used and its political implications. In effect, the white social scientist is in a dilemma; he must be willing to purport the black perspective or be censored from the research community. Williams concludes that, as an educator, she is not concerned with the white researcher, that her allegiance "must stand with those members of the Black community who no longer will allow forces outside the Black community access to information on . . . Black children" (p. 7).

Some blacks in Boston have already adopted a particularly strong antiresearch position, according to Roscoe C. Brown (1971), director of Afro-American affairs at New York University. Black residents of Boston, with black social scientists, have established a Community Research Review Committee. The CRRC insists on

1. Continuously screening and approving researchers studying the black community.

2. Involving black staff, consultants, and also a black coinvestigator in *all* phases of the research.
3. Being paid 10 percent of the total budget of research projects.
4. Screening and approving (or disapproving) findings before they are submitted to any agency or journal.
5. Paying any consultant required to review the report or present an alternative interpretation out of research project funds.

There is no question that blacks have reason to be sensitive about the analysis and interpretation of research data concerning their schools and communities. Clearly, they have the right to rebut reports that may be inimical to the interests of the black community; however, some CRRC stipulations border on black censorship. They imply that white social scientists should not conduct research in the black community, or at least that they should be allowed to do so only under the watchful eye of an "inside" social scientist who is willing to slant findings to accommodate black community interests. Both implications have political ramifications. Black community activists could gain control of the information disseminated from ghetto areas. As Caro (1971) suggests, general antagonism toward the social scientist is also linked to the political ambitions of the minority activist: "The independent social scientist who does poverty research is a potential competitor for the activist who would like to control the flow of information from poverty areas" (p. 99).

Further complicating the picture is the recent appearance of several black, privately owned research and consulting agencies which emphasize the black experience of their personnel as qualifying them to conduct research and evaluation in the ghetto. Not only are these agencies profit-making schemes to cash in on the "relevancy" of blackness, but their technical and research qualifications may be questioned. Writes Record (1973c):

> . . . lacking in significant research experience, and staffed by hardly minimally qualified blacks, these agencies seek contracts with organizations operating programs or engaged in research which involves data gathering in black areas. It is not clear how such agencies could or do help except by limited public relations work and by placing a black sign of approval on a particular subject. One suspects that such "research and consulting" is only still another "hustle" that sharp black operators are laying down in a situation in which significant amounts of money are involved. Again, one must note, however, that if black hustlers have gotten into the research racket, they have plenty of examples of whites to follow [p. 30].

Stent (1973), one person who has exercised her privilege as a black researcher to form her own agency and is presently making a handsome profit, provides us with an example of the rhetoric that is used to advance the cause of these black firms. She claims that black researchers and consultants can often merge their skills with their "cultural heritage in such a way as to widen the cracks in the white-washed walls of opportunity" (p. 2). She denounces integration as a "peculiarly egotistical policy . . . from the white man's perspective" (p. 2), condemns standard tests and the tracking of students as "technological racism" (p. 7), and claims that black researchers should serve as "community resource agents . . . and agitators" (p. 10). She then opens the door to a new profit-making scheme for black researchers by claiming that they are "increasingly vital in the consultation process with white administrative personnel" in black and white schools because of their racial insights which white researchers lack (p. 10). In other words, blacks are supposed to have a monopoly on the data-gathering process in the ghetto because of their blackness. She also advocates that black researchers expand profits at the expense of white researchers. Her statement that black social scientists "challenge those who cling to the supremacy of their 'scientific' authority" connotes that formal qualifications and research abilities no longer count in the black community or for black social scientists, and that blacks must develop their own social science derived "from their black experience" (p. 11). For Stent and many other black spokesmen, it seems that blackness and ideology are more important now than professional skills and scholarship. In effect, it seems that, because some black consultants and evaluators lack research and statistical abilities, they discount formal qualifications as irrelevant and recognize color and ideology as important substitutes.

In this connection, Record (1973b, 1973c) points out that a growing number of critics of conventional research—in which personal biases are minimized and objectivity is honored—insist that black social science cannot afford the luxury of conducting reliable and valid research: the politically partisan researcher is fast becoming the only person acceptable to many voices within the black community, not the researcher with integrity. A selective process has now come into play where expertise is based on race and ideology and not on research skills. As Glennan (1973) asserts, a growing number of social scientists have sacrificed integrity and candor, and use highly questionable procedures, in their haste to develop new models and concepts for social science.

These trends are making it increasingly more difficult to conduct research or discuss frankly several topics related to race both inside and outside the university. If certain sensitive topics are researched or discussed, according to Record (1973c), Scriven (1970), and Wilson (1972), a great deal of turmoil and, in many instances, even violence follows. In particular, white social scientists, even those with partisan views that favor blacks, are finding it extremely difficult to conduct research in the black community or to explore racial issues in an objective manner.

As the efforts of the blacks to control research in the black community increase, fewer white social scientists will be conducting this research. In addition, many universities and foundations, while they have not formalized and made public arrangements with black spokesmen, seem to have implemented an informal arrangement so these blacks can control funds and approve almost all research concerning blacks. Most professors and foundation workers are unaware of this growing trend; and, perhaps because of their naïveté and the pressure from black spokesmen, we can expect it to continue. There is even the possibility that the federal government may require a high percentage of blacks on research teams and a black research director or co-director for all federally funded projects in the black community. Such a policy would certainly be in line with affirmative-action programs which require percentages and quotas and new federal guidelines in proposal writing, research, and evaluation which now give special attention to minority applicants. Unless the research community takes a firm position to maintain its integrity, research on blacks may be undertaken only by members of that group; and it is highly probable that the data will be censored and its validity suspect. The published "findings" will amount to nothing more than black ideology and propaganda.

What is to be said of the black perspective in social science? It is safe to say that what is happening in social science research in race relations today is not social science or research, but political ideology and self-serving propaganda. While I understand why blacks are using social science research to advance their own purposes, or—more accurately—transforming it into black ideology and propaganda, I cannot condone this trend. Many people are afraid to speak out: I am not responsible for their behavior. Despite the fact that social science research must be concerned with honest observations of what is actually happening, most black social scientists are unwilling to speak out because their first loyalty is not to social science but understandingly to other members of their race, and many white social scientists who would normally speak out are intimidated in class and on campus and believe it is best to leave well enough alone. In this connection a number of summary items should be mentioned.

First, the charge, made frequently, that white social scientists are conservative and racist is a ridiculous one, given the political and social dispositions of most social scientists. If anything, most social scientists professionally love poor and minority groups, adopt their causes and find reasons to justify their demands (even at the expense of unpoor and white groups), romanticize their culture, rationalize their pathologies, and are sensitive to what kinds of research they disseminate about them.

Second, overemphasis on prejudice encourages blacks to define all their problems in terms of white "racism," when many other factors influence human conditions. The pretense that blacks are the victims of the white man's hate and greed oversimplifies reality and leads to futile and even destructive policies and to the nonadoption of other policies that might do some good and be fair to *all* groups.

Third, the reasons for high crime rates, persistent unemployment despite training programs, IQ differences between blacks and whites, broken families, and the like are difficult to measure. Not only are the causes difficult to define and detect, because of the complex and multiple nature of human variables, the effects are difficult to disentangle from the causes. Whatever factors are defined, they should not be lumped into a single, all-encompassing, variable such as race or racism. Such lumping at best connotes a simplistic approach, not a sophisticated analysis of contemporary society. Social science research, on the other hand, is equipped to identify causes and effects, as well as the interaction process, by multivariable analysis.

Fourth, there is something called social science, a body of knowledge, a methodology which is free of politics and ideology and can be used to collect and disseminate data, and to report and make recommendations for purposes of social policy. When a social scientist undertakes research or manipulates data to conform to a preconceived bias or ideology, in effect, when he conducts research for purposes of developing or expanding a specific policy or strategy, his work is no longer research in that the data are nonobjective and are used to promote dogma. When a social scientist undertakes research to promote one idea, "to tell it how it is," to produce only positive findings, he is propagandizing, not searching for knowledge.

Fifth, when loyalty to one's race and the extent of one's racial experience and the nature of one's political views take precedence over loyalty to truth, when social scientists are forced to show fidelity to a prescribed political ideology in order to conduct research or collect data, we have at best the misuse of social science and research. At worst, we have old-fashioned censorship and authoritarianism rather than academic freedom and democratic principles.

Sixth, when scholarly and scientific principles are ridiculed as "irrelevant" or as expressions of "racism," and then are replaced by qualifications based on race or knowing the "truth" about blackness, it is time for the research community to openly take a stand and question the legitimacy of the new twisted science. When academic freedom is curtailed under the guise of political necessity or simply because of fear of personal abuse or safety, an uncivil and totalitarian effect is introduced into the field and must be stopped. When social scientists of one color are considered politically or ideologically "pure" while those of another color are considered alien and lacking in "racial spirit," we have entered the dangerous arena of reverse German racism. In effect, we are dealing with the political and racial concept of "racial soul," once expounded by some German theorists as *Volkseist.*

Seventh, differences in opinion among social scientists cannot easily be resolved. As a result, schools of thought evolve and infighting between adherents of different ideas continues, with readers being allowed to make up their own minds. Social science methods are another matter, however. While there may be several acceptable methods for conducting research, there are certain basic principles that should be followed. The researcher's ability to find the true relationships between causes and effects will depend on his having a good initial idea of the whole range of possible conditions effecting the problem, and on his ability to construct a valid method for analyzing these. The better the social scientist understands these basic processes, despite his opinions about the problem, the less likely he will be to make mistakes. But a researcher's being unable to study certain variables that are sensitive, being forced to interpret data in only one way to coincide with a partisan stance, or being more concerned with opinion than with method may render his "findings" unacceptable and as propaganda.

Eighth, all social scientists, except those conditioned by political masters and driven by political ideology, believe that they can operate only in an atmosphere of freedom. They must not have imposed upon them dogma or censorship which limits what can be done or expressed in science or social science, as for example, that from which Galileo or Sevetus suffered. Although the research community exercises a critical and even subjective control through its societies, professional journals, and informal groups, it does permit differing opinions. Ideas and theories are continually discussed, criticized, and revised at meetings and in journals. Various ideas are advanced, compared, and synthesized into new visions and understandings. Although this freedom is somewhat restricted when the topic is race, there is still the attempt to permit differing views and interpretations which the black community is sensitive about and has been successful in stifling when it deems it unacceptable.

Ninth, the job of the social scientist is to question all sacred cows, even those that are highly visible and anxiety-provoking. It follows that maintaining the status quo is self-reinforcing and creates stagnation, and that being unable to pursue certain assumptions or areas of research retards legitimate research and prevents the formation of reform policies. The present barriers that confront the social scientist in the black community create a political, self-interest black view and limit legitimate social change for *all* groups. The social scientist can play an important role in providing data to lower the barriers against social change and social policy reform by his unrestricted and uncensored exploration of relevant problems; however, he can only study these problems and conduct his research if he has the freedom to collect and disseminate data.

Tenth, social scientists are best qualified to remove social barriers created by their own thinking, as well as those resulting from the pseudo realities of society and social policy. They have the ability to promote thinking and research in previously ignored areas and to bring new light to current conditions. In other words, society can change if social scientists are permitted to question many aspects of current social policy. It would seem necessary that they do just that, and to do it they must be permitted the right of inquiry and given academic freedom; in fact, a democratic society thrives when social scientists operate under these conditions. If they are restricted, if they operate under censorship, we are forced to rely on false information, and the social foundations of this society are threatened.

Eleventh, social scientists are rarely put in charge of social action programs or social policy, but their work is used to evaluate the results of these programs and policies. The role of the social scientist is to collect data and report findings in an honest and nonideological way; in turn, his ideas and results should be taken into consideration by program directors and policy makers. The trouble is, program directors and policy makers often have little understanding of social science research and often use such data in a way not justified by the actual findings. Social scientists need to be honest in reporting their findings and to write their findings in such a way that they can be understood by program directors and policy makers (as well as by lay people); otherwise, their work will be either ignored or misused. That some social scientists have been corrupted into becoming profit-making entrepreneurs and quack propagandist activists in part illustrates the growing politics and hustle in black power and lends a particular urgency to the need for other social scientists, especially black moderates, to expose this practice.

Twelfth, most of the public and many of the policy makers do not have the time, training, or occasion to read through, much less understand, the technical literature on social behavior. They rely on professional analyses. Since most of these social analysts are liberal, the public receives a slanted view of the facts involved and not always the total picture. The views of the liberal-black community, the silence of many other social scientists and academicians, the one-sided coverage in the newspapers and popular magazines, the increasing reluctance of social science journals to publish sensitive findings, the increasing refusal of universities, foundations, and the federal government to support research in sensitive areas while encouraging and funding liberal and black-controlled research—these are all signs of political ideology to which research and social policy has become hostage. This is a trend we can no longer afford, because of the loss in honest inquiry and legitimate reform.

Conclusion

The black perspective in social science is advocated by a significant number of liberals and blacks and must be understood for what it is at the present; it is a strategy that seeks to:

1. Persuade researchers to explore issues in which blacks are interested.
2. Postpone, if possible, comparative research between blacks and whites in sensitive areas.
3. Ensure that research concerning blacks is cleared by black research committees.
4. Ensure that research concerning blacks is checked at interim stages and that the findings are approved before they are disseminated to the public or published in a professional journal.
5. Have researchers "tell it like it is" about black history and culture, meaning that they present blacks in a favorable light.
6. Conduct research and disseminate data that coincide with preconceived biases and serve black self-interests.

7. Oversimplify by attributing the problems of blacks to the "sickness" of society, or deny that possible problems exist within the black family structure.
8. Deny that conditions among blacks have improved markedly.
9. Use, if needed, invalid research methods to advance political beliefs and ideology.
10. Claim that only blacks know the "truth" about other blacks and therefore are the only ones qualified to conduct research in the black community.
11. Reject qualified white researchers as "alien," "irrelevant," and "racist" and argue that they do not belong in the black community—certainly not alone or, if they are directing a research project, without a black co-director.
12. Restrict academic freedom and promote censorship under the guise that morality demands that certain issues not be discussed, regardless of the possible truth.
13. Prevent criticism of the black community, regardless of the possible objectivity of the criticism, even to the extent of intimidating the researcher, professor, or speaker.
14. Use social science research or, more accurately, subvert its principles to develop a "liberation" strategy which is basically propagandistic and fosters black ethnocentrism and antiwhite attitudes to unify blacks.

It must be recognized that, given the kind of data with which the social sciences deal, disagreement is not only healthy but necessary, indeed vital for social science to refine explanations of social phenomena. Because of the complexity of the social sciences, each researcher worth his salt learns the significance of a point of view, and learns to judge data in relation to the author's point of view and his own. Sometimes the author and reader may have a similar way of looking at the world, and in other instances they may disagree. Over the long time and sometimes even within a short time, certain points of view show themselves as capable or incapable of explaining the phenomena they purport to explain. I believe that the views expressed in this chapter will start taking on greater relevance and stand the test of time, especially as the black perspective in social science increases in tempo and other social scientists sense a growing feeling of intimidation in their own college classrooms.

Postscript

a. Hostility to concepts of scholarship and research in the field of race relations continues to grow against social scientists who refuse to follow the radical/militant philosophy. As of late 1973, HEW published a 346-page report which detailed an extensive control system over "improper" research and "social risks" in all federally-funded grants and contracts. In effect, the social scientist is now forced to limit his choice of topics and research boundaries if he wishes to obtain money for research. At the same time at Harvard University, Gerald Lesser's follow-up study on differing patterns of thinking among Chinese, Jewish, Puerto Rican, and black students has been withheld from publication because the earlier study showed differences among these groups, even when income was held constant. Professors at Berkeley University have established review policy which prohibits research that seems damaging to the reputation of a social or racial group. Arthur Jensen's research lies behind the controversy. Professors at Columbia University are reaching a showdown on a similar issue which may limit research.

One of the first universities to establish a research screening panel was Stanford University, mainly as a reaction to William Shockley's research. Shockley has had to go to court to defend his right to conduct research and discuss his views on genetics, and to maintain his tenured teaching position. He continues to be savagely criticized in professional journals and organizations and is often denied the right to publish or speak. Universities also restrict him in expressing his ideas. In the last four months of 1973, Harvard University cancelled a debate between Schockley and Roy Innis of CORE, largely because of protests from the Black Law Students Association. Dartmouth students took matters into their own hands and prevented him from speaking by applauding continuously during his appearance. Even at Staten Island Community College, opposition by some members of the student senate and Black Students Union prevented Shockley from speaking; the previous speaker in the seminar was Justice William O. Douglas, noted for his liberal views, and the next was Bobby Seale, chairman of the Black Panther Party. Both speakers were permitted to espouse their views.

Most distressing is the half page advertisement that appeared in the Sunday *New York Times* (October 28, 1973), "A Resolution Against Racism," which was signed by more than 1,000 professors. The resolution denounced Eysenck, Herrnstein, Jensen, and Shockley for their views on standardized testing and intelligence, and condemned their ideas as "master-race" and "Nazi-like." The resolution also (1) called upon academicians to adopt measures to eliminate classroom racism, (2) urged professional organizations and societies, colleges and universities, and editors of professional journals to refuse to disseminate racist research, (3) advocated that those who express racist ideas be denied the legitimacy provided by academia, and (4) advocated the organization of activities to eliminate racist practices.

Bearing in mind the emotionalism and politics resulting from "racist" research, and reading between the lines, we note the implications of these four points. First, the measures to be taken are not specified and could include witch hunts and vigilantism. Point two connotes clear censorship. The next point implies that those who fail to espouse or diverge too far from the liberal-black party line may be fired—unless they temper or curtail their views. The final point, bearing in mind the current controversy over "racist" research, could include irrational or extreme activities. Like most contemporary data on the subject, the whole tone of the resolution ignores the fact that racism, today, can be a two-way process. The resolution ends with a call to a "National Conference on Racism and the University" at New York University with the implied purpose of organizing further activities to eliminate individuals on campuses across the country who espouse racist ideas.

We overlook the fact that the personal denunciations and name-calling fail to grapple with the methodology of the research and the related policy implications. Questions of what is racism, who is a racist, how value judgments effect social science data, and how political motives interact with the charge of racism should be explored. These questions need clarification before tainting others for conducting "racist" research, advocating censorship under the guise of social responsibility, or urging that someone be discharged from academia because of his research. Indeed, it is questionable whether those who criticize the findings of Jensen, Shockley, etc. have read, much less understand the data. It is doubtful if these critics, especially the students, have the social scientific background and statistical knowledge to analyze such issues, or any good reason for believing that the radical left/black militant commitment to free inquiry is nothing more than politics and another form of intolerance and hostility of the corrupt society they condemn.

Without alluding to the First Amendment, those who don't want to hear or read someone's ideas don't have to; those who want to challenge someone's views can (in a civil tone); but those who try to suppress a specific viewpoint give it credence and encourage the trappings of a cause. On the other hand, those who wish to suppress data are politically motivated and constitute a grave danger to academia; they encourage (1) censorship, (2) fear, (3) a mono-interpretation of research and development, (4) illegitimate, or at best restricted, scholarship, and (5) fraudulent public policy. In short, the search for knowledge and solutions becomes limited to the popular view and exclusive ideological position.

The social scientist must be free to develop theories and test hypotheses of his (not society's or those of a political or social pressure group's) choosing. This means that research not in vogue should be permitted. Unless social scientists are free to pursue their research in their own ways, the data so desperately needed about social problems will be slow in coming, or it will be deceiving. Without trying to separate the roles of researcher, critic, and activist, those who formulate public policy must realize that empirical findings—not ideologies—offer the best answers for current problems.

The conflict that seems to arise today is between the norms of social science and the norms of politics. Scientists should be committed to public revelation of what they learn; those who are politically motivated are committed to norms of secrecy and selective publicity. Social science demands a full disclosure of the facts; politics works on the basis of partial disclosure. When politics, not scientific findings, take precedence over what can be discussed in print or in public, certain problems will be ignored and there will be a distorted policy-making impact.

If we regard the acquisition of scientific knowledge about people as necessary for solving social problems, then it is difficult to rule out knowledge that may be sensitive. If deception and fraudulent schemes are the main objectives, then there is good reason for ruling out potential research or research findings that constitute a challenge. The social scientist is a competitor among his own profession and with others in the effort to establish an interpretation of society. The scientist represents a threat to politically-motivated interpreters of reality, and he is being told that certain things are best left unsaid. Regardless of who is "right," which is a value judgment, all parties to a controversy are obligated to present their cases to the public with fullness and fairness, and to permit the public to enter into discussions on policy which affect them.

Notes

1. For example, the *New York Times* (October 1, 1972) compiled a list of colleges and universities receiving federal support in fiscal year 1971. The top 50 recipients received between $18 and $90 million that year. Heading the list were Massachusetts Institute of Technology; University of Minnesota; University of Michigan; University of Wisconsin, Madison; University of Washington; Stanford University; Harvard University; University of California, Los Angeles; University of California, Berkeley; Columbia University; and Howard University—each receiving more than $50 million per year. Although there has been a reduction in federal funding since 1971, the institutions of higher learning are under greater pressure to hire and promote minorities regardless of formal qualifications (see chapter 2) or risk the possible loss of federal monies. Indeed, many graduate schools and schools of medicine would fold in a few years without federal funds. As J. Stanley Pottinger, former head of HEW's affirmative-

action program, said in a 1972 west coast speech: "We have a lot of power and we are prepared to use it."

2. See chapters 2 and 5.

3. See chapter 5.

4. See chapter 2.

References

Armor, David
1972 "The Evidence of Busing." *Public Interest*, Summer, pp. 90–126.
Banfield, Edward C.
1970 *The Unheavenly City*. Boston: Little, Brown.
Billingsley, Andrew
1970 "Black Families and White Social Science." *Journal of Social Issues* 26:127–42.
1972 "Forward." In R. H. Hill, *The Strengths of Black Families*. New York: Emerson Hall.
Blackwell, James, and Morris Janowitz, eds.
1973 *The Black Sociologists*. Chicago: University of Chicago Press.
Bonaparte, Tony H.
1973 Article in the *New York Times*, February 4, sec. 3, p. 9.
Brown, Bob B.
1969 *The Experimental Mind in Education*. New York: Harper & Row.
Brown, Roscoe C., Jr.
1971 "How to Make Educational Research Relevant to the Urban Community—The Researcher's View." Paper presented at the Annual AERA Conference, New York, February.
Caro, Francis G.
1971 "Issues in the Evaluation of Social Programs." *Review of Educational Research* 41:87–114.
Clark, Kenneth B.
1969 "Letter of Resignation from Board of Directors of Antioch College." In *Black Studies: Myths and Realities*, ed. B. Rustin, pp. 32–37. New York: A. Philip Randolph Educational Fund.
Deutsch, Martin
1969 "Organizational and Conceptual Barriers to Social Change." *Journal of Social Issues* 25:5–18.
Draper, Theodore
1970 *The Rediscovery of Black Nationalism*. New York: Viking Press.
Edwards, Harry
1971 *Black Studies*. New York: Free Press.
Glazer, Nathan
1969 "Ethnic Group and Education: Towards the Tolerance of Difference." *Journal of Negro Education* 38:187–95.
Glennan, Thomas K., Jr.
1973 "National Institute of Education: A Personal View." *Educational Researcher* 2:13–16.
Hare, Nathan
1972a "The Battle for Black Studies." *Black Scholar* 3:39–47.
1972b "The Sociological Study of Racial Conflict." *Phylon* 33:27–31.

Herrnstein, R. J.
  1973 "On Challenging Orthodoxy." *Commentary,* April, pp. 56–62. Reprinted from *Commentary,* by permission; Copyright © 1973 by the American Jewish Committee.
Kilson, Martin
  1971 "Memo on Direction of Reforms in Afro-American Studies Curriculum at Harvard University." November, pp. 11–12.
Ladner, Joyce
  1973 *The Death of White Sociology.* New York: Random House.
Lahnston, Anton T.
  1973 "The White Researcher in the Black Community: A Dilemma." Paper presented at the Annual AERA Conference, New Orleans, February.
Moseley, Francis S.
  1972 "The Urban School: Too Late for More Change." *Phi Delta Kappan* 54:559–64.
Moynihan, Daniel P.
  1968 "Sources of Resistance to the Coleman Report." *Harvard Educational Review* 38:23–36.
  1969 *Maximum Feasible Misunderstanding.* New York: Free Press.
  1972 "The Schism of the Black Family." *Public Interest,* Spring, pp. 3–24.
New York Times
  October 1, 1972.
Obradović, Sylvia M.
  1972 "Community Perspectives on Educational Research in Black Communities." Paper presented at the Annual AERA Conference, Chicago, April.
Ornstein, Allan C.
  1972 *Urban Education: Student Unrest, Teacher Behaviors, and Black Power.* Columbus, Ohio: Merrill.
  1973 "Research on Decentralization." *Phi Delta Kappan* 54:610–14.
Patterson, Orlando
  1971 "Rethinking Black History." *Harvard Educational Review* 41: 297–315.
Podhoretz, Norman
  1973 "The New Inquisitors." *Commentary,* April, pp. 7–8. Reprinted from *Commentary,* by permission; Copyright © 1973 by the American Jewish Committee.
Record, Wilson
  1972*a* "White Sociologists and Black Studies: A Very Preliminary Report." Paper presented at the annual conference of the Pacific Sociological Association, Portland, April.
  1972*b* "Who Is Impartial?" *Time,* August 7, pp. 46–47. Reprinted by permission from *Time,* The Weekly Newsmagazine; Copyright Time Inc.
  1973*a* "Can Sociology and Black Studies Find a Common Ground?" Paper presented at the Black Cultural Forum, Portland State University, February.
  1973*b* "More Than a Matter of Color." Paper presented to the annual conference of the American Sociological Association, New York, August.
  1973*c* "Some Implications of the Black Studies Movement for Higher Education in the 1970s." Paper presented at the Annual AERA Conference, New Orleans, February.

Riesman, David
    1970 "Reservations about Black Power." In *The Transformation of Activism,* ed. A. Meier, pp. 155–62. Chicago, Aldine.

Rose, Caroline B.
    1965 *Sociology: The Study of Man in Society.* Columbus, Ohio: Merrill.

Rustin, Bayard
    1969 "Introduction." In *Black Studies: Myths and Realities,* ed. B. Rustin. New York: A Philip Randolph Educational Fund.

Scriven, Michael
    1970 "The Values of the Academy." *Review of Educational Research* 40: 541–49.

Shanahan, Judith K.
    1973 "The White Researcher in the Black Community: A Dilemma." Paper presented at the Annual AERA Conference, New Orleans, February.

Shanker, Albert
    1969 "The Real Meaning of the New York City Teachers' Strike." *Phi Delta Kappan* 50:434–41.

Sizemore, Barbara A.
    1972 "Social Science and Education for a Black Identity." In *Black Self-Concept,* ed. J. A. Banks and J. D. Grambs, pp. 141–70. New York: McGraw-Hill.

Sowell, Thomas
    1973 *Black Education: Myths and Tragedies.* New York: McKay.

Staples, Robert E.
    1971 *The Black Family.* Belmont, Ca.: Wadsworth.

Stent, Madelon D.
    1973 "Researchers, Consultants and Urban Schools." Paper presented at the Annual AERA Conference, New Orleans, February.

Stone, Chuck
    1972 "The Psychology of Whiteness vs. the Politics of Blackness." *Educational Researcher* 1:4–6, 16.

Vontress, Clemmont E.
    1970 "Black Studies—Boon or Bane?" *Journal of Negro Education* 39: 192–201.

Wattenberg, Ben J., and Richard M. Scammon
    1973 "Black Progress and Liberal Rhetoric." *Commentary,* April, pp. 35–44.

White, Mary A., and Jan Duker
    1973 *Education: A Conceptual and Empirical Approach.* New York: Holt, Rinehart & Winston.

Williams, Barbara I.
    1973 "The White Researcher in the Black Community: Black Perspectives." Paper presented at the Annual AERA Conference, New Orleans, February.

Wilson, James Q.
    1972 "Liberalism versus Liberal Education." *Commentary,* June, pp. 50–54.
    1973 "On Pettigrew and Armour: An Afterword." *Public Interest,* Winter, pp. 132–34.

chapter 5

Black Nationalism

This chapter explores the rise of black nationalism and the accompanying decline of integrationist sentiments among many blacks. Next it examines briefly the relationship between race and crime, especially that between black nationalism and the use of violence as a political tactic. Most important, the reader should note that the two terms "nationalist" and "integrationist" are general terms; not all groups or actions can be equated with nationalism or integration.

Black Nationalism versus Integration

In the mid-1960s, when many social, political, and legal gains were being won by blacks, the civil rights movement took on a noticeable change for a small but growing number of blacks. This group became less trusting of whites and less concerned with the major goals of integration and began to be outwardly hostile toward whites and to express a desire for black nationalism. The slogans of equality and justice changed to slogans of black pride and power, and the concept of integration began to connote white "assimilation." Within a few short years, there was a sense and surge of black consciousness, black control over black institutions, black politics and culture, and black revolution.

The black nationalists tend to be younger, and are accused by integrationists of not knowing their history and being ignorant of recent black advances through the civil rights movement. The integrationists point out that black violence—especially the riots and the rise of Panther-like organizations—the demands for community control, and the subsequent ouster of whites from the black community are causing white backlash and strengthening conservatism. The integrationists see the nationalists as hustlers, out to frighten the white power structure so as to increase their own green power; they accuse them of being hypocritical, resorting to rhetoric rather than seeking reform, and of setting back the black cause. They accuse the nationalists of not understanding real power, which is not based on the barrel of a gun but on the democratic process whereby ethnics gain power through the political system but respect the rights and interests of other groups. Finally, the integrationists point out that blacks are a minority and need white friends and allies in coalition politics: any other strategy is nihilistic and suicidal.

The nationalists reject integration because it depends on the good will of whites who, they claim, are bigoted and cannot be trusted. They view the integrationists as tools of the white structure; furthermore, black nationalists contend that the integrationists are crippled by rejection of self and of blackness. They insist that it is the integrationists who are politically naïve, too moderate, and that black gains can best be made through threats of or actual violence, by getting rid of white power influences, and controlling their own institutions. Integration, they claim, means that blacks will remain a minority surrounded by a hostile majority. They assert that people do not surrender power, that it must be taken away from them: traditional and democratic methods do not apply to blacks, so force must be used if necessary.

It is the nationalists who have recently gained the momentum and influence over many blacks, especially the youth. They have produced swift changes but have alienated whites to the point that they are beginning to lose some of their liberal allies. Black nationalist gains in popularity and influence at the expense of integrationists are evident in the increase in sales of books written by Frantz Fanon, Malcolm X, Stokely Carmichael, H. Rap Brown, Eldridge Cleaver, and Angela Davis, and the corresponding decline in sales of books written by Roy Wilkins, Martin Luther King, Jr., Whitney Young, Jr., Louis Lomax, and Bayard Rustin.

The difference between the nationalists and integrationists is somewhat illustrated by table 5.1. Although the overall concepts, nationalism and integration, can be considered as a dichotomy, the people listed under each concept do not necessarily reflect a bipolar view; rather they lean toward the respective concept. Blacks are compared with selected fields of endeavor according to their philosophies: those in the middle column are seen by the nationalists as symbols of white servitude, white "assimilation," white stories of success, and integration according to white standards; those in the righthand column are seen as symbols of black independence, black identity, black stories of success according to black terms. Those persons in the right colum have gained popularity and respect among black nationalists and an increasing number within the black community.

Further evidence of nationalist gains in stature and influence can be seen in the decline of such groups as the National Association for the Advancement of Colored People (NAACP) and the Southern Christian Leadership Conference (SCLC), and the shift in philosophy and tactics of such previously integrationist organizations as the Council of Racial Equality

(CORE), Student Nonviolent Coordinating Committee (SNCC), and the National Urban League—a shift in the direction of confrontation, community control, and black power.

Table 5.1

BLACK HEROES: INTEGRATIONISTS VERSUS NATIONALISTS

Basis for Comparison	Integrationists	Nationalists
Early integration methods	George Washington Carver	Frederick Douglass
Self-help methods	Booker T. Washington	Marcus Garvey
Early NAACP leaders	A. Philip Randolph	W. E. B. Du Bois
Early 1960 leadership	Martin Luther King, Jr., Civil Rights	Malcolm X, Separation
Boxing star	Joe Louis	Muhammad Ali
Actor	Sidney Poitier	Jim Brown
Poet	Contee Cullen	Imamu Amiri Baraka
Playwright	Langston Hughes	Melvin Van Peebles
Historian	John Hope Franklin	Lerone Bennett
Economist	Thomas Sowell	David H. Swinton
Psychologist	Kenneth B. Clark	Alvin Poussaint
Sociologist	E. Franklin Frazier	Nathan Hare
Lawyer	Robert L. Carter	Haywood Burns
Congressman	Edward Brooke	Julian Bond
Clergyman	Ralph Abernathy, SCLC	Jesse Jackson, Jr., PUSH
African leader	Haile Selassie	Kwame Nkrumah

A dramatic and recent illustration of the gain in black nationalism at the expense of the philosophy of integration is seen in the ouster of the militant Reverend Jesse Jackson from SCLC, the subsequent decline of SCLC, and the rise of power of Jackson and his Organization PUSH. According to the *Chicago Tribune* (July 26, 1973) and the *New York Times* (July 22, 1973), Reverend Ralph Abernathy resigned tentatively as president of SCLC and blasted blacks for giving lip service to Martin Luther King's dream for integration and white coalitions. Abernathy pointed out that SCLC was in debt and that middle-class blacks were no longer donating sufficient money to the organization.

Even more disturbing is the NAACP's current school policy change by the Atlanta branch—by far, the most influential and prestigious branch in the South. The *New York Times* (July 22, 1973) reports that the 1973 NAACP's plan in Atlanta deemphasizes integration in favor of black control of the schools. The national office has ruled that the plan was contrary to policy and 46 officers of the Atlanta chapter were suspended for refusing to repudiate their position. Indeed, the plan sets a dangerous trend for other black integrationist organizations of surrendering the struggle for integration if it is at all possible, given white resistance. Elsewhere the *Times* (July 15, 1973) said, "Some NAACP officials feel that the fight with the Atlanta branch involves the very future of the organization which sees itself as 'the last civil rights organization that still believes in integration' " (p. 3).

Only a few weeks after the plan was announced, it was cited in four federal district courts in which white segregationist pressure groups tried to limit student integration: Brooklyn, New York; Dayton, Ohio; Grand Rapids, Michigan; and Knoxville, Tennessee. At the same time, the former integrationist organization, CORE, is fighting the NAACP and blocking the U.S. Supreme Court approval of city-suburban school integration.

Also apparent is the rise of a number of black militant organizations that preach violence—and worse. These include:

1. Revolutionary Action Movement (RAM), headed by Robert F. Williams, living in exile in Cuba, and consisting of a number of black college-educated youth in a few large cities, some of whom were recently charged with plotting the murder of integrationists such as Roy Wilkins and Whitney M. Young, Jr.
2. US, headed by Mualana Ron Karenga, an organization that seeks a nationwide national struggle or revolution based on the philosophy of Marx, Fanon, and Mao.
3. Negro Action Group (NAG), modeled by Jesse Gray, which displayed street agitation and violent tactics, as well as nationalistic, antiwhite philosophy, during the I. S. 201 and Ocean Hill–Brownsville controversy in New York City, and even refused to cooperate with CORE, which was integrationist and interracial at that time.
4. Republic of New America (RNA), a small organization which has received wide publicity because of its demands that $400 billion in reparations be paid to blacks and that five southern states be turned into a sovereign black nation and its numerous shootouts with the police in the North and South.
5. Black Panthers, a nationwide organization originally bent on destroying the oppressive "amerika" and killing white "pigs" (policemen), most of whose original leaders—among them are Eldridge Cleaver, Huey Newton, Bobby Seale, Bobby Hutton, and Fred Hampton—have either been exiled, jailed (some acquitted), or killed in shootouts with the police.

The black nationalist trend has been apparent as a nationwide move-ment since the first black power conference in Newark, New Jersey, in 1967. This was a four-day conference from which whites were barred. Moderate black leaders, such as Reverend Martin Luther King, Bayard Rustin, Roy Wilkins, and Whitney Young, were absent; and a nationwide unified and militant black power movement was outlined. The resolutions that were passed rejected whites and integration, promoted black political power and ideology, and called on nonwhites of the world to unite in their struggle against their white "oppressors." By 1972 the nationalist trend had become more influential. When the black caucus was held in Gary, Indiana, black moderates and integrationists felt it necessary to attend. They were out-voted, however, and the 3,000 black delegates passed, among others, several anti-integrationist and black ideology resolutions. A general antiwhite feeling prevailed over the entire conference, and the NAACP representatives refused to endorse the resolutions.

If one closely examines the literature of such black nationalists as Marcus Garvey, Frantz Fanon, Malcolm X, Stokley Carmichael, Eldridge Cleaver, H. Rap Brown, and Angela Davis, one finds many passages that espouse a philosophy and a strategy that coincide with the national socialism of Richard Wagner, Friedrich Nietzsche, Oswald Spengler, Ernest Jünger, Leopold von Ranke, Martin Heidegger, and Carl Schmitt. Even though black nationalism and national socialism were born in different countries at different times, their philosophies and strategies, as outlined by these authors, run parallel in their reliance on military virtues, in their rejection of compro-mise and tolerance, in their claims of victimization, in their glorification of hatred and violence, and in their efforts to transform their community or na-tion into an armed camp to wage war.

Similar views between both nationalist groups include the rejection of individual rights for the good of the movement, where noise, violence of language, conflict, and the collective strength of the movement shout down the individual. There is the belief that the ends justify the means, and there is historical justification of the ends and means. There is the application of dialectic history, making war appear as a normal manifestation of nature. War is envisioned along racial lines, where there is the inevitable victory of one race over another. In fact, there is the belief that war is inescapable and even psychologically healthy. Western civilization is rejected as evil, decadent, corrupt, and oppressive. The movement is geared toward toppling Western civilization and creating a new and utopian civilization. The law protects the enemy (and the weak) because it was devised by them. There is growing im-patience with reason, compromise, and slow progress; these democratic pro-cedures are rejected as tools of the enemy. There is the appeal to followers as bearers of racial ideas of pride and power. The teaching of art, history, literature, etc., become methods for mobilizing and educating followers. Racial slogans and rhetoric replace facts and reason. Self-sacrifice, defiance of the enemy, and conflict are enhanced. There is an appeal to myths, especially of superhuman qualities; the Nordic superman is replaced by the black superstud who puts down "whitey." There is the glamour and glorification of primitive heroism; military warriors are exalted. The individual does not count; he is multiplied by the number of his brothers, comrades, or soldiers. Fists, salutes, handshakes, arm bands, clothing (uniforms), hair styles are important symbols of pride, comradeship, and group solidarity. There is the preaching of self-sufficiency and the elimination of everything alien.

The above comparisons have been somewhat arbitrarily chosen, and many more comparisons could be made. The idea is to limit the comparisons to prevent overkill. Each idea has been expressed by one or more of the recognized black nationalist and national socialist authors. The total views are not those of one author but are a composite of the views expressed by all the authors in each group. It is important to recognize that the number of active black nationalists is small, although many others may espouse the above philosophy on an intellectual basis. Similarly, it is significant that the majority of blacks reject these authors, despite past discrimination and continuing segregation; however, it seems that the influence of the black nationalists is growing.

There are several fundamental differences between the black nationalist and national socialist movements: The black movement is an attempt at building identity and strength among a relatively disorganized group, at least a group that was disorganized in the 1960s, in comparison to advocating nationalism mainly to gain a majority for repressing others. The former is limited by the fact that it lacks the two most important things in American politics, the dollar and the ballot; the latter's goals were unlimited, and it was able to expand beyond the boundaries of the nation in which it began. Whereas both groups seek to avenge the past, the blacks represent a clear minority while the national socialists represented the German people or nation seeking to rectify history. The black nationalists cannot appeal to the mass of Americans, whereas the German nationalists not only could appeal to the German masses but eventually even came to represent them. Both movements are driven by their dynamism, even to self-destruction. Both glorify racial pride and denigrate Western values. Both emphasize conflict and warfare to a high degree. One difference lies in the fact that, while the black nationalists can drive whites out of the black community and even many cities, they cannot drive them out of the United States. The national socialists could conquer the minds of the German people, but thinking they could rule the world was absurd—a fanatical and nihilistic wish—just as it is absurd for blacks to argue that they can unite oppressed whites and youth in the United States or that two-thirds of the world's population are colored and will rise up together to conquer the white world.

To think of a coordinated uprising with the Third World or colored people of the world uniting against whites, which is often heard in the black rhetoric, is at best fantasy and at worst nihilistic. The Reverend King (1967), in his last book before his death, summed it up:

> . . . young American Negroes, who are predominantly
> involved in the Black Power movement, often quote
> Fanon's belief that violence is the only thing that will
> bring about liberation.
>
> Anyone leading a violent rebellion must be willing to
> make an honest assessment regarding the possible
> casualties to a minority population confronting a
> well-armed, wealthy majority.
>
> Arguments that the American Negro is a part of a world
> which is two-thirds colored and that there will come a
> day when the oppressed people of color will violently
> rise together to throw off the yoke of white oppression
> are beyond the realm of serious discussion.
>
> [The] advocates of violence . . . are blatantly illogical. . . .
> They fail to see that no internal revolution has ever
> succeeded in overthrowing a government by violence
> unless the government had already lost the allegiance
> and effective control of its armed forces. Anyone in
> his right mind knows that this will not happen in the
> United States. In a violent racial situation, the power
> structure has the local police, the state troopers, the
> national guard and finally the army to call on, all of
> which are predominantly white.
>
> It is perfectly clear that a violent revolution on the
> part of American blacks would find no sympathy and
> support from the white population and very little from
> the majority of the Negroes themselves [pp. 55–59].

The ideas and tactics of the black nationalists connote the surrender of the suburbs to whites.[1] In other words, blacks gain control of their communities and of the major cities; they gain control of the ghettos and the decaying cities of America—and it is becoming doubtful that life is worth living in them. The cities have become plagued (and it seems to be worsening) by inadequate schools; growing pollution and population density to the danger level; traffic jams and the decline of public transportation; rising welfare rolls; deteriorating housing; crowded slums and physical rot; increased crime, violence, and drug addiction; the flight of industry and jobs, along with the flight of the middle-class tax base; municipal overburden and unbalanced budgets; angry municipal employees and even angrier taxpayers. The suburbs, on the other hand, represent almost the opposite situation, or at least their problems are much smaller.

The concept of black nationalism rejects white coalitions and the federal government in favor of a black-controlled ghetto and eventually a black-controlled city. Indeed, black nationalists fail to recognize that we are all in this society together and we must learn to live in this society together, or at least in peace; that no minority group can realistically reject the almost 90 percent majority who control the dollars and the votes. By the same token, the federal government has the resources and muscle to help and favor poor and black Americans and has been doing so with increasing tempo since the War on Poverty and civil rights movement. Legislation and enforcement of nondiscriminatory orders have been implemented on a national scale by the federal government. Since the mid-1960s, the federal government has poured billions of dollars yearly into programs connected with housing, medical care, education, jobs, and business loans to blacks. The recent revenue sharing program, although criticized for too little money for the cities, highly favors the cities—where the black population is concentrated.

At this point, it might be appropriate to repeat the words of three black social scientists: Thomas Sowell, an economist; Martin A. Kilson, a political scientist; and Bayard Rustin, a labor union and civil rights leader. First Sowell (1971) points out that black militants are more interested in being paid off than in helping blacks, and that the white Establishment is willing to make the "payoff" to keep a false peace. Similarly, other concessions are made to blacks, including winking at violence, to appease them and maintain the system. He contends that people in authority and policy makers are more concerned with alleviating militant tactics and "getting immediate problems off their backs than with long-run consequences of their decisions. This has led to the . . . 'payoff' society, in which the comfort, peace and good conscience of 'responsible' decision makers takes precedence over the interests of society." The payoff exists in many institutions of society, especially where "the decision makers can pay off with other people's money." Places such as schools, universities, poverty programs, and other governmental jobs are good examples where the payoff is rampant. According to Sowell, the payoff can also take the form of "exemption from the necessary standard of society, including society's prohibition against violence." A certain amount of violence is permitted by decision makers "to buy off more serious inconvenience with strategically placed concessions" (p. 4).

Kilson (1973) claims those who believe in and preach black militant ideology are frauds, and either are caught up in their own slogans and rhetoric or do not believe in what they espouse, implying that they merely use their ideology for selfish purposes. He writes, "The problem with black [youth] . . . is that they are too caught up in ideology. Most people who deal in ideologies believe only ten percent of it, at most. But blacks . . . want to believe ninety percent of their own ideological bullshit" (p. 48).

Rustin (1972) asserts that black power has been destructive and detrimental to blacks, infesting political and economic progress with ideology, fragmentizing the civil rights movement which once included the majority population of America, into "a powerful legacy of polarization, division and political nonsense." He contends that many black militants are either in exile or have turned into capitalistic entrepreneurs. "They created a fantasy view . . . of mass revolutionary potential," matched by their political naiveté. They failed to understand that the majority of blacks are not revolutionists; rather they have middle-class aspirations. Today, blacks suffer from the excesses of black militarism. The 1960s gave promise to a civil rights movement "committed to broad change and able to draw the support of a decisive majority." The movement is now splintered into various "racial, ethnic, sexual, age, and psychological lines," each vying against one another for its interests and ascendancy. Rustin puts the major blame for the decline of the civil rights movement and black-white coalition politics on the militants as well as on many black moderate leaders who refused to challenge the black power leaders. The most dangerous result of black power, he claims, is "the new tribalism it engendered" (pp. 18–19).

What can blacks gain by resorting to a black nationalist strategy? At best, they can and will gain control of their community, even the large and medium-sized cities of the nation. This they can do, however, without resorting to antiwhite slogans, terror tactics, violence, and the rejection of compromise, tolerance, and individualism. The population trends keenly illustrate their growing strength; they need not polarize this country and risk white reaction, which is often oversimplified as racism.

According to the 1970 census, blacks make up 11.1 percent of the country's total population, but in the cities the percentage is much higher. The figure is 21 percent for all central cities, and in the 12 largest cities it is 28 percent. In 9 major cities, more than 40 percent of the population is black, and 4 other cities already have a black majority, the highest such majority being in Washington, D.C., where blacks make up 71 percent of the population. In still other cities like New York and Houston, if we combine the black population with the brown population, the nonwhite percentages approach 50 percent.

The urbanization process within the last 20 years has been so dramatic that, in 1970, 58 percent of the blacks lived in the central cities, compared with 28 percent of the white populace. Since 1950, the cities have added 10 million people, mostly black, and the suburbs have added 35 million people, the overwhelming majority being white. The greatest exchange of city-suburban population shifts occurred in New York and its surrounding suburban areas: nearly 2 million blacks and Puerto Ricans moved into the city and replaced nearly 2½ million white middle-class residents fleeing to suburbia.

By 1970 there were 64 million people in the cities, mainly ghetto nonwhites and a few white rich and unmarried young desiring the excitement and social opportunities of the inner city, and the white ethnics mainly living in the outer city. Seventy-six million people lived in the suburbs, and 63 million lived outside the metropolitan area mainly in rural places. Between 1960 and 1970, the black population in the suburbs increased approximately 1 million, bringing the total to about 3.6 million. Because the white exodus to the suburbs was so large, the 1 million blacks who also moved to the suburbs went somewhat unnoticed by many people. The percentage of blacks in suburbia rose from 4.3 percent in 1960 to 4.7 percent in 1970, less than 0.5 percent, and still totals less than 5 percent (Ornstein 1972; U. S. Bureau of the Census 1971).

The black population is growing at a significantly faster rate than the white population. Between 1960 and 1966 the white population grew 7.6 percent and the black population jumped 14.4 percent, almost twice as much. In 1950 the blacks made up 10 percent of the total U.S. population; by 1960 they represented 10.5 percent; by 1970 11.1 percent. In 1965, the black fertility rate was 1.46 greater than that for whites. By 1970, whites had achieved zero growth, but any talk about blacks reducing their birthrate was branded as genocide. By 1980 it is estimated that blacks, given no major changes in variables, will make up 13 percent of the population (*New York Times,* September 24, 1972; U. S. Bureau of the Census 1971; U. S. Riot Commission 1968).

By 1985 the black population will rise to about 30.9 million, gaining an average of 7.7 percent per year. Keeping in mind the growing black fertility rates, the declining white fertility rates, and the present population shifts from the cities and to the suburbs, it is estimated that blacks will comprise between 31 and 36 percent of the population in the central cities in 1985, a gain of 10 to 15 percent over 1970 figures. These figures are for the nation as a whole; the increases will be faster in the major cities, and 11 more will become over 50 percent black; these include New Orleans, Richmond, Baltimore, Jacksonville, Gary, Cleveland, St. Louis, and Detroit in the mid- and late 1970s, and Philadelphia, Oakland, and Chicago by 1985. Again, unless there are major changes in population shifts, the suburbs ringing these cities will remain largely white.

Experience shows that the black school enrollment in these cities will exceed 50 percent before the total population reaches this level. For example, in 12 of these cities, blacks already constitute more than a majority of those students in the public elementary schools. Reasons for this are that the black population is younger and that many white children attend private and parochial schools. If present trends continue, many additional cities will have a black school majority by 1985: these include Atlanta, Buffalo, Cincinnati, Dallas, Hartford, Harrisburg, Indianapolis, Kansas City (Missouri), Louisville, New Haven, and Pittsburgh.

In short, from 1950 to 1970, the black population rose 6.5 million, and 86 percent of this rise took place within the central cities. The majority of white population growth is occurring in the suburbs; the central cities received only 2.5 percent of the total white population increase within this 20-year period. From 1960 to 1970, the white central city population actually declined 1.5 million. The 12 largest central cities contain 33 percent of the total U.S. black population; these cities are New York, Chicago, Los Angeles, Philadelphia, Detroit, Baltimore, Houston, Cleveland, Washington, D.C., St. Louis, Milwaukee, and San Francisco (U. S. Bureau of the Census 1971; U. S. Riot Commission 1968).

The population shifts in the United States mean that the cities are being drained of their middle-class tax base, while being burdened with less affluent and poor residents. This increasing population concentration calls for greater expenditures for every kind of public service: education, health, police and fire protection, sewage, parks, and so on. The resulting financial plight of the cities is seen as a national problem and is reflected in the expansion of federal assistance to the cities, which reached $10 billion in fiscal year 1967–68, and the federal revenue-sharing program, which was recently enacted into law. This one program alone calls for federal handouts of $5.3 billion in 1972, going up in annual increments of $300 million until it reaches $6.5 billion in 1976.

The program unquestionably favors the cities over the suburbs, even though suburban communities are beginning to feel the pinch of providing services along with paying increased taxes. For example, the city of Chicago received in 1972 a check for more than $69.3 million, while all suburban units in the state of Illinois received grants totaling only $28.1 million, even though the suburban population is slightly larger than the city population (*Chicago Today*, September 27, 1972). In New York, of the total $393 million passed on to local governmental units, $248 million went to New York City (*New York Times*, October 1, 1972). Based on a complex formula which includes such factors as population density, poverty, and taxes levied, approximately two-thirds of the revenue share goes to the cities. Also the wealthier suburbs receive less than the poorer suburbs. For example, the richest suburb in the Chicago area is Kenilworth with a median income of approximately $35,000. In 1972 it received only $9,826, while the all-black Robbins, one of the poorer suburbs, received $113,500—nearly four times more per capita (*Chicago Tribune*, October 14, 1972). Scarsdale, the richest suburb in New York state, with a median income of approximately $30,000, received ten times less money than Mt. Vernon, which is approximately 30 percent black and much poorer but has only three times as many people (*New York Times*, October 1, 1972).

The above population trends illustrate the growing political power of blacks, regardless of ideology. This growing political awareness is also evidenced by the recent transition of some members of the black nationalist movement—from confronting the system to working within it to gain power. Even the Black Panthers have exchanged many of their guns for ballots: they have spearheaded registration drives and diverted their energies to grass roots politics. Black nationalists in general have become politically active in most large and medium-sized cities in the North, especially in New York City, Chicago, Detroit, Baltimore, St. Louis, Cleveland, Gary, and Newark. In California, Erika Huggins has been elected to the Berkeley Community Development Council, but Bobby Seale was an unsuccessful candidate for mayor of Oakland; both Panthers were on trial for their lives in Connecticut in 1971. Other Panthers or militants in California have won 6 out of 18 positions on the 1971 West Oakland Model Cities governing board, 14 seats on the

Berkeley antipoverty board, and 3 out of 9 seats on the Berkeley City Council. Another Panther, Elaine Brown, is now (1973) running for the Oakland City Council. Furthermore, as previously mentioned, black nationalist groups controlled the 1972 nationwide black caucus in Gary.

The change in tactics of the Panthers is illustrated by the Erikson and Newton (1973) debates. Originally booked for a series of confrontations, the conversation is gentle and there is the absence of adversary spirit. In the conversations, Newton, the present Panther chief, points out that the Panther party today has come to realize that black nationalism is inherently no improvement over any brand of nationalism. He attempts to reconcile black militancy with the Marxist tradition of a revolutionary class. Although he does not repudiate the Panther's violent tactics of the early and middle 1960s, rather he claims it was "historically necessary and valid," he does claim that it is now possible to bring about a revolution without violence—or without bringing down "amerika." The shift of opinion is apparent, from destroying the system to possibly working within the system.

The black activist who urges a nationalist view now is prating a dated and dangerous position, popular at the time when the Black Panther and black fist emerged as symbols of the new direction of the civil rights movement. Population and voter registration trends inform us that black nationalist tactics, besides increasing social tension, are unwarranted.

Black Nationalism and Black Crime

When one attempts to make cross-jurisdictional or longitudinal comparisons of crime, or a combination of both, one faces a difficult task. The reason is that definitions of offenses and recording procedures often differ from county to county and from state to state, and frequently change over a period of time. Also, law enforcement records and statistics are sometimes manipulated for political effect and to win public support for the police. If the desire is to lessen fear, purse snatching can be classified as larceny or criminal mischief. If the desire is the opposite, most purse snatching can be classified as robbery. Similarly, it is difficult to know whether a change in the number of arrests reflects a change in the crime rate or changes in police behavior and enforcement tactics. The difficulty inherent in evaluating crime statistics is compounded by the fact that a tremendous number of crimes are never reported to the police. Exactly how many go unreported depends on what expert or panel one quotes. As our expert panel, we will refer to the President's Commission on Law Enforcement and Administration of Justice (1967), which indicates that the actual number of forcible rapes is more than 3½ times the number reported; the number of burglaries, 3 times that reported; and the number of aggravated assaults and larcenies of over $50, more than twice the number reported. Also, it has long been recognized that a great many of the minor crimes, such as petty delinquency and shoplifting, never come to the attention of the police; hence, changes in the reporting behavior of victims may also cause variations in crime statistics.

What most observers of crime seem to agree on is that crime is heavily concentrated in urban areas and especially in densely populated and low-income areas. Population concentration and degree of urbanization do not, however, explain all crime rate variations. For example, the President's Commission (1967) reported that Los Angeles has the highest number of re-ported rapes of any city in the country but ranks only twentieth in the number of reported murders. Chicago has the highest rate of robbery but a low rate of burglary. New York City ranks fifth in larcenies of $50 or more, but fifty-fourth for larcenies under $50. We know that youths under 25 commit the greater percentage of crimes, or at least are arrested 47 percent of the time; however, we also know that much youth crime is committed by males as an expression of their masculinity. And, according to Banfield (1970), Hacker (1973), and Wilson (1973), we also know that a greater percentage of crimi-nal offenders are black, even when age and income are held constant. There are other studies, however, that indicate no difference by race when class is controlled.

According to these three authors, crime trends are heightened by the fact that juveniles and criminals have learned through experience that an infraction can be committed with little or no penalty. There is little chance of being caught, and when caught, the penalties are negligible. For example, in New York City the probability of arrest for a black youth gang member for involvement in an instance of potential violence is about 0.04 if he has average skill and about half that if he is quite skillful. Even when arrested, because the courts are overcrowded, lighter penalties are common. Thus the probability of being caught is low, and the penalty, if caught, is light. While it is supposedly common knowledge that more blacks are convicted in pro-portion to whites because of the interaction effect with race and income, the individual (black or white) still realizes that crime pays.[2]

One of the most important facts is that all but 10 percent of crimi-nal cases must be disposed of by plea bargaining, a tactic that inevitably re-sults in considerably lower sentences. Moreover, if stiffer sentences were mandatory for a larger number of offenders and these people were tried, the system would break down altogether. The promise of a lower sentence is usually the only incentive for pleading guilty. For example, Wilson (1973) reports that, between July 1963 and July 1966, only 3 percent of the 13,555 persons indicted in Manhattan (one of the five boroughs in New York City) were convicted, and almost 80 percent of those convicted had pleaded guilty. In one middle-sized nonurban county in Wisconsin, 94 percent of the con-victions were the result of a guilty plea, and it made little difference whether the offender was represented by a lawyer or not. Says Kaplan (1973), "If even 20 percent of defendants had to be tried, there would be chaos" (p. 69).

Again, New York City helps illustrate the point. Hacker (1973) indicates that the city courts can handle no more than 600 felony trials per year, and that the entire state has less than 22,000 beds for prisoners. Yet, in 1972, 434,303 crimes were reported in that city. This number includes

78,865 auto thefts, 78,202 robberies, and 1,691 murders. (Remember, these are only *reported* crimes: it is estimated that nearly one million crimes were committed in New York City during that year.) Slightly more than 19,000 were arrested for robbery in that city, which means that less than 3 percent could be brought to trial: if 3 percent of those arrested for robbery were brought to trial, there would be no time to try other serious cases, such as those involving murder.[a]

In Chicago, the more serious the crime, the better the chances of the defendant being set free by the courts. The Chicago Crime Commission (1973) pointed out that the chances are 9 out of 10 of being found guilty if the defendant was indicted for stealing a television. But if he's on trial for murder, the chances are 2 out of 3 that he will walk out of the courtroom a free man. Similarly, only 2 percent of armed robberies are punished by convictions. Of the 405 reported homicides in the first six months of 1973, there were 450 arrests on murder charges, but only 53 convictions. Most rapes are not reported. Of the 678 that were reported in this six-month period, there were 280 arrests, but only 53 convictions. The report concluded that "either the police are arresting innocent people, or the courts are being too lenient with real criminals" (p. 3). In either case, the criminal who engages in murder, armed robbery, or rape realizes that even if he is brought to trial, he stands an excellent chance of walking out of court free. Moreover, if his lawyer feels his chances of being found "not guilty" are not good, there is always plea bargaining for purposes of reducing the sentence.

The point is that increased penalties are at best peripheral, at worst inimical, to actually punishing a substantial number of offenders who are caught. According to Wilson (1973), sentencing has very little to do with achieving some social objective: the overwhelming need in busy jurisdictions is to clear crowded court dockets and to avoid the time and expense of a trial. It is a sad irony that the more crime increases, the more pressure on court calendars increases, the greater the chances the sentence will be reduced through plea bargaining; the more serious the crime the easier it is to be freed, and the less criminals need fear severe penalties for committing crimes. Hence, a vicious and increasing crime cycle is perpetuated.

That the number of violent crimes committed by blacks is high hardly needs to be repeated. Blacks make up about 11 percent of the U. S. population, yet more blacks than whites were arrested for crimes of violence in 1970—105,000 versus 96,000. This means that the crime rate among blacks is about 10 times higher than that among whites. Whether one wishes to interpret these figures as a barometer of white racism, and nothing else, probably depends on one's biases and political thinking.[b]

In the past, there was sufficient evidence that blacks were likely to assault other blacks. In fact, the U. S. Riot Commission (1968) reported that the odds that a resident in a black neighborhood would suffer physical assault were 13 times greater than those for a resident in a white neighborhood. The trouble is, however, that the recent crime reports in many cities show that

these assaults are beginning to spill over into white neighborhoods. Writes
Hacker (1970):

> The poor [and most blacks are poor] have more fatherless
> families, more free-wheeling children, and seem less com-
> mitted to civil properties.

> As blacks arrive in a district and whites depart, such terri-
> tory becomes more susceptible to burglary and assault.
> Once even a few blacks begin to reside in an area, there
> faces become part of the local landscape and members of
> their race who are not residents find it easier to make
> criminal forays into the zone [p. 77].

Glazer (1972) points out that a large portion of black children grow
up on the streets, resentful of authority by virtue of being poor and black, influenced by the rhetoric that claims black crime is a political act, and that as
neighborhoods become integrated many of these youth, because they are
prone to delinquency, will

> exhort money from [white] children at school, beat them
> if they don't provide any, break the windows of the neigh-
> borhood stores, rob from them, attack the elderly for money
> or sport [p. 27].

It can be debated whether the increase in black crimes toward whites
is solely related to their increased contact with whites, as Hacker and Glazer
suggest,[c] or whether some of this increase is related to the rise in black militancy and the race rhetoric of "victimization" and "oppression." Nevertheless,
these twin trends now lead many young blacks to claim they have license to
break the law. Indeed, several autobiographies and revolutionary tracts have
urged them to do so. Authors of such works include Eldridge Cleaver, who
claimed the right to rape white women; Huey Newton and Bobby Seale, who
once claimed the right to kill the "fascist" police; H. Rap Brown, Julius Lester,
and more recently Angela Davis, who urged that "whitey" be killed and that
the American "racist" system be overthrown by force. Not only do these black
spokesmen influence many black youth, but their rhetoric is reinforced by
newspapers such as the *Black Panther* and *Black Liberation Front,* which commonly interpret black crime against whites as a heroic and revolutionary act.[d]
    What is even more disturbing is the fact that few responsible black
leaders are willing to speak out against black criminal offenders because of
the risks of personal censure and communal friction (Sowell 1973; Starr 1973).
Even worse, a small number of these leaders actually applaud the situation because of the heightened focus on blacks and the feeling of black pride (*Education News,* October 16, 1967). It is interesting that the increase of black
crimes directed toward whites coincides statistically with the rise in increased
black militancy as well as with the riots of the middle and late 1960s (Banfield 1970; Hacker 1973; Moynihan 1969). What is important, also, is that

black crime and rioting have been indirectly endorsed—at least excused—in two million copies of the Kerner report, the liberal assessment of black violence which claims that white "racism" is to blame.

For some observers, the situation has reached a crisis, and recently prompted each of the three leading news magazines to feature a special crime report within a three-month period. *Newsweek* (December 18, 1972), *Time* (February 19, 1973), and *U. S. News & World Report* (November 13, 1972) reported that, while crime remains most highly concentrated in the ghetto, it has long since been spilling over into white neighborhoods and is increasingly directed against whites. The special reports of these three magazines show rising black crime and terror have included political assassinations, skyjacking (now sharply curtailed through extra surveillance at airports), rioting, armed robbery, physical assault, and random murder. The reports frequently used the term "terror" and pointed out that terror was inflicting fear on the cities and suburbs, and even blackmail on the U. S. government. More and more, these crimes were becoming politically acceptable and even justified as revolutionary tactics. Combined, the three news reports suggest several reasons for the rise in crime:

1. Sensational television programs and movies that appeal to the criminal and susceptible element.
2. The hesitancy of police to use force when it is justified because of civil rights pressure.
3. Predictions of violence and crime by civil rights leaders and political officials which somehow make the acts more explainable and so more acceptable.
4. The leniency of and over crowdedness of the courts.
5. The new opinion that black crime is a way of protesting injustices.

According to Sowell (1971):

> We have reached the stage in the condoning of violence where the question may reasonably be asked whether the forbidding of violence by a particular group . . . is not an act of discrimination. We have seen unions grow powerful through the use of violence and the implied threat of violence. . . . Now the same "right" is being claimed by . . . ghetto dwellers and assorted political and vigilantes of the left and right [p. 4].

Similarly, in her extensive studies on violence, Arendt (1972) noted:

> It has become rather fashionable among white liberals to react to Negro grievances with the cry, "We are all guilty," and Black Power has proved only too happy to take advantage of this "confession" to institute an irrational

"black rage." Where all are guilty, no one is; confessions
of collective guilt are the best possible safeguard against the
discovery of culprits [p. 48].

We have even reached the stage where we now sometimes read about
black systematic killing of white people and the increased murdering of policemen. For example, one of the most visible events in the long string of black
militant activities since 1962 is the formation of the De Mau Mau group. A
requirement for initiation into this group is the killing of a white person. The
Chicago Daily News (October 16, 1972) reports that the group has some 300
to 400 members in Chicago, Gary, and Detroit, and 3,000 to 4,000 across the
nation. Most of these are black war veterans, and their existence was brought
to the attention of the public when eight members were accused of murdering
nine white suburbanites in the Chicago metropolitan area. This was followed
by the sniper killing of six whites and the wounding of ten others in New
Orleans by a black Navy veteran who was supposedly linked to the Black
Liberation Army, an offshoot of the Black Panthers, whose numbers are unknown (*New York Times,* January 8, 1973). Although the body of one
sniper was found, some police and witnesses insist there were two or three
gunmen. A black hotel maid who encountered a gunman was told not to
worry as the shooting began: "We're not killing blacks today, just whites.
The revolution is here."
    While most blacks were appalled by these two incidents, *U. S. News
& World Report* (January 22, 1973) cites several psychologists who claim
some militant and criminally inclined blacks regard these killers as heroes to
emulate. Although the NAACP denies the existence of any conspiracy against
whites, a growing number of black militants warn that such incidents will increase. Unquestionably these incidents are not common occurrences, but they
do influence many gang- and delinquent-oriented youth. Moreover, many
whites feel this neutralizes the unrelated reminders by blacks of the KKK
lynchings some 50 years ago.
    In the same vein, the *New York Times* (January 26, 1973) and *U. S.
News & World Report* (January 22, 1973) report that war on policemen has
rapidly increased, and there is growing conjecture among many policemen
and law enforcement officials that it is linked with black nationalist groups.
Both news sources cite FBI statistics which show that in 1971 as many as 126
policemen were targets for killings, more than double the figure in 1968, about
the year in which the civil rights movement started to take on black nationalist
characteristics. Between 1970 and 1973, over 100 officers have been killed each
year: 100 in 1970, 126 in 1971, 112 in 1972, compared with 60 in 1968 and
48 in 1962. Ambush attacks have become a growing menace. Between 1970
and 1972, a total of 53 police officers were killed from ambush, and several
hundred have been wounded. The latest figures before the *U. S. News* article
went to print were that 13 policemen were slain in December 1972 and that,
in the first 11 days of 1973, 7 more were killed. In New York City, within

a one-week period between January 20 and 27, 1973, eight policemen were shot and two were killed. In the following two-week period, the *New York Times* (January 29, February 4, 11, 1973) reported that eight other police-men were wounded and one killed in ambush incidents. All of these New York City shootings were attributed to black militants, and most of them to ten members of the Black Liberation Army. Similar incidents were re-ported in other large cities during the same time period, including the death of two white policemen in Milwaukee and two more in Chicago (*Chicago Tribune,* February 10, 11, 1973; *New York Times,* February 11, 1973).

Since the summer of 1971 police killings in California, Michigan, New Jersey, and New York and shootouts in St. Louis and Charlotte, North Carolina, have been accompanied by messages to police and press supposedly from Black Liberationists (*New York Times,* August 26, 1973). In this con-nection, the *New York Times* (January 26, 1973) and the *U. S. News & World Report* (January 22, 1973) quote numerous high-ranking police officials in more than a dozen major cities who insist that there is an organized conspiracy against police. While the cop on the beat is likely to believe this idea, other police officials and almost all nonmilitant civil rights leaders play down this idea and insist there is no evidence to support it. Whether there is a definite conspiracy or not is difficult to assess; nevertheless, policemen are cautious and worried about becoming marked targets and are hampered in the per-formance of their duties by the cry of "police brutality."

In the meantime, the overall crime figures seem to have continued to soar since the civil rights movement transformed into a more militant trend. According to the FBI, the three most violent crimes have steadily increased during the 1960s into the 1970s and reached record proportions in 1972. Forcible rape was up 35.4 percent from the previous year; aggravated assault, 9.6 percent; and murder, 15.3 percent. The remaining four crimes that go into the FBI index all involve theft of property and have decreased slightly because they have been made more difficult. For example, the drop in auto-mobile thefts is largely credited to the steering wheel and transmission locks that have been mandatory on new U.S. cars since 1970 and the added option of a siren to ward off would-be thieves. Shoplifting is apparently going down (although most of it is never reported) because of increased store security. However, it is the violent crimes, especially the police killings, prison riots, and sniper shootings, which make the headlines on television and in the papers. The media repeatedly show that both the greater number and the overwhelm-ing percentage of violent crimes are committed by blacks.

Although it is difficult to discuss these trends in public without being denounced as a "racist" or "Tom," or without having the discussion diverted to the "sickness" of society, the majority of whites do not forget the boasts—of course, most of it is rhetoric—of the Black Panthers in the 1960s and the De Mau Mau and Black Liberation Army in the 1970s about slaying "fascist pigs" and white "racists." Most whites do not forget the re-lease of black militants accused of murdering policemen in many cities and their acquittal in cities across the country—from New York to Los Angeles, from New Haven to Oakland. The majority of Americans resent the liberal support given black crime and rioting in reports like those of the Kerner, McCone, McKay, and Scranton commissions, which make a mockery of the public's search for protection from crime and freedom from danger. The white majority resent being told by Yale's liberal President Kingman Brewster or by black militant Angela Davis that blacks cannot get a fair trial in America unless, in effect, the verdict is "not guilty." The majority of whites do not forget the picture of a judge with a shotgun taped to him taken only moments before it blew off his head, or the subsequent release of Angela Davis and her being proclaimed a heroine. They do not forget the killing of three auto workers in a Chrysler plant in Detroit and the subsequent release of the black worker accused of the crime on the grounds that he was a victim of white "racism."

Whites are beginning to piece together the idea that the system black militants denounce as "oppressive" and "racist" is the same system that frees them in the courts and in many cases has led to their increasing influence and wealth—through the sale of black revolutionary books and autobiographies, and fees of up to $1,500 for speaking to college audiences.

These black criminals and black militants may be heroes to many black youths and even to white radical youths, but to the majority of whites they are only using the system as a platform to sell their books and make speeches at a large profit. Their behavior, slogans, and symbols may appear continuously on television and in the newspapers, but the majority of whites resent what they see and read about the rise in black nationalism and concurrent rise of black crime. Black militants use the word "political repression," and want Americans to believe them on simple faith. They do not want freedom: they have it. They want power and use these slogans as a unifying tool, a means to their end.

Black hero worship of those who commit crimes against whites and the psychological need to put down "whitey" are keenly illustrated in new new black movies and plays. A few years ago it was almost impossible to see a black-oriented movie, unless it starred someone like Sidney Poitier. And prior to this period, the movies about blacks depicted Amos 'n' Andy, Stepin Fetchit, and Rochester in eye-roll, grinning, lazy roles. But now the movie industry has discovered that the black audience will line up and fill the movie houses to see pictures that glorify black crime and violence. "Bone," "Cool Breeze," "Farewell Uncle Tom," "Hammer," "Hitman," "Is the Father Black Enough," "Legend of Nigger Charley," "Melinda," "Savage," "Shaft's Big Score," "Slaughter," and "Super Fly" all have a common theme: black criminals, dope pushers, prostitutes, pimps, and killers with enormous sexual prowess and the ability to put down "whitey."

For example, "Bone" goes to the limit, playing on the fears and fantasies that whites have held about blacks. The hero, a strapping black, shows up one morning in a Beverly Hills swimming pool and demands of its white owner his money or wife. Although the would-be rapist has second thoughts about the wife, the wife has to seduce him. She apparently likes him so well that both plot to do away with the husband. As Knight (1972) writes, "One can readily understand the glee in the black communities at this kind of representation of black supremacy" (p. 101). In "Super Fly," a black cocaine dealer outwits the police, the Mafia, and the people and escapes with a half million dollars. Not only did this movie gross $11 million during the first two months after its release—more than any other movie, black or white, was making at that time—it also stimulated some young blacks in Los Angeles, Chicago, and New York City to commit robberies along the same pattern as that developed by its hero. His wide-lapelled midi-coat, wide-brimmed hat, and neck adornings were considered fashionable by both ghetto youths and gangs and other black young adults for more than a year after the movie ended its run.

One constantly hears that whites are to blame for these movies. True, these movies are supported by white investors, but they would stop investing in these movies if the turnouts and profits stopped, if blacks did not take pleasure in seeing them. Also, many of these movies are written, filmed, and directed by blacks; in the final analysis, blacks are putting these movies together. In fact, this is one reason many black intellectuals support these movies: they represent black opportunity and black business. The *New York Times* (December 17, 1972) ran a feature article and asked ten prominent black figures in the movie industry and the civil rights movement for their views on these movies. Eight of the responses were favorable and can be summed up as follows: these movies (1) provide blacks with an opportunity to enter the movie industry; (2) bolster black pride and depict antiwhite sentiment and blacks putting down whites, which the audience wants to see; (3) portray blacks as witty, intelligent, strong, and handsome; and (4) provide a counterstereotype to the white film image of the docile, lazy, ignorant, smiling black. Only Junius Griffin, president of the Hollywood branch of the NAACP, and Roy Innis, national director of CORE, criticized these movies. Griffin pointed out that the movies glorified and justified black criminals as "super-studs," and that the constant bombardment of such images on the minds of children would influence them adversely. They did not contribute to building constructive and healthy images of black people. Innis went further and branded the movies as portraying black "psychopathic superdudes,"[3] more sick then the John Wayne movies, which glorified violence but still stressed positive virtues.

The same themes are portrayed in the recent plays of black nationalists from LeRoi Jones (Imamu Amiri Baraka) to Melvin Van Peeples. Blacks are romanticized as pimps, dope addicts, studs, prostitutes, revolutionists against white America—all ghetto stereotypes—"freaks" rather than middle-class or normal people. Writes Hill (1972), a black critic:

> It was bad enough when the white man insisted on presenting us in this light. Now the black man is exploiting

his own people. The black man is producing plays and films of one image . . . to come and pay money and see yourself from a [ghetto] viewpoint and no other.

By doing this, blacks in control of the arts are being as racist as the white man they hate so much for having done it to them for so many years [p. 38].

In the meantime, whites are told they are unable or have no right to judge black literary works, not only films and plays, but also poems, essays, and books. Most whites respond to these movies (in most instances without seeing them but after having read about them) as part of the antiwhite, pro-black nationalist movement in America. These movies only increase white fears of black crime and violence.

All these trends come together: the high incidence of crime among blacks; the increase in violent crimes directed toward whites; the growing argument that there is no such thing as black crime, that it is a revolutionary tactic which contributes to the "liberation" struggle; the news media, which repeatedly remind audiences that crime is out of control; and the recent movies that glorify black criminal behavior and antiwhite sentiment. In this respect, *Time* (March 26, 1973) considers this nation to be the most crime-ridden of any industrialized society, and one whose crime problems are fast becoming unsolvable. The *New York Times* (March 11, 1973) reports that crime is the number-one issue haunting the American populace, requiring steadily increasing outlays of both public and private dollars for more police-men, tougher locks, brighter street lights, and longer jail sentences. Reports *U. S. News & World Report* (November 13, 1972), "All kinds of alarms and other protective devices are being developed for businessmen and home-owners," and if the trend continues, we will be manufacturing and buying " 'bulletproof pajama sets in full color,' " claims one business representative (p. 49). The *Saturday Review* (April 21, 1973) points out that fear of being robbed or burglarized has created a brand new billion dollar industry, that of keeping people safe, or at least making them feel safe. And a 1972 Gallup poll indicates that one out of every five suburban residents had been the vic-tim of burglary, mugging, or robbery—crimes committed mainly by persons from outside their communities. Thus suburbanites no longer feel safe, and it is expected that by 1980 homeowners will be spending $500 million each year on protection. The above *World Report* (November 13, 1972) and the *New York Times* (August 5, 1973) report the cities are even more frightening: people live in total fear—fear of deserted streets, fear of the evening, in an atmosphere of suspicion, and with a loss of confidence in police protection. In this connection, recent mayoral elections (between 1970 and 1973) in the five largest cities (among other major cities) among other themes have stressed law and order. In fact, former Mayor Lindsay of New York, one of the most noted symbols of liberalism, asked the U. S. government for $7 million in 1973 to increase the city's fight against crime (*New York Times,* September 9, 1973). And crime is even considered to be a major problem in perhaps the two most liberal "islands" in the country, where the intellectuals of the Upper West Side of Manhattan and in the Hyde Park section of Chicago espouse their liberalism in the daytime and fear walking alone in the evenings, where it is the norm for women to wear whistles and carry sprays to help protect themselves against potential assaults (*Chicago Tribune,* August 20, 1973; Starr 1972). Understandably, *Newsweek* (December 18, 1972) calls America a "fortress," where crime is out of control and concern about property loss is far superseded by "fears of physical violence, which includes the thief killing without provocation in the act of stealing. . . . The emotional atmosphere is further charged by race [which is seen by whites] in terms of black against white" (p. 31).

And President Nixon in 1973 felt no embarrassment about claiming Americans had been misled in the last decade by some reformers who felt that "the criminal was not responsible for his crimes . . . but that society was responsible." He contended "the only way to attack crime in America [was] the way crime attacks people—without pity." He recommended a get-tough program for fighting crimes which included stiffer sentences, life imprisonment for anyone with a previous drug record who was convicted of selling more than four ounces of heroin or morphine, capital punishment for federal offenses such as skyjacking, kidnapping, and assaulting a federal officer, and an end to the use of the insanity defense.

Despite the U. S. Supreme Court decision in 1972 that capital punishment was unconstitutional as presently applied, the fears of white America have resulted in the National Association of Attorneys General's overwhelming endorsement of restoration of the death penalty and leaving it up to the states to decide how it should be applied. This has been followed, beginning in 1973, by the reinstatement of the death sentence in several states for offenses such as rape, kidnapping, skyjacking, assassination of public officials, killing of police officers, and murder connected with robbery, rape, arson, kidnapping, or sexual abuse of a child. Several governors have already introduced legislation to adopt mandatory life sentences for convicted adult drug pushers, and Congress is debating legislation to restore the death penalty for many federal offenses. In the meantime, many black spokesmen claim the new laws are directed at blacks and connote black genocide—part of the rhetoric of denial.[e]

Conclusion

With the rising wave of crime and violence in America, we are approaching—or more accurately, regressing—to medieval times when the workers, then called peasants, toiled by day and returned at night to the castle for protection against marauding bands, only now the locked and guarded apartment or private house has replaced the castle. Fears of crime and loss of safety overlap with black crime, and the distinctions become blurred as black nationalism increases. As the trends overlap, the fears of white America become simplified into one common fear, a fear of blacks which finds expression in resisting integration. Writes Glazer (1972):

> If those who know truly that they search for safety are
> denounced for being racist, are they not to conclude that
> the only way *not* to be a racist is to accept living with
> personal danger? Does not the confusion grow when
> liberals and black organizations argue that the people
> escaping from crime are really trying to escape from
> the presence of blacks? [p. 27]

As white fear of blacks intensifies and resistance toward integration increases, the black integration movement loses its credibility and the black nationalist movement gains in credibility among blacks. In turn, integration among blacks is denounced, and black crime toward white society is legitimatized among extremists. Thus a cycle has developed where the trends of black nationalism, crime, and resistance toward integration are promoting white backlash and further polarizing the nation. In fact, it is not uncommon to hear that armed groups in both black and white areas are patrolling their communities.

As liberals and conservatives inflate their philosophies, as black crime toward whites seems to increase, and as black leaders brand white fears as "racism" and denounce stiffer penalties as black genocide, the nation becomes more polarized. There are those who say that law and order are just code words for bigotry and repression, and there are those on the opposite side who say the time has come to get tough with lawbreakers. In the meantime, it becomes more and more difficult to distinguish between rhetoric and reality, especially as black-white racial trends and behaviors overlap.

Postscript

a. Rape still remains the easiest crime to get away with. Only 1 out of 4 cases, it is estimated, are reported to the police in New York City. In the first six months of 1972 there were 613 first-degree rape cases, (this does not include attempted rape) in which some disposition had been made in the city. In 342 cases, the charges were dismissed. There were acquittals after trial in 14 others; another 110 were still pending. Of the 147 who were convicted, 74 were convicted on lesser charges, 51 were released on some form of probation, 13 were released after being fined, and only 9 were sentenced on the original charge. ("New York City Police Departments Criminal Justice Liaison Division" in the *New York Times,* November 13, 1973.)

b. It is true that a large segment of the white population equates blackness with criminal behavior. It might be comforting to the liberal rhetoric if we could assert that black Americans do not really commit much crime, but in fact they do. However, this data is impaired by the harsh fact that blacks in our society traditionally and up to, say, 1970 have been discriminated against at every level in our political, economic, and social process. The resulting frustration and the lack of faith in the system is hard to judge, but they are factors to consider when comparing black and white criminality. (This is somewhat illustrated by the fact that crime rates among blacks from Africa and the Caribbean are several times lower than those among black Americans born in this country.) Black crime rates also reflect the fact that blacks are concentrated in those sectors of the American population that show high crime rates for individuals of all races. Moreover, they are heavily represented in lower income, educational categories, and high-risk, young adult age (15–25 years old) groups which correlate with criminal behavior. We cannot be absolutely sure what black crime rates would be like if this population was distributed in different categories and the frustration factor was nullified, but it is highly probable that the statistics would be substantially altered.

We also know that there is a great deal of hidden and upper middle-class crime that society reacts to in the same way—occupational offenses such as larceny, bribery, and tax evasion—as it reacts to crimes defined as violent or anti-social. *Past* studies have also shown that blacks are more likely to be arrested, prosecuted, and convicted than whites who commit the same crime. It has also been found in some communities that the racial membership of the criminal and victim has also influenced the intensity of law enforcement, where black on white offenses were considered most serious, and where there was an underreaction to intraracial offenses and white on black offenses within the larger society. *Present* trends, which combine gradual recognition by whites of the legitimacy of black complaints and the growing trend of reverse discrimination in all sectors of society, cannot help but substantially reduce or possibly invert these differentials in the administration of criminal justice.

c. It is difficult to ignore the spill-over factor; as integration in schools and society proceed, and as blacks increasingly come into contact with whites, we may expect an increase of black aggressors on white victims, especially if racial tensions increase and normal avenues of asserting masculinity remain beyond the aggressor's reach. Quite apart from the fact that no people are "basically criminal," many of the fears of white America are real. Not only is white, middle-class society pretty cool to the use of personal or mass violence as a means of solving human problems or avenging social justice; whites also look for other methods of accommodating or mediating differences. This is often not an acceptable mode of moral behavior for a black young adult from an inner-city ghetto. At some point, he confirms his morality and avenges past discrimination by beating the hell out of somebody or by committing an act which society defines as violent. Moreover, the cry of "racism" and the guilt syndrome of white America glare at the white victim as a defense tactic in the courts, just as these manifestations are used to advocate political and social justice for past wrongs. We are reaching the point where we blame the victim for the mistake of being in the wrong place at the wrong time, rather than convicting the criminal.

d. It is important to emphasize that the author is discussing a small but influential group of extremists. By an ironic turn of events, the civil rights movement has been the generator of this group, where politics and criminality are combined and justified under the banner of revolutionary slogans. As the civil rights movement pushed along the battle for black recognition and equality of citizenship, it acquired the trappings of racial pride which ranged from Negro History Week (a moderate view) to the Black Liberation flag and racial chauvinism (an extreme position) of which separation and withdrawal were the mildest manifestations. The most egregious tone of the black revolutionary movement is expressed in hatred of and criminal behavior against whites, as well as the philosophy in which the interests of blacks and whites in America are seen to be so antithetical, that the thrust of revolutionary fulfillment is based on and encourages black malice against white America as an equalizer for the past. Although this interpretation may be construed as "racist" by some critics because the author is white, a number of black leaders, ranging from John A. Morsell, Executive Director of the NAACP to Charles V. Hamilton, the noted militant sociologist at Columbia University, have expressed somewhat similar views.

e. Society is disturbed by the fact that criminal behavior is completely out of control. We feel something must be done if we are to preserve the social fabric of our society—indeed, if we are to preserve ourselves. At the same time, we feel afraid and impotent, and there is a dangerous combination of receptiveness to extreme and repressive appeals. We must remain alert to real dangers, not hysterical ones, and our assessments must be informed and frank. While we need to increase our anti-crime energies in a rational way, we must also devise basic long-term efforts to ameliorate the conditions that lead to crime.

Notes

1. See chapter 1.

2. On the other hand, there is data that suggest that black defendants fare better than whites. For example, in Chicago a black person indicted for a serious crime is more likely to (1) be found not guilty, (2) have his case dropped by the state, and (3) get a lenient prison sentence. A white person if sentenced, however, is more likely to be put on probation than is a black person (*Chicago Sun–Times,* September 18, 1973). The black reaction was one of denial, "absolutely impossible." a similar response for income parity and other trends which reveal marked improvement from past years.

3. Sadly, the black moviegoer rarely gets the opportunity to see middle-class blacks, or the average black person. Although most civil rights organizations object to these new movies, they do not picket or demonstrate against them. Rather they have used them to advance quotas in the movie, television, and advertising industries; establish film scholarships for black college students; put a portion of the profits into black-owned banks; and provide business loans for blacks to buy and operate their own movie houses and concessions. They have also established a review board and demanded to be allowed to screen all films at the script stage with the expressed intention of

presenting positive images of minorities. This last demand is interpreted by many observers as a license to censor and has, at present,
been shelved, but the other demands were being put into operation
in 1973.

References

Arendt, Hannah
    1972 Quote in *U. S. News & World Report,* November 13, p. 48.
Banfield, Edward C.
    1970 *The Unheavenly City.* Boston: Little, Brown.
Chicago Crime Commission
    1973 News article in the *Chicago Tribune,* September 17, p. 3.
Chicago Daily News
    October 16, 1972.
Chicago Sun-Times
    September 18, 1973.
Chicago Today
    September 27, 1972.
Chicago Tribune
    October 14, 1972.
    February 10, 1973.
    February 11, 1973.
    July 26, 1973.
    August 20, 1973.
Education News
    October 16, 1967.
Erikson, Erik, and Huey P. Newton
    1973 *In Search of Common Ground.* New York: Norton.
Glazer, Nathan
    1972 "When the Melting Pot Doesn't Melt." *New York Times Magazine,*
        September 10, pp. 12–13 ff. © 1972 by The New York Times Com-
        pany. Reprinted by permission.
Hacker, Andrew
    1970 "The Violent Black Minority." *New York Times Magazine,* May 10,
        pp. 25 ff.
    1973 "Getting Used to Mugging." *New York Review of Books,* April 19,
        pp. 9–14.
Hill, Marshall
    1972 "Letter to the Editor." *New York Times Magazine,* September 10,
        p. 38. © 1972 by The New York Times Company. Reprinted by
        permission.
Kaplan, John
    1973 Quote in *Time,* March 26, p. 69.
Kilson, Martin A.
    1973 Quote in S. Monroe, "Guest in a Strange House." *Saturday Review,*
        January 13, p. 48.
King, Martin L.
    1967 *Where Do We Go from Here: Chaos or Community?* New York:
        Harper & Row. pp. 55–59.
Knight, Arthur
    1972 "Black Can Be Beautiful." *Saturday Review,* September 16, p. 101.

Moynihan, Daniel P.
1969 *Maximum Feasible Misunderstanding.* New York: Free Press.
Newsweek
1972 "Living with Crime, USA." December 18, pp. 31–36.
New York Times
   September 24, 1972.
   October 1, 1972.
   November 12, 1972.
   December 17, 1972.
   January 8, 1973.
   January 26, 1973.
   January 29, 1973.
   February 4, 1973.
   February 11, 1973.
   March 11, 1973.
   July 15, 1973.
   July 22, 1973.
   August 5, 1973.
   August 26, 1973.
   September 9, 1973.
Ornstein, Allan C.
   1972 *Urban Education: Student Unrest, Teacher Behaviors, and Black
      Power.* Columbus, Ohio: Merrill.
President's Commission on Law Enforcement and Administration of Justice
   1967 *Task Force Report: Crime and Its Impact—An Assessment.* Wash-
      ington, D.C.: U.S. Government Printing Office.
Rustin, Bayard
   1972 "The Failure of Black Separatism." *Newsweek*, November 13, pp.
      18–19.
Saturday Review
   1973 "The Burglar in the Bushes," April 21, pp. 36–40.
Sowell, Thomas
   1971 "Violence and the Payoff Sociology." Unpublished.
   1973 *Black Education: Myths and Tragedies.* New York: McKay.
Starr, Roger
   1972 "The Lesson of Forest Hills." *Commentary*, June, pp. 45–49.
   1973 "Prisons, Politics and the Attica Report." *Commentary*, March, pp.
      31–37.
Time
   1973 "The Irregular Economy." February 19, pp. 36–40.
   1973 "Debate Between Rhetoric and Reality." March 26, pp. 68–69.
U. S. Bureau of the Census
   1971 *Census Population, 1970.* Vol. 1. Washington, D.C.: U.S. Govern-
      ment Printing Office.
U. S. News & World Report
   1972 "Behind the Rise in Crime and Terror." November 13, pp. 41–49.
   1973 "A New Drive Against Killers of Police." January 22, pp. 26–28.
U. S. Riot Commission
   1968 *Report of the National Advisory Commission on Civil Disorders.*
      New York: Bantam.
Wilson, James Q.
   1973 "If Every Criminal Knew He Would Be Caught." *New York Times
      Magazine*, January 28, pp. 9, 44 ff.

chapter 6

The Overlooked Majority

In this chapter, we will discuss the overlooked majority, that is, white members of the working and middle classes, and the rise of ethnicity. These people are forgotten and disaffected middle Americans. They work hard, are not poor, but feel ignored and discriminated against by the government and excluded from affluent society. Most of them live in the gray, outer areas of the cities or in the modest suburbs of America. They belong to mixed religious and ethnic backgrounds. Ignored in the 1960s, they are becoming the focus of the 1970s: ethnicity has assumed a new popularity in the mass media, in colleges and universities, in local, state, and national politics.

Forgotten Americans

We have pointed out nationwide attention has been focused on the plight of the cities and their schools, with special emphasis on the inner-city dweller and student. This socioeducational trend has corresponded, to a large extent, with the shift of the civil rights movement to the North and the impetus gained from the Johnsonian War on Poverty across the nation. As citizens and educators, we should be gratified at this widespread interest in a long-neglected segment of the population; however, while the plight of the inner-city and disadvantaged populace has been stressed and their culture romanticized, the working and middle classes have been largely ignored. Between 150 and 175 million members of these classes—depending on how you count them —live in the outer cities and modest suburbs of America. As Galbraith (1958) pointed out, there are millions of people, the overwhelming majority of Americans, who live between Harlem and Scarsdale, Roxbury and Wellesley, and Hough and Shaker Heights, and, if this author may add, who live between

Detroit's East Side and Grosse Pointe, Chicago's South Side and Kenilworth, and Watts and Beverly Hills.

The term "middle" American has been loosely defined, but it is often used to describe a member of the majority working or middle class.[1] When these middle Americans have been the subject of interest, they have usually been criticized and ridiculed. Once, at the turn of the century, they were treated with compassion and understanding in the literature of the muck-rakers (Ida Tarbell, Lincoln Steffens, Upton Sinclair, and Theodore Dreiser) and the socioeducational reformers (Jacob Riis, Max Eastman, Jane Addams, and John Dewey). This was the era when America was changing from an agrarian to an industrialized nation, and there was an urgent but short-lived mood of criticizing the deficiencies of machine civilization and highlighting the plight of those who labored in mines, in factories, and on farms. But the era ended with the U. S. entry into World War I, and John Chamberlain could entitle his survey of the preceding decades a *Farewell to Reform*.

Today, the working-class man is mainly portrayed in the literature as a beer-drinking, drum-and-bugle type who is anti-intellectual, antipeacenik, and antiblack and marches to the tune of "God Bless America." Similarly the book-of-the-month clubs and college bookstores are flooded with popular and "scholarly" commentaries about the decadence and decline of the middle class, with its plastic world of Howard Johnson restaurants, green stamps, and rows of brick houses. Its people are supposedly chain-smoking, pill-gorging, gin-guzzling, bed-hopping frauds. Another book about working-class and middle-class stereotypes is an invitation to a yawn, and is likely to illustrate the intellectual snobbery and sometimes spiteful bigotry of these authors. While the poor and the black have innumerable authors sympathetic to their cause—commentators who are part of the culture of the intellectual, liberal, and black "swinging protest" movement—the unpoor and unblack have few full-time popularizers, few contemporary heroes, and few writers who are sensitive to their concerns and needs.

The media and liberal reformers often lump these people together not only as middle Americans, but also as the silent majority. They are con-sidered quaint at best, most of the time awkward and bigoted. They are not worth listening to, and the media does not pay attention to them, because they are silent. They are silent, not because they have nothing to say, but with only a few exceptions in some areas of the country, they are voiceless and powerless, unorganized, forgotten and silenced by inaccessible power that shapes their destiny.

Ethnic groupings represent the key personal relations which sustain many of these Americans. With the exception of religious institutions, the only place in urban America where one is likely to find a sense of community is among ethnic groups. According to Gans (1968), about 60–75 percent of the people in urban areas, both working and middle class, have considerable contact with immediate and extended ethnic neighborhoods—in city and sub-urban areas. The ethnic community, according to Gordon (1964), provides the security and effective association in the context of the extended family. There are many viable ethnic communities, although many outsiders view them as slum or depressed areas; just as many outsiders wrongfully perceive almost all minority communities as slums. Many urban planners make no provision for the types of housing facilities or gathering places which ethnics look to as a source of their sense of community. Urban renewal displaces these people in the same manner as poor and minority groups are bulldozed. The tenements and rooming houses, taverns and clubrooms, the boccie ball area, the neighborhood grocery store, the night spots, etc., often come down when urban renewal goes up. Indeed, urban planners seldom take into account what the community considers as essential to its needs and integration.

While a wide variety of statistics are offered by experts about the number of ethnics, one rough estimate is that there are 40 million, what the U. S. census calls "foreign born." This number almost triples when we add their sons and daughters and then their children who were born in America—one or two generations removed from the original Irish, Italians, Poles, Greeks, and Germans. While most of the foreign born are classified in the working class, most of the American born ethnics are one or two steps removed from their parents on the mobility ladder and are nearly evenly distributed among the working and middle classes.[2]

Trying to describe these middle Americans is more than just describing ethnics. Many of them have no distinct ethnic identity. Describing them is really like trying to describe America itself; and while there is both good and bad in this country, certainly most of what is here is good, especially when compared with the rest of the world. If we look for these people, we find them almost everywhere. Although their culture and background are extremely diverse and different, they share common attitudes and behaviors; they have in common that they do the right things—obey the laws, work hard, pay taxes, go to church, fight the country's wars, seek a better education and opportunities for their children—but the right things do not seem to be paying off these days.

These are the yeomen and hardworking people of America, the Bill Smiths and Joe Taylors who built this country and who power it forward. Writes Schrag (1969), the middle American "was once the hero of the civics book. . . . Now he is the 'forgotten man,' perhaps the most alienated person" (p. 29). These working- and middle-class people put into office such presidents as Thomas Jefferson, Andrew Jackson, Abraham Lincoln, Franklin Roosevelt, and John Kennedy. They supported the New Deal, the New Frontier, and the Great Society labor–civil rights coalition, only to realize finally that these programs had benefitted them less and less while benefitting the poor and the black more and more. According to Isaacs (1972), these are men and women "with deep and [grave] problems of their own, trying under great pressure to defend what they have won by hard work and still trying to achieve the American dream as they still dream it" (p. 75). Hoffer (1972) contends these people have been poor for all or most of their lives, "and now [they're] being preached at by every son of a bitch who comes along" (pp. 29–30). Writes Ribicoff (1972), "These men and women look back upon the humble origin of their families in America, and they say: 'We did it without federal grants. Why can't blacks? Why should they have all the special treatment' " (p. 30). And Schrag (1969) points out that these people know that their options and mobility are limited; they "cannot imagine any major change for the better, but [they] can imagine change for the worse" (p. 31).

Indeed, there is little recognition of the Bill Smiths and Joe Taylors of this country, the majority Americans who barely make it from week to week, taxed and squeezed to the breaking point, unable to keep up with inflation, and almost always broke after their bills are paid. These are the Americans whose sons died in Vietnam and who now need desperately to believe that America was right, who cannot send their children to college except with the help of scholarships, which it is almost impossible for ordinary students to obtain. These people believe in the system, but receive few rewards from it; in effect, they are trapped by it into low-paying jobs, installment buying, monthly mortgages, small pensions, and low social security benefits.

Since the last decade, these working- and middle-class groups have been asked to shoulder the burden of social reform, to integrate their schools and neighborhoods. Now they are being told that hard work and ability no longer count, that quotas must be enacted and minority workers hired and promoted before them, regardless of individual qualifications. They have been asked by those who are comfortably well-off to pay the social debts due the poor and the blacks. Indeed, the intellectual elites and affluent Americans have generally gone untouched and unburdened by the reforms of the 1960s and early 1970s, while the not-so-well educated and near poor have paid the bulk of the bill for increased welfare checks and enlarged poverty programs.

The integration issue, aside from the practical problems involved, is symbolic of how the liberal-intellectual and wealthy elite impose social reform on ordinary people against their customs and beliefs. Many whites are afraid that the buses will bring the problems of the ghetto to "their" schools[3] and expose their children to the social ills that blacks have had to cope with and which have turned many of their schools into "blackboard jungles." Similarly, opposition to fear of low-income housing is linked to fear of crime that will come with high concentrations of low-income and minority groups. Many whites moved away from the inner city for the sake of their children's education and for their own safety and particularly reject the idea of having some liberal who patronizes them, or some judge they did not elect, tell them they must send their children into ghetto schools or must cope with the increased crime rates, while these elites—if they have children—send their own children to private schools (in effect, white segregated schools) and live in expensive neighborhoods, often away from minority groups and buffered by layers of working- and middle-class groups.

Neither this forgotten majority nor the electorate at large can play a substantial role in influencing the policies implemented by so-called reformers. A few nonelected liberal bureaucrats now tell the white majority they must be penalized because they are white, while most of the policy makers themselves and almost all of the wealthy remain untouched by their quotas and reverse discrimination practices. According to Steinhart (1972), "A persistent question remains: are the goals and purposes of any group of experts necessarily similar to those of the population at large?" (p. 18)

Some parallel trends are apparent in education. The oversimplified stereotypes, the portrayal of the so-called wicked "system" and its "care-takers," the naïve proposals, the end-all solutions, the unreasonable demands, the inflammatory rhetoric, and the racial name-calling at best are repetitious and at worst often mask real issues and oversimplify solutions to complex social and educational problems. In the same vein, the central educational issues are often oversimplified into one "relevant" issue, the noble struggle of the poor and the black, while teachers and schools are blamed as the causes of their learning failure. In the meantime, working-class and middle-class students are largely ignored in the educational literature. When they are discussed, they are, like their parents, stereotyped. They are described either as "street corner" adolescents who manage to get their C's, finish high school, and then go into the army or get married and have a few children, or as a bunch of protected and striving youth who are pressured by parents obsessed with having their children make good grades and get into college. To be sure, there is very little in the literature, especially in comparison to the "underdog" literature of poverty and blackness, that notes the cultural and ethnic diversity of these middle-American students, their different abilities and cognitive patterns, their personality attributes, their various aspirations and goals, the different educational and occupational routes the different ethnic groups choose, and so on—in short, their life styles—what it is like to grow up in Astoria, New York; Bridgeport, Connecticut; Lombard, Illinois; Des Moines, Iowa; or Whittier, California. There is little recognition that there are hundreds of thousands of students who are not poor, but from working-class and middle-class families who are in desperate need of educational assistance. As House Rep. Albert Quie (1973) from Minnesota points out, as many as 27 percent of children from families with 1970 yearly incomes between $8,000 and $12,000 need assistance in reading and as many as 23 percent need help in mathematics.

Many of these students feel brushed aside by governmental and educational reformers who are preoccupied with the problems of so-called disadvantaged populations. They feel victimized by the new double standards in education: compensatory educational programs geared for the inner-city populations which overlook slow readers in outer-city and suburban schools; construction of new schools in ghetto areas but not in working-class neighborhoods where the old buildings are often equally dilapidated; lower college admission requirements for members of racial minorities but not for ordinary students from middle America; admissions rules that favor minority students trying to get into college or into law or medical school but mitigate against students from middle America even though their academic qualifications may be higher; attenuated grading standards for minorities and cries of racial discrimination if a teacher or professor trys to apply the same grading standards to all students in an effort to maintain excellence. They resent the fact that middle-American students cannot obtain many scholarships, loans, and jobs on campuses because these monies are mainly earmarked for minority students.[4] Their feeling that they can no longer obtain equal treatment in school and in other sectors of the country is illustrated by a growing number, even of those with ethnic names, who claim on application forms that they are part black or Indian and tell reformers to go to hell or prove otherwise.

More and more, the rising demands of the inner-city population, and especially of black Americans, are coming into conflict with the higher expectations of the working and middle classes. According to Gans (1972), we are entering a period where almost everyone has increased expectations. Inevitably, there must be "conflict over how these expectations are to be met and just whose expectations are to be met first and foremost" (p. 45). The white working class, and now even the white middle class, observe blacks organizing and making gains at their expense, even favored by private and public institutions, while they and their children are being ignored and even subjected to reverse discrimination. The more precarious their economic situation, the more menaced they feel and the more they are beginning to question whether a rewarding working-class or middle-class life in America is still possible. If anything, they feel they are the victimized group by virtue of the climate of change; they are beginning to question if they can still get a fair shake in today's society. This group, whose members have been economically threatened most or all of their lives, having to moonlight to make ends meet, watching increased taxes and inflation gobble up their remaining dollars, managing to save just enough money to keep one step ahead of the bill collector, many living not too far above the poverty level where the loss of a job for six months or a serious illness in the family presents the threat of impoverishment, sees black political and economic gains made mostly by new rules and artificial standards as eroding their rights, job opportunities, and life-styles.

These frustrations and fears result in growing demands for equality for white ethnics. Thus we have the revival of tribalism and the new cries for "Italian Power," "Irish Power," and "Polish Power." The citizenry demands greater police protection and harsher penalties for criminals. As previously mentioned in chapter 5, many mayors in our large cities are getting elected on law-and-order platforms. An increasing number of housewives from New York City to San Francisco (and it is difficult to find two more progressive and cosmopolitan cities in the country) picket and demonstrate with their suburban counterparts against busing and scattered-site public housing, where only a few years ago white America seemed willing to accept integration. The recent popularity in the North of George Wallace and other New Populists who reflect similar sentiments without a southern drawl is symptomatic. And there is the landslide victory of Mr. Nixon, considered by many critics to be one of the most unpopular presidents in the twentieth century, which may be credited to the overwhelming support of middle Americans.

All these trends can be simplified as an expression of white racism and backlash, which is often implied in the liberal and black rhetoric of race relations; but the mood of middle America is more complex. These people see themselves as men and women in the middle, footing the major tax bill while government policies continue to favor the poor and the rich, feeling besieged, neglected, and trapped by dull jobs, small wages, and lack of chances for better employment. They see that their hard-earned pay is little more than what welfare recipients get and buys them less and less. They are trying to defend their fundamental rights, the concept of equal opportunity, the sanctity of work, and the stability of their family. They are expressing a wistfulness for the "old values" of respect for decency, authority, education, merit, and hard work that seem to have gone awry.

It is easy for blacks, at least militant blacks, to voice their grievances on television and in newspapers and professional journals; however, it is extremely difficult for whites to express their grievances. They are not supposed to have grievances, and when they do express their needs and concerns, they are often denounced for their white backlash and prejudicial attitudes. Black problems are often defined in terms of white "racism" and the "sickness" of the larger society, even when there are other factors to consider; and white problems are often defined in terms of their own "racism" and "rationalizations." Blacks and other minorities can claim "prejudiceness" and "bigotry" and as a result get different treatment (more accurately, more lenient treatment) than whites. This double standard is recognized by both blacks and whites, but the latter become defensive in dealing with this strategy.

In the vernacular, Schrag (1969) describes the feelings and plight of the Bill Smiths and Joe Taylors of America. A guy in the streets of Boston says, "I'm working my ass off." There's no place for his kids to play; he is up to his head in bills. "I'm supposed to bleed for a bunch of people on relief." In New York, a person who drives a truck for the Post Office during the 4 PM–12 midnight shift and drives a cab between 7 AM and 2 PM and sells radios on the side is ready to fight. He claims, "The colored guys work when they feel like it." Half the time they don't even show up to work. "One guy tore up the time cards," and nothing happened to him. "I'd like to see a white guy do that and get away with it."

To another person, the black child represents "trouble in school," who gets special treatment that his kid never received. With disdain, he states that "their fucking mothers are all on welfare." The black child means "a change in the rules, a double standard in grades and discipline." In Chicago, a widow with three children is unable to get a college loan because she earns $7,000 a year; the money is reserved for the poor and those on welfare. In Newark, the head of an Italian vigilante group contends that whites in his area cannot get jobs: "we have to hire Negroes first." The median income in Irish Boston is $5,100, but it is hard to convince a community worker that a white person "who is not stupid or irresponsible can be poor. Pride still keeps them from applying for income supplements or Medicaid," but it does not prevent them from resenting those who do. In Pittsburgh, Polish Americans earn about $5,500, and many fall below the poverty level, but "the governmental programs are nonetheless primarily directed to Negroes."

Schrag points out that "black power is supposed to be nothing but emulation of the ways in which other ethnic groups made it. But have they made it?" Across the country, from town to town, city to city, in greyhound terminals, beach bungalows, supermarkets, barbershops, bowling alleys, etc., white frustration is evident and people say, "Somebody has to say no." Backlash is associated with the many white ethnics "whose members have themselves a [doubtful] hold on security of affluence." Furthermore, for every ethnic, there are "a dozen American-Americans," beyond ethnic identity, who are just as angry and alienated by programs mainly geared for minorities and by preferential treatment given to them. The manifestations are similar, almost everywhere—"race, taxes, welfare," and law and order (pp. 28–32).

Senator Abraham Ribicoff (1972) from Connecticut describes some of the causes of conflict between blacks and white working-class people. He contends that the latter group feels that its government "has brushed them aside," that politicians and social reformers are only interested in the problems of "blacks, youths, and other troublesome minorities." These blue-collar workers feel they are "a forgotten class." They are beginning to think in terms of white unity. If blacks can think "in black-versus-white terms, why shouldn't we do the same?"

The blue-collar worker feels trapped by rising costs. For most of them, hospital costs are a constant worry. As many as 24 million Americans are not covered by hospital insurance; more than 75 percent lack surgical insurance. "A major sickness or illness can wipe out their personal savings and put them into debt." They realize, however, the poor do not pay for medical or hospital treatment. They resent the fact that compensatory education is mainly geared for poor and minority children. "Academic standards are lowered" for minorities to permit them to go to college, but are not lowered for ordinary youth. "Most working-class people retire and live at or near poverty level." In 1971, as many as one out of four aged Americans lived in economic squalor, "a rate of poverty twice that of our society." Many of these people were too embarrassed to register for federal assistance, yet "a substantial number of able-bodied blacks refused to work and collected welfare."

As the social, welfare, and educational programs continue to favor minorities, "men and women who once thought of themselves as tolerant [and] progressive . . . now have become resentful and bitter." Why be tolerant or progressive? If you are, reform overlooks one's needs. Ribicoff concludes that "protest is important"; however, we either make it or decline together as a society. This means no group "can be downgraded or forgotten" (pp. 28–33).

Newsweek in 1969 commissioned the Gallup organization to survey the white working-class and middle-class population. Gallup interviewed 2,165 adults, 61 percent of whom earned incomes between $5,000 and $15,000, a large enough cross sample to make a detailed analysis and accurate generalizations. The special report indicated that "all around the country . . . whites feel increasingly free to voice their hostility." The average American is staunchly opposed to black militant and violent tactics. As many as 63 percent believe that the police should have "more power to curb crime." Sixty-eight percent contend that dangerous suspects who might commit another crime before trial should not be permitted to post bail, and 85 percent contend that black militant and college demonstrators have been treated too leniently. The average American is afraid to walk the streets alone; he is afraid for his life.

The middle American "is convinced that Negroes actually have a better chance to get ahead . . . than he does and that any trouble blacks suffer are probably their own fault." Across the country, the feeling is that blacks are well organized and getting almost everything at the expense of white working- and middle-class Americans. There is the sense of "the ultimate victim," the victim being the average white American. One Washington official admitted that more programs were needed "for Mr. Forgotten American," as he put it. "Foundations and think tanks have primarily been concerned with . . . minorities."

Resentment toward blacks is increasing, based not on racism as is often claimed by black spokesmen, but by "recent progress for Negroes—particularly in jobs, education, and housing . . . partly at the expense of the [white] middle class." Moreover, the liberal-black rhetoric has changed from equal opportunity to "the concept of reparations for years of discrimination," an idea that the average American rejects as pure reverse racism. The feeling is that the black American is infringing on the rights of the middle American, asking for more than he is entitled to. As many as 40 percent of the whites interviewed believe that blacks have the advantage in getting financial help for buying homes, a good-paying job, or a good education, and 65 percent contend that blacks receive "preference in unemployment from the government." Though blacks claim it is ludicrous, a great proportion of whites are convinced that "police and the courts give blacks especially lenient treatment." The oft-repeated claim was that "whites don't have the rights that Negroes do." There is the feeling that reformers are "making them [blacks] think that [whites] owe them jobs and . . . housing, food, money, for nothing" (pp. 29–33).

In general, the survey found that most middle Americans were not antiblack, but were opposed to the methods used by blacks to make gains in jobs and education and in other sectors of society. Black gains were being made while the governmental, business, and educational institutions were discriminating against whites. Furthermore, this author contends that the situation has drastically escalated; the same whites, if surveyed today, would

find the deck even more stacked against them and their individual rights further curtailed in lieu of rising group rights and racial quotas.

Buckley (1973) describes the change of sentiment in New York
City, once considered to have a majority of tolerant and reform-minded
urban dwellers. "The white working-class and middle-class voters are near the
flashpoint of rage." They see themselves burdened by $2.5 billion a year in
welfare payments, earmarked mainly for minorities and a goodly number who
are ineligible but still receive payments. This cost comprises 25 percent of
the entire city budget. Added to this cost is a host of other services—hospitals,
courts, poverty programs, and so on—as well as the "incalculable cost of the
crimes they commit." Fear of the night hangs over the city. The polarization
is intense: "the white middle and working classes" on one side, "and the minorities and their allies among the limousine liberals" who are financially secure enough to preach the "gospel of reform" [my quotes] to the white
majority (p. 12). To a large extent, the present situation in New York minus
the size sounds like so many other cities in America.

Only a very naïve person or one propelled by leftward ideology
would view growing white resentment toward blacks as merely an expression
of racism. To go on seeing the masses of whites as exhibiting bigot and backlash sentiments, without trying to understand their problems and grievances,
only gives fuel and substance to continuous racial hostility and alienation in
this country. To go on viewing middle Americans as nonexistent and unnews-
worthy is not only unfair and spiteful, but permits local, state, and federal
governments, as well as liberal policy makers, to ignore the vital interests of
this majority populace. Political and social reformers must pay attention to
all groups, including the 150 to 175 million members of the white working
and middle classes, the "muscle and heart" that keep this country moving.

We need also to be concerned with and to help middle Americans
because they are essentially important to the bios and vitality of this country:
without them the country would collapse. They build our skyscrapers and
bridges, mine our minerals, grow our food, unload our ships, run our railroads,
pave our roads, drive our trucks, teach our children, police our streets, and
fight our fires. They do not steal; they do not collect welfare even when they
are entitled to it; they do not riot or threaten the system with violence; they
do not make a lot of money. These are the people that liberals and blacks
know very little about and yet they have lumped them together and stereotyped them as "racists" and "bigots." Despite more than a decade of prosperity, these middle Americans lack economic affluence: they are still very
close to layoffs, strikes, plant reductions, tax squeezes, inflation, and now reverse discrimination.

The Jewish teachers of New York City, the Irish teachers of Boston and Chicago, the Polish teachers of Buffalo and Detroit, and the German
teachers of Milwaukee and Minneapolis all have one thing in common with the
social workers, restaurant owners, policemen, firemen, construction workers,
insurance salesmen, secretaries, and housewives in Pittsburgh, Cleveland,

Birmingham, Denver, Dallas, and Los Angeles. The question that unites middle Americans throughout the country: What the hell have the local, state, and federal governments done for them in the last 15 years? And this is coupled with a growing hostility toward liberals and blacks whom middle Americans see in an unholy alliance to take away what they have earned through hard work and education by employing a double and relaxed standard—even preferential treatment—for blacks in all social, judicial, economic, and educational institutions. Thus middle Americans feel that a small minority have run roughshod over the majority, where the majority must surrender their interests and needs to those of the minority, where they must suppress their feelings in public or run the risk of being denounced as "racists." In the meantime, blacks are able to vocalize their demands because of their so-called victimized status, and they have sufficient liberal and government support to enable their demands to be met first—and at the expense of middle Americans.

Despite the fact that most of these middle groups are less educated and articulate than liberals, they sense the liberals' resentment of them and that the claims made on behalf of blacks to justify black advancement are implicitly denied to whites. Not only are whites supposed to be held back, lest their "greed" and "racism" impede black progress and black "liberation," but whites are also not supposed to state their needs and interests without running the risk of being called racist. Not only are standard tests considered biased and to be scrapped as criteria for making decisions for graduate school entrance and job hiring and promotions because blacks as a group score lower than whites on these tests, but racial justice now demands that minorities be pushed ahead despite their scores. Only blacks seem to have political rights; and, they can appeal to the consciousness of America as "oppressed" people when voicing their demands while whites are at best considered immoral for questioning these black demands.

According to Hitchcock (1973), blacks in Harlem and South Side Chicago have the right to veto construction of state or federal buildings or a university gymnasium, but whites in Forest Hills or Northwest Chicago cannot veto low-income housing. Blacks in large cities have the right to control their own schools and discharge white teachers and administrators, but white parents are labeled racists if they attempt to exercise the same rights under local control. Blacks can demand separate schools and separate community institutions, but whites who seek neighborhood schools and their own ethnic community organizations are branded as "racists" and "bigots." Blacks can promote pride and power in local schools, colleges, and universities with what sometimes boils down to antiwhite slogans and ideology, but whites are often considered "racists" if they question some of the black power rhetoric and venting backlash sentiment if they seek "Italian power" or "Polish power." Fear of crime and opposition to low-income housing are seen as white rationalizations, but black hostility and violence toward whites is considered justified as a political tactic by some liberals and blacks. Militants like H. Rap Brown, who was convicted of intent to riot; Eldridge Cleaver, who boasts about raping white women; and George Jackson, a convicted killer, are heroes and considered "chic," while George Wallace, Ronald Reagan, and Frank Rizzo are seen as fascists. Manifestations in Carnesie and Rosedale, Gage Park and Cicero, and Pontiac and Grosse Pointe are labeled white bigotry, but the riots in Watts, Detroit, and Newark are justified as expressions of black frustration. As Hitchcock (1973) points out, "The rhetoric of the oppressed is always accepted at face value; their grievances are what they perceive them to be; their motives are exactly what they claim," while the grievances, motives, and fears of whites are considered to be racist sentiments (p. 66).

The Rise of White Ethnicity

Sennett and Cobb (1972) found, in a series of interviews with 150 white working-class residents from Boston, that these people grow to despise themselves, precisely because they are workers with limited opportunities, and that they internalize society's negative judgment on their attainments. On the other hand, the authors contend that members of the middle class are also plagued by class injuries, are crippled by the pursuit of success which they never quite obtain and are dissatisfied with their jobs. Sennett and Cobb conclude that the two classes lack a political organization and a coherent class solidarity which could sustain the combative self-consciousness found in the European working class and bourgeoisie society and its political parties. It is this lack of class and political consciousness which makes the white working and middle classes impotent and powerless today in comparison with the black workers who have economically and politically organized around race.

Thus the fears and frustrations of middle Americans result not in the growing political and economic class consciousness of workers or bourgeoisie society, but in the revival of tribalism and white ethnicity. The growing problems and concerns of white working- and middle-class America are beginning to coincide with the increased momentum of cultural pluralism and ethnic politics. These twin trends are reflected in the growing popularity of ethnic writers such as Geno Baroni, Andrew Greeley, Barbara Mikulski, and Michael Novak. For example, Baroni (1972) points out that public policy in the 1960s overlooked white ethnics in designing programs to restore urban America, to eliminate poverty, substandard housing, depressed schools, and racial discord. "Problems of American society were defined . . . almost entirely within the context of poverty and race," not in terms of the total society, "thereby making it impossible to deal with social issues as the distribution of resources, rights, and privileges among different groups." The ethnic factor is sparked by an untenable economic situation, where ordinary Americans have been "ignored and castigated by the establishment. It is a revolution of self-assertion that will utilize new techniques of . . . community organization, community development, and legislative action to make power felt at the polls" (p. 4).

Baroni points out that social reform has ignored and alienated working-class and middle-class populations, and has forced them to pay a disproportionate amount of the social and monetary costs of such reform. Similarly, the ethnics have come to resent the Archie Bunker stereotypes, the movies like "Joe" which portray the working man as anti-youth and antiblack, and the liberal contention, found in the Kerner report and elsewhere, that they are the cause of the cities' ills. White ethnics should no longer pay for America's guilt: they did not bring racism with them; they found it here.

As America redefines itself, part of the political and economic struggle will include the ethnic factor. Baroni contends that a new agenda for the 1970s "must go beyond the civil rights" struggle and consider the legitimate needs of the poor and near poor, racial minorities as well as ethnic minorities. "Urban ethnics, white, black, and Spanish-speaking, should not be enemies" (p. 10). They are all being oppressed by special interest groups and politicians, and they share a common destiny by virtue of their needs and concerns. "We summon ethnic people across the country to rise up in a new urban populism —demanding decentralized control and recognition of the pluralistic quality of neighborhood living" (p. 11).

Reverend Andrew Greeley (1972) declares that the ideas of assimilation and the melting pot are absurd. It is not wrong for ethnics to define themselves as Italian, Irish, Polish, and the like. The black pride phenomenon expresses the desire of a minority group to define its heritage and culture and is considered legitimate by American intellectual elites. White ethnics also seek to keep alive something of their past in the larger American context. Writes Greeley:

> Since it is assumed that most ethnic groups ought to vanish (except for Jews, blacks, Spanish-speaking Americans, and American Indians), and since it is also assumed that most ethnic groups have no contribution to make, it is scarcely worth learning anything about them. Italians provide pizza, Poles provide Polish jokes, and the Irish provide corrupt politicians. The Greeks, the Latvians, the Slovaks, the Slovenes, the Luxembourgers, the Armenians? Well, they're all going to go away, too. The blunt truth is that many members of those elite groups who read the *New York Times* and the *Washington Post*, and also *Commentary* and the *New York Review of Books*, know more about Nigeria than about the Northwest Side of Chicago, and have a much better understanding of the issues facing Britain in its entry into the Common Market than of the issues facing American Poles and Italians. The myths that the hard hat supports the war and the white ethnics are racist are myths that persist in the face of overwhelming statistical evidence to the contrary, in part because the opinion-making intellectual and political elite really don't think it worth the effort to learn anything about the alleged hard hats and racists [pp. 289-90].

Greeley asserts that ethnicity is considered a racist cop-out by many liberals and blacks. The liberals feel it leads to provincialism and particularism, in effect, connoting their own bigotry and lack of tolerance toward diversity. Most blacks label ethnicity as white backlash, failing to admit that the new consciousness of ethnics is in part "based on the fact that blacks have legitimized cultural pluralism as it has perhaps never been legitimized before" (p. 291). If it is all right to be proud of being black, why is it not all right to be proud of being Italian or Irish? Is it blacks alone who have the right to assert pride and power?

Mikulski (1972) points out that American ethnic neighborhoods are rarely appreciated: they are either castigated by politicians and policy makers or romanticized and patronized by intellectuals. There is more to Little Italy than garlic bread or about Germantown than Wiener Schnitzel. "The family structure, the ethnic organizations, the political clubs, the relationship between school, church, and leading institutions form the community" (p. 55). It is not bricks or European recipes, but how people work and live with each other and the institutions they create that form the fiber of their culture and neighborhood. "One of the problems with ethnic neighborhoods is that they have always been considered the other side of the tracks. Being 'put down' . . . eroded our spirit [and] battered our sense of security" (p. 56). The result was that many ethnics who could afford to move, moved to the suburbs. Those who were left behind (mainly the elderly and the near poor) found the banks unwilling to lend money to the outer cities because they were "transitional areas." Thus, many ethnic neighborhoods have lost their vitality and have become targets for speculators, block busters, and urban renewal planners. "These invisible bureaucrats . . . think they have all the answers; that they are enlightened and we are reactionary. . . . They're so hung up in their organization charts, they forget they're organizing for people, people who live within a family and a family that lives within a community." You have to plan things that youth, the family, or the elderly can appreciate. "Now those guys wouldn't even know what a boccie ball is" (p. 57). Ethnics have been ignored by Republicans and taken for granted by the Democrats. They have been either overlooked or exploited by local politicians, and they have been forced to organize to protect themselves from unwanted freeways and truck traffic through their residential neighborhoods. People organize around economic, political, and social issues, and ethnicity can be used to organize effectively to deal with these issues on a local and national basis. "Ethnic pride and ethnic consciousness could provide a richness to this America that we really don't have now" (p. 60). The ethnic spirit is going to change America. Mikulski sees it as "both the agony and the hope of the country as we move into the 21st century" (p. 61).

Since their arrival, says Novak (1972), ethnics have been made to feel unenlightened, stupid, immoral, backward, and ashamed of their heritage. The WASP superculture has pressed a new and alienating life-style on ethnics. America is not a melting pot, and it is time to understand and appreciate the diversity of her ethnic elements; it is time for a new culture and politics based on ethnic pluralism and pride.

The grievances of white ethnics can no longer be overlooked. "When muggings and robberies reached the educated and the affluent, some finally recognized that the cries for law and order are not identical with 'prejudice' " (p. 7). The phrase "white racism" has become for the Left what "communism" was for the Right, an indiscriminate scare word which prevents honest discussion and legitimate reform. Reformists can no longer afford to overlook ethnic diversity or devise programs for blacks only. "While ethnics welcome black gains, their persistent question is why the gains of blacks should be solely at *their* expense" (p. 14). The failure of reformers to note the white ethnic factor has caused ethnics to consider political coalitions, and they hold the swing vote in the presidential elections in the 1970s.

Resentment of social class, economic privilege, and educational advantage is also a pervasive emotion among ethnics. Observes Novak, "The Left is exhausted; it has no more to offer" ordinary Americans. To ethnics, "the style of the Left seems decadent. . . . There is not much evidence that the liberal wing of the Democratic party respects the culture, the values, the dreams, the hopes of ethnic peoples" (p. 18). The intellectual elites and left wing of the Democratic party must revise its stance; it must "hear [ethnic] voices and accents against which for too long it has closed its ears." If it does not revise its policies and "enter into a give-and-take with working people and ethnic interests," blue-collar and ethnic Americans will side with the emerging Republican majority (p. 38). (The 1972 election proved Novak to be astute in his judgments, as white ethnics switched their vote to the new Republican majority.)

There is nothing wrong with ethnic pride and culture, nor with black pride and culture; but just as black pride and culture turned into black power and black racism, we can expect similar political and racial overtones in the rise of white ethnicity. Most ethnic and black spokesmen admit that ethnicity and race are interrelated with public policy, but few if any are willing to publicly admit to the excessive prejudices and discriminatory practices that often accompany the fever of pride and culture.

Liberal and black leaders have good reason to fear white ethnicity, but then the liberal-black orthodoxy has given rise to it. Whites are beginning to take the cue from blacks; they are also starting to think of their own ethnicity and solidarity to advance their political and economic considerations. Toth (1972) asserts that were it not for the ethnic stereotypes and slurs, the ethnic jokes, and the Italian parades on Columbus Day or the Irish parades on St. Patrick's Day, who would know that ethnics exist? Sure, a few of us dine at Greek and Hungarian restaurants, but the ethnics are unblack, unpoor, unrich—considered a bore—thus, the nation has overlooked and alienated them.

Brown and Feinstein (1972) maintain that ethnics were told not to cling to traditions. Even worse, the melting pot myth dislodged their culture; now they must turn for identity back to their heritage which is rooted in their family and community and organize politically to advance their own priorities. The authors point out that our national policies have drifted into false assumptions, categories, and programs developed by people whose experience is antithetical to that of ethnics. Even political figures who have ethnic origins usually no longer represent ethnics, but have surrendered their ethnic identity and are no longer a part of the same community from whom information is sought and for whom decisions are made. The authors contend that ethnics must have their own power to make the decisions that affect their lives.

Ethnic leaders such as Toth (1972) and Mikulski (1972) feel that ethnicity is rooted in the community, that the community must develop and control its own institutions in dealing with other groups and larger national institutions. Ethnic communities must not be destroyed, and decisions about these communities must no longer be made by outsiders, political bureaucrats. The time has come to rethink our democratic concepts and to advance the concept of ethnic pluralism. Brown and Feinstein (1972) also assert the importance of not permitting one group to define the fate of another. Citizen participation in the form of ethnicity is important at all levels of government, and it is now, they believe, the most important issue in contemporary America.

Novak (1972) and Toth (1972) declare that ethnics have descended into near squalor and have become refugees in a hell of smog, pollution, and decaying neighborhoods because they lack an ethnic and political consciousness. Similarly, they have allowed themselves to be exploited by technology and bureaucracy, as well as by liberal-black rhetoric. They have become powerless, and have thus been taken for granted and overlooked by local and federal policies in the 1960s. They have been silenced by a faceless, inaccessible, incomprehensible governmental power that has shaped their destinies. Who speaks for the ethnics? Only ethnics! They must politically organize and form coalitions as ethnics.

Thus the new ethnicity is transformed from pride to power, from a cultural dimension to a political dimension. In this new ethnocentrism, we see the seeds of new American divisiveness. The immediate question to be faced in talking about ethnicity in the 1970s is whether this leads to pluralism, as some ethnic leaders say, or to separatism and further polarization. As blacks claimed black pride and culture were and still are healthy and necessary, ethnics make similar claims for Polish pride and Polish power. As blacks transformed this new identity into a political and ideological movement, so may we expect ethnics to follow suit. As black separatism, control, and racism have become justified slogans and tactics, we may expect comparable trends among ethnics. The possible excesses of white ethnicity should be clear: (1) balkanization of communities and fragmentation of the country, (2) group quotas extended to Italian quotas, Greek quotas, Croatian quotas, and so on to complement black quotas and the upshot of other minority quotas— possibly even youth quotas and homosexual quotas[5]—and (3) a surge of white coalitions to counteract black power and a new form of white racism to neutralize the recent rise of black racism.

As ethnics regain their identity and make political and economic
demands, they will probably go the same route as the black movement, baring
the accumulated resentment and frustration that have been building up toward
blacks. As the black movement opened up the pathologies of black hatred
toward whites—most of it suppressed for generations and now spilling over—
we can expect white fears and prejudices to be vented against blacks and other
ethnic minorities. Isaacs (1972) takes a dim view of such a reassertion of
ethnic separateness:

> . . . the appeal here to the Middle Americans is to *depolar
> ize* on social issues and to *repolarize* ethnically. This may
> make beautiful music in the heads of some of these com
> posers, but it has to be played out loud to hear what it
> actually sounds like. . . .

> The drummers who beat this drum march down any num
> ber of separate roads, and each can be playing a bright
> and satisfying tune full of love and peace and enhance
> ment until two such roads intersect, which they usually
> do. Then, the record shows, there is invariable trouble at
> the crossroads. . . .

> It is clear enough that a great reordering of identities is
> going on among all kinds of Americans. It is clear that in
> the great confusion of time, a certain lunging back into
> the tribal caves is one way to find, maybe, the emotional
> security that seems to have disappeared everywhere else.
> It is a time when new meanings of *American-ness* are being
> made. It is surely a complicated and profound happening.
> But we still know very little about it. . . .

> We do not know how far the ethnic factor, as such, ap
> pears in the pattern of disaffection and disarray that now
> grips so many among them. . . . We do not know how
> marginal these stirrings are or how deep they may go, how
> they turn up among the generations, how ethnic concerns
> survive in the old, how far and in what forms they touch
> the young.

> . . . suspicion and mistrust are not . . . inevitable. If they
> can be eliminated . . . ethnicity enriches life. Unfortu
> nately, . . . no one has yet figured out the formula for
> doing so. . . .

> It appears, then, that the "new pluralism" as conceived
> [now] requires (1) a new formula for keeping ethnic
> groups from tearing each other limb from limb as they
> have done from time immemorial, and (2) a new for
> mula . . . which will reshape our society . . . with some
> safeguards—remnants of the American creed. . . .

> The shadow [of these problems appears] in the proposals
> now before Congress . . . for establishing "ethnic heritage

studies" in schools with federal funds. . . . The details
vary, but the essence of the matter has to do with setting
up separate ethnic-studies programs—like the black-studies
programs which inspired the whole idea—under the control of the separate ethnic communities to teach young
ethnics about their ethnic heritage. Sounds reasonable,
doesn't it, just like the black-studies programs? But the
same questions hold: just who will represent the "community"? *Who* will decide what is to go into each program? Which Hungarians, for example, will decide what
version of contemporary Hungarian history is to be
taught. . . . And what kind of pressure will this system
apply, in the public domain, on the child whose family
has other ideas about its own or any other ethnic background? We have already had enough experience in
"black studies" and "community control" to see what
innumerable cans of worms are opened up by *this* one. . . .

In its private domain any religio-ethnic group is free to
establish schools and publish literature and propagate any
version of its view of life that it wants its young to learn.
But not in the public domain. Obviously we do need to
correct, revise, and expand all that is taught about American history and American life . . . [but] this has to be
done under public auspices and public control, with an
obligation to respect scholarly standards, comparative criteria, and the presence of the endlessly differing versions
there are of all this material [pp. 75–78].

It is perhaps a good thing that new patterns of ethnic self-esteem
and mutual respect are being shaped to replace some of the old stereotypes.
But the danger is that the resurgence of group identity will lead to group conflict. While we may not have a melting pot, we do not need a balkanized
country, one where each ethnic group asserts its own demands and wages a
miniwar against the others. We should not expect the new ethnicity to promote peace: it never did in Europe and it never did in the cities and within
the labor movement of America. Just as black ethnicity has enhanced racism
and polarization, white ethnicity is most likely to do the same. In a world of
tribal identity, the Catholics, Jews, Italians, Irish, Poles, and Greeks are bound
to protect their own vital interests; and if this country is fragmented along
ethnic lines, those who can expect to lose the most are those who are not
members of local and forceful groups—and perhaps blacks, if white groups
form coalitions in terms of race.

Trying to alleviate some of the above fears, Friedman (1972)
writes:

. . . a close reading of the work and a knowledge of the
activities of the New Pluralists indicates that we are asking
many of the same questions. . . . We are aware that the
idea of ethnic identity carried to an extreme can turn
into ethnocentrism and reduce communities to warring

turfs. . . . Without exception, I believe the New Pluralists are strongly opposed to substituting group rights for individual rights with the consequent lowering of standards and the destruction of the merit system. . . . Resurgent ethnicity is good because it has forced all Americans to redefine who and what they are. . . . It is also good because every person needs to have or recover or acquire a self-respecting acceptance of his own origins, but when some of us press for ethnic studies in the schools to help gain such pride it becomes a "me-too knee jerk response" to the black-studies phenomenon. Incidentally, why is it that when blacks quite legitimately sought, and still seek, racial pride and identity, their action is not questioned (though, of course, the techniques they use have been widely criticized), but when other religious and ethnic groups ask for the same treatment, they are suspect?

Understanding the deep interests of the groups involved in the struggle and working out the necessary compromises and accomodations to achieve both peace and progress have been the underlying methods by which we have made a multi-group society work. . . .

. . . the New Pluralism [offers a] more accurate picture . . . of the group [it presents] as well as the common nature of our society [and] an opportunity . . . to recreate the older coalition of ethnics and working-class whites with blacks and liberals. . . . We have helped to consign the white ethnics to the eager arms of reactionaries who are only too willing to play on their fears. In short, I believe that understanding and acting upon the New Pluralism offers liberals a chance to regain credibility with large segments of the American public who have turned away from us [pp. 8–10].

Indeed, Friedman defends his position well, that the new ethnicity will facilitate cooperation and social progress rather than destructive fragmentation. The trouble is, he is advocating an idealistic position, the same position originally argued by most blacks until their movement gained momentum and resulted in bitterness and frustration among white individuals and groups whose interests and rights were denied. It is wishful thinking, absurd logic, to assume that the liberal-black orthodoxy can unite white ethnics when the latter see the liberals and blacks as combining against them and as responsible for their increasing economic and social plight. It is doubtful if a broad coalition can be built among liberals, blacks, and ethnics when the latter are being driven toward a conservative stance. It is fine to advocate an ethnic identity and an ethnic studies program, like black identity and black studies, but most of us already recognize the danger inherent in "telling it like it really is," presenting super heroes, a minority interpretation, that these cultural needs become transformed into political demands and ideology and excessive nationalism.

I am not expecting all readers to agree with my analysis,[a] the way they respond will reflect, to a large degree, their own biases and ideologies. We all read and react to data through a filtering process based on judgments and opinions. I am asking the reader to recognize the needs of and seek to understand both the poor and the unpoor, both blacks and whites, not to concentrate on the needs of one group while overlooking another group, not to perpetuate reverse discrimination or any form of discrimination at the expense of another group. Indeed, it is difficult to convince middle America that the government should continue to favor the poor through compensatory and relief programs and the rich and the super-rich through tax privileges and loopholes, while they continue to carry the heaviest burden of the tax bill. It is difficult to tell the man caught in the middle that he is wrong to feel his own problems are being neglected in favor of poor or black America.

On the issue of race relations in America, the reader would be a fool to hope that "the good old days" could be preserved. They were never good for blacks or for the country; they never should have been tolerated, much less preserved. While we should support equal opportunity for all Americans, we cannot ignore the interests and concerns of the majority groups in America, much less continue to discriminate against them. Such a procedure, if continued, can only promote bitterness, frustration, and hostility—and possibly the demise of democracy. We are all in this society together, each with his own aspirations and interests to protect, and we commit an injustice when we try to solve the problems of one group at the expense of others.

To each generation, it usually seems that "it can't happen here." Well, I think it can, and if it does the revolution and the withering of our freedoms will not come from the poor or blacks or Third World groups; the political alteration will be a counterrevolution, not through violence but votes. And if we go by opinion polls and election returns, we are a conservative people, and have been becoming more so each year for the past ten years. The first note of conservative upsurge was sounded by Goldwater's backers in 1964, but was largely overlooked because of Johnson's landslide victory. The Nixon victory in 1968 showed the increasing conservative impulse, although there was a sizable middle constituency that was willing to accept change addressed to particular grievances, if it was realistic and attainable without social and economic upheaval and without violence. However, the Nixon landslide victory of 1972 reflected the growing disenchantment of middle Americans with black demands, black political organization, and black achievement at their expense. It is difficult to predict the future, but current trends indicate we may have a near right-wing government by the end of the decade.

The masses may be deceived and exploited, but political education has not brought them too much awareness on this score. While they may not realize how the system has deceived them, and how very little of the material rewards they obtain, they still cling to a stalwart Americanism—and part of this Americanism is the right to make oneself heard at the polls. It is doubtful if their political muscle will be directed at the rich (the 1.5 percent of the nation that owns 32 percent of the privately owned wealth) or the super-rich (the 0.5 percent that owns 25 percent of the private wealth holdings);[6] their middle votes seem to be directed at black Americans, because the latter groups are challenging their economic position. On the other hand, American wealth is an outgrowth of working-class and middle-class values, where there is reward for education, hard work, savings, and enterprise. This orientation, coupled with the increasing rhetoric of race relations, is driving these so-called racists and cretins into the hands of "folk" heroes and politicians who prate a rightest philosophy.

Thus witness the concurrent fever of the New Populism, which may be analyzed as part of the ethnic trend to counteract the problems and fears of middle America. It is present in law-and-order themes of many newly elected mayors, in the upsurge of anti–school desegregation in the platforms of many congressmen, in the recent popularity of George Wallace and other "grass roots" politicians who appeal to the forgotten man, and, as previously mentioned, in the overwhelming 1972 victory of President Nixon, whose major support came from middle America.

In the late 1960s we saw two of the most liberal mayors in the country, Jerome P. Cavanagh of Detroit and Richard C. Lee of New Haven, become the victims of black-white polarization and choose not to run again.[7] Thomas G. Currigan, former progressive mayor of Denver, gave up in midterm, and former Mayor A. W. Sorensen of Omaha confessed he had "gone through three-and-a-half years in this racial business" and he had had it. And in Minneapolis, liberal Mayor Arthur Naftalin was defeated by Charles Stenvig, a policeman and law-and-order candidate. At that time in Boston, Louise Day Hicks, who stressed the average man on the streets and promised to hold the color line in the schools and city, was barely defeated for the mayoralty by Kevin White who has now refused to implement school integration even though it is statistically feasible with a school population which is 26 percent nonwhite and 74 percent white,[8] and would involve minimal busing compared with that required in larger cities such as New York, Chicago, and Los Angeles. In the same vein, Newark's Tony Imperiale, a construction worker and karate expert, and Minneapolis's Antonio Felicetta, a labor union official, both became instant "folk" heroes for their stand against blacks and welfare recipients. Imperiale was elected to the City Council, and Felicetta was appointed to the City Commission on Human Relations.

The New Popularism continued full steam in the 1970s. Frank Rizzo, the former police commissioner, was elected mayor of Philadelphia on the basis of his law-and-order platform and his promise to fire liberal School Superintendent Mark Shedd, which he did. Rizzo won by 58,000 votes and became Philadelphia's first Italian-American and second Catholic mayor. In Los Angeles, Sam Yorty was reelected mayor after waging a campaign with heavy racial overtones against the favorite black candidate. Granted, he lost the 1973 mayoral election with the same strategy, but his successful opponent,

Thomas Bradley, emphasized his police career. Furthermore, the same racial type of campaign was waged in San Francisco, more precisely against school busing, and led to the election of Joseph Alioto. And in Chicago, Richard J. Daley has been elected mayor four times, in the most recent election by the largest majority—74 percent—over liberal candidate Richard Friedman. Daley's people just below him continue to sell real estate and insurance in their fiefs and his committeemen continue to be involved in scandals and mis-appropriation of funds, yet Daley remains supreme, "King Richard" as he is often called in Chicago, the prototype New Populist. In the meantime, in New York City, the Athens of liberalism, John V. Lindsay appeared to be a loser if he dared run again for mayor and decided to bow out before the 1973 primaries. Abraham Beame won the mayoral election on a platform that expressed the sentiments of the middle American.

The reelection of Nixon must be weighed in terms of some hard facts. This is the same man who lost the presidency to John Kennedy in 1960 and the California governorship to Edmund Brown in 1962, and who almost lost the presidency in 1968. Yet the figures for 1972 were indeed im-pressive: he won a 17 million vote majority, 49 states, and 521 out of 538 electoral seats, while his party lost both houses of Congress. In a frenzy of ticket-splitting unprecedented on a national scale and involving more than 40 percent of the voters, the people turned their backs on Republican candi-dates for Congress and state houses and overwhelmingly cast their vote for Richard Nixon (who appeared to represent middle America and the mainte-nance of the social order) and registered their disdain for the policies of George McGovern (who appeared to represent liberals and blacks and the overthrow of the social order). Nixon polled 60.8 percent of the popular vote, second only to Johnson's 61.1 percent in 1964. It was the worst defeat in his-tory for a Democratic presidential candidate, beaten even in his own state.

The choice was as much an endorsement of Nixon's accomplish-ments as a condemnation of McGovern's policies of increased taxes and quotas at the expense of middle America (*New York Times*, November 9, December 14, 1972; *Saturday Review*, December 9, 1972). In traditionally Democratic strongholds, Nixon either ran neck and neck with his Democratic challenger or won. Never before in history had a Republican candidate come even close to sweeping the South, much less collecting all of its electoral strength. Analysis of the votes cast in sample districts in large cities across the country showed that the white ethnic groups who usually vote Democratic had switched to Republican. This was especially true in the Roman Catholic areas. Even the Jewish vote, noted for its liberalism, departed sharply from 4 to 1 for the Democratic nominee in 1968 as against 2 to 1 for the Demo-cratic nominee in 1972, an indication that some of the ethnic liberals also have become disenchanted with the social reform policies of the 1960s.

Nixon picked up votes in working- and middle-class areas which he did not in 1968 and reversed voting trends in key industrial and populated states such as New York, New Jersey, Pennsylvania, Michigan, Illinois, and Texas. Much of Nixon's majority appeared to come from the 9 million people who voted for Wallace in the 1968 presidential race and the 25 million people who voted for Wallace (more popular votes than were received by any of the three other candidates) in the 11 states in which he campaigned during the 1972 Democratic primaries. Nixon picked up virtually all of the Wallace vote, and much of it came from the working class. In fact, the figures showed that the blue-collar block went to Nixon 3 to 2, an unheard-of accomplishment for a Republican candidate *(Chicago Tribune,* November 8, 9, 1972; *New York Times,* November 8, 9, 12, 1972). In fact, the Democrats lost the Catholics, the labor unions, the ethnics, and the South—all Democratic strongholds—as well as the suburbs and big business, women and youth. When these facts are considered in the light of ticket-splitting, and we have an indication of the voting mood that prevailed throughout the country in 1972, the outcome represented a personal victory for Nixon as much as an expression of growing conservative sentiment.

Many of the people who voted for Nixon were the same people who were once part of the liberal-black coalition of the 1960s, who championed social reform and reform-minded presidents, who have been ignored by the left orthodoxy of the Democratic party, who reject the programs and pieties of the liberal-black establishment, and who are fearful of a worsening economic and social status as blacks continue to receive special attention and preferential treatment. Indeed, the major issues of the election—crime, busing, quotas, taxes, and domestic spending—may be considered antiliberal and antiblack. Even the minor issues, such as marijuana and amnesty, reflected a liberal-conservative controversy, helped elect Nixon, and provided a clear indication of the emerging Republican majority. Watergate might dampen Republican hopes in 1976, but the growing conservative element of the nation will probably remain with us.

It is important to add that 9 out of 10 voters are unpoor and 9 out of 10 are unblack. Altogether, 80 percent of the voters are neither poor nor black; they are middle Americans. The youth, young adults between the ages of 18 and 24 years, represent about 12 percent of the voting population. For most of them, the 1972 presidential election was their first time to go to the polls, and the majority of this group voted along conservative lines and supported Nixon. As for women, they do not vote in blocks. In 1960 as many as 54 percent voted for Nixon, and in 1972 about 60 percent voted for him. If anything, the majority of young adults and women are neither outspoken college radicals nor feminists, but are middle Americans and vote accordingly. In fact, most young adults do not go to college but are either members of the work force, unemployed, or are in the armed forces; and with all due regard to female activism, most women are not aspiring career women but are housewives or single women who are working temporarily while seeking a husband and a permanent career of marriage and raising children.

In the same vein, Scammon (1972) characterizes the American voter as working class and middle class. It would be wrong to call great sections of the American electorate the poor, in the sense of the statistical definition. They belong to other interest groups, mainly the elderly and ethnic groups. As for the youth vote, 25 million potential voters are under 25, but 50 million over 50—and their turn out rate is higher. Actually the median age of the voter in 1972 was about 45 years. Ninety percent of the voters are white, and the white ethnic voter makes up the majority of the population. As his values and way of life become threatened, "a good deal of new ethnic political vitality may be sensed" (p. 118). And in light of contemporary events, one might say that the ethnic value system is being threatened and thus we can sense the rise of ethnic politics and a new conservative mood in America.

Understanding the Liberal Intellectual

The overwhelming number of intellectuals are liberal and, as previously indicated, extremely sympathetic to the poor and the blacks, often viewing them as underdogs and oppressed groups while categorizing the unpoor and unblack as "bigots" and "cretins." This analysis, while it may be somewhat generalized, represents the intellectual desire to be fashionable and "chic," to romanticize poor and minority groups while villifying the majority group.

As Riesman (1966) points out, the liberals and intellectuals exhibit a general snobbery toward the working-class and lower middle-class world of construction workers, policemen, firemen, social workers, teachers, and other civil servants. In recent years, this snobbery has been expressed as a nasty and spiteful bigotry toward these hardworking, decent people and in their frequent romanticization of the violence and vitality of the poor and the black. Moynihan (1969) similarly contends that too frequently these liberals and intellectuals have expressed only contempt for the working and lower-middle classes, while exhibiting great compassion for the poor and the black. One reason is, these elite academics and writers came of age in the 1950s, during complacent times, and experienced minimum suffering and maximum security. Alter (1972) puts it in another but similar way: many of these liberal reformers have been assimilated into a culture of "swinging protest," where the idea is to root for the underdog, be antiestablishment, and vent their "disdain for the TV-trapped masses of lower-middle and working classes" (p. 69).

Hitchcock (1973) claims the intellectual perceives middle Americans as backward and pathological, a major obstacle to their plans for reform. While the poor and the black are accorded sympathetic attention and their demands are deemed to be just, the consensus of whites is perceived as unjust and racist. Intellectuals justify black advancement at the expense of middle Americans on the basis of their own partisan snobbery and dislike toward the masses.

In terms of ethnicity, Novak (1972) points out that intellectuals are unaware of their own biases in describing ethnics. They tend to feel morally superior to these people and do not realize how much they impose their own views of the world upon working and ethnic groups. Despite ideological differences, they believe solidly in the superiority of their culture—the world of progress, efficiency, and science. They tend to reject ethnic groups as "foreign," not "truly American," backward, and uncivil, and vent their contempt toward these groups. Because it is difficult today to be antiblack in public or in print, they continue to denounce white ethnics who do not fit the mold. Similarly, Baroni (1970, 1972) asserts that liberal intellectuals tend to blame middle Americans for almost all the ills of society, while overlooking their own prejudices and the gross injustices of those who manage America's political and economic life. More and more, liberals use "white racism" as a stick with which to beat down ethnics and working Americans, although the Harris and Gallup polls and the National Opinion Research Center surveys continuously reveal that "native" Americans have the most prejudicial attitudes toward other racial and religious groups. And, Hamilton (1972) points out, liberals exhibit all the preconceived biases and distortions about middle America that they blame the working and middle classes for having toward blacks. Survey after survey show that the liberal judgments about the racial attitudes of the majority populace are complex and do not clearly support their original thoughts about so-called racist middle America. Such selective perceptions and continuous misreading of the evidence give rise to the antagonism felt by middle Americans toward liberal intellectuals and worsens the communication gap between these groups. Failure to describe the total picture, to recognize the problems and conditions of working- and middle-class Americans, and to realize they too are concerned with equality and human decency is a form of intellectual spite and prejudice of which the liberal-intellectual community is frequently guilty.

Yet another reason for the disdain expressed by intellectuals toward middle America is advanced by Shils (1972). He points out that most of them feel a revulsion for their own societies and for the institutions and people that rule them. Intellectuals are indispensable to any society, and the more complex the latter, the more important the former. While they serve society, they also denounce and deride it because of their moralistic and utopian attitudes. From time to time, a national effort such as the war against Hitler unites them even with the masses and integrates them into society as a whole, but no such singular purpose has existed for the past 30 years. Thus an entire generation of intellectuals, most of whom are liberals, has felt free to stress the imperfections of society (and of the people who make up that society) while at the same time struggling to win prestige in the society they reject. Similarly, they must choose between either serving the technological-corporate structure with little regard for the means or ends it seeks or serving theories, ideologies, and (underdog) philosophies, thus giving them a reason for their existence.

Shils objects to ideological politics because of its obsession with totality, animosity, and separatism and its impractical destructive and devisive tendencies. Rather than ideological politics, he describes the need for "civil politics," politics carried on by ethical and sensible men willing to accept responsibility for the consequences of their sentiments and actions, by people who are willing to tone down the rhetoric and deal with facts, people who recognize that virtues and evils are often intertwined. The trouble is (according to this author), many intellectuals have few virtues but only sentiments to express. They switch from Communism to anti-Communism, from isolationism to internationalism and back to isolationism, from rejecting the poor to romanticizing them, from espousing equal opportunity to rejecting it in favor of equality of results. Indeed, they would be hard pressed to state exactly what theoretical thread underlies their apparent confusion.

The college professor often considers himself liberal, or an intellectual. He has much to learn about the lives and feelings of ordinary Americans. Perhaps one way to begin is to compare one of the Bill Smiths who works in a factory on a mundane assembly line with Professor Jones. Writes Levison (1972):

> . . . the professor would begin to understand how a factory worker feels if he had to type a single paragraph—not papers—from nine to five, every day of the week. Instead of setting the pace himself, the professor's typewriter carriage should begin to move at nine and continue at a steady rate until five. The professor's job would be at stake if his typing did not keep up the pace.
>
> For permission to go to the bathroom or to use the telephone, the professor would have to ask a supervisor. His salary, $16,000 for a full professor, would be cut by $9,000 and his vacations reduced to two weeks a year. He could also be ordered to work overtime at the discretion of the company, or lose his job. If unlucky, he might have to work the night shift. Finally, if he faced the grim conclusion that his job was a dead end, his situation would then approximate that of an unskilled young worker in a contemporary auto factory [p. 38].

There is something in the smoldering anger of the working class, and even of the middle class, that is perhaps incomprehensible to many professors. Even though this anger is not fully understood by most intellectuals, it can no longer be ignored or dismissed as the ingratitude of a group of "racists," "clods," or hopeless Archie Bunkers.

Some liberal intellectuals who have traditionally been on the side of blacks are beginning to lose their enthusiasm for the black cause because the black power movement explicity denies the basic liberal ideological commitment to equality and univeralism, to the theory that ethnic and community differences should be eliminated or absorbed in order to create a harmonious and smooth social order. There is growing recognition—at least in private and it is beginning to surface in some of the popular liberal magazines such as *Commentary, Dissent, New Republic, New York Times Magazine, Public Interest,* and *Saturday Review*—that black militancy and demands violate many of the traditional liberal tenets: individual civil liberties, property and personal safety, the right to fair employment, the concepts of individual merit and equal opportunity, and the belief in integration. A small but growing number of liberals are grappling seriously with the recurring evidence of preferential treatment of blacks at the expense of whites. The facts that most of the liberals in this country are employed at various universities, that their own job security and promotions are affected by reverse discrimination, that academic freedom and the right to free inquiry on the topic of race have been curtailed, and that many of them have been pronounced "irrelevant" by a small number of black militant students have lessened their commitment to the black movement.

According to Fein (1970), over the years liberal commitment supported a number of myths or ideals that did not correspond with reality. They supported the idea of the melting pot, a utopian concept of universal brotherhood. They embraced the idea that white America should become color-blind and judge people as individuals and not on the basis of skin color: white people ought not to pay attention to color, and black people ought to disregard their own blackness. It is debatable if these approaches were viable; nevertheless, the black power–black nationalist movement connotes the rise of color consciousness, even to the point where black narcissism breeds black racism. This movement encourages the establishment of quotas favoring blacks in hiring on university campuses and throughout the job sector, thus subjugating the rights of the individual to those of a group. This policy represents a return to judging people on the basis of heredity and color, an idea liberals have long rejected. Black power and community control connote polarization rather than harmony, parochialization rather than secularization, segregation rather than integration, reverse discrimination rather than nondiscrimination—all of which profoundly contradict liberal concepts and philosophy.

Most liberals still identify with the black cause for moral reasons; but those who remain attached to it and so tacitly condone an increasing number of violations of the civil liberties, property, and personal safety of the majority population may best be described as masochistic or guilt-ridden, or both. As Berger and Neuhaus (1970) contend, the identification of white liberals with the black movement, which includes violence and antiwhite philosophy, connotes their own personal problems. Similarly, their abject submission to the demands of blacks, no matter how unjustified some may be, requires guilt, and if there is no guilt, it must be invented. Only the guilty are morally justified in enjoying punishment. Thus, according to this author, some white Americans—whose relations with blacks have been overwhelmingly sympathetic and perhaps self-destructive, both politically and sexually—

have confessed to the worst sins of "racism" and have dealt with their guilt
problems through injurious behavior. Similarly, they have condemned other
whites as hateful toward blacks and attributed *all* the problems of blacks to
white malice. According to Corbally (1972), these liberals are ready to accept
the blame for every shortcoming of which white society is accused, but then
they further decide that, for every shortcoming of which society is accused,
they must find within their professions someone other than themselves who is
really to blame. In this vein, they often accuse anyone who disagrees with
their analysis and "reform" policies of being antiblack.

People who get vicarious thrills from being whipped should persuade
their spouses or lovers to oblige them, but should not involve all of society in
their punishment. There is no such thing as collective or inherited guilt; it is
merely part of the victim strategy of blacks which feeds on the personal inse-
curities of whites. For those readers who accept a collective or inherited guilt
for white sins committed against blacks, Jonas's (1970) analysis is relevant.
Collective guilt means that every member of a group is automatically guilty
for the sins and crimes committed by an individual member. Thus every white
person is guilty of oppressing blacks. Inherited guilt means that the children
of the guilty (and the grandchildren and so on) are guilty of the crimes committed by their ancestors. But if collective guilt is valid, then all blacks are
guilty of the horrible deeds of those African chiefs who sold their own people
into slavery. Or, more recently, if I may add, they are all guilty of the violence
and terror tactics committed by a few black militants such as the De Mau Mau
group or Black Liberation Army, and they are all guilty of the ruthless killings
and "Hitler-like" policies (*New York Times* statement, December 10, 1972) of
General Idi Amin's Second Republic of Uganda who stripped 75,000 Asians
of their property and savings, sent them into exile, and mass murdered those
who remained. Similarly, with inherited guilt: Since many white-black unions
have produced offspring during our history, the majority of people classified
as blacks have some white ancestors or does their black ancestry neutralize
the guilt of their white ancestry? Do only white genes transmit guilt?

I was four years old when the atomic bomb was dropped on Hiro-
shima and cannot be held accountable for the decision to make or explode it.
Such thinking can be applied to our black-white history. I am not responsible
for slavery, and I cannot be held responsible for my white ancestors. In fact,
like millions of white ethnics, my grandparents were immigrants from Europe;
and like many other people who came to America at that time, they were es-
caping from hundreds of years of authoritarian rule, serfdom, pogroms, and
frequent imprisonment in Eastern and Southeastern European countries. The
parents and grandparents of many other readers came to America to escape
the famine, unemployment, and endless wars of other parts of Europe and
Asia. Our grandmothers and grandfathers did not own slaves, and for the
reader whose ancestors owned slaves, he is not responsible for his ancestors'
behavior when they were adults and he had not yet been born. We cannot
be held responsible for events over which we had no control, and we should
not be called upon to pay for the sins of others, or to share their guilt.

By the same token, I cannot take credit for the 1954 Supreme Court decision which outlawed *de jure* segregation; likewise, I am not guilty of massacring the residents of a Vietnamese village or of assassinating Reverend Martin Luther King. I did not testify before the Supreme Court, nor did I help plot the war strategy or Rev. King's murder. To hold white society or the nation responsible for some act performed on the other side of the world by some frightened soldier, or performed in Memphis by some fanatic who killed in the name of hatred, is nonsensical; it is equally as absurd to blame all blacks for Eldridge Cleaver's rapist acts, or for the skyjacking of an airplane to Algeria in the name of power to the Third World.

Guilt by association, collective or inherited, being held responsible for someone else's behavior—this chain of guilt has no end. It means that every reader is guilty of something he did not do; moreover, it means that his unborn children can be held guilty of any sin the "victim" wishes to manufacture. Those who have the problem of guilt, and the people who benefit from it, continue to maintain the rhetoric. Indeed, it is difficult for the majority of Americans to question this logic of guilt with someone who is possessed by it or receives new "rights" because of it without being held in suspicion, or worse, denounced as a "racist."

On still another level it is important to remember that racial arrogance and exploitation based on race have been practiced by all races—white, black, brown, yellow, and red. Colored races, whether Asiatic Mongols, brown-skinned Aztecs or Egyptians, or black Bantus have been great conquerors and have, on the whole, treated their subject races with greater cruelty than that shown by whites toward nonwhites. In India, prejudice has separated people into castes based solely on heredity and color, the lowest caste being the "untouchables." As the Germans regarded themselves set apart from other white people, the Japanese claimed racial superiority over other yellow people, in fact, over all other people regardless of their race. For thousands of years, ancient China maintained a wall to keep out foreign races who were considered inferior.

Blacks in this country fail to recognize that white America fought among themselves to free blacks from slavery, that it is presently discriminating against whites to make up for past discrimination. No nation, no civilization, has set in practice this type of internal "reparation policy." Perhaps we all fail to recognize that racism is a global phenomenon, practiced by all groups—white, black, brown, yellow, red. Any group that possesses political power tends to subordinate other groups, not necessarily because of race per se, but because of political and economic benefits. If the dominant-subordinate groups are divided along racial lines, then the dominant group sometimes exhibits racial power behavior. In this country, whites in the past have been the power group. If the dominant-subordinate groups were reversed, the direction of racial power behavior would be reversed, and examples of this reversal are evident in the rise of black power and community control, whereby the white person is at an extreme disadvantage and where his due process is often denied. It is indeed fascinating that most blacks deny that this new trend is a form of racist behavior; rather they usually claim it is only politics, because this is a more acceptable excuse.

According to Berger and Neuhaus (1970), no collective group—not the nation, state, or a movement of any kind—can automatically enmesh the individual just by virtue of his being assigned membership in it. This is a simple truth, but it seems that it must be repeated in these times. In the same vein, I refuse to be tainted by feelings of guilt by virtue of being assigned membership in an educational or political institution, in a white group, in society, or in the nation. Imaginary guilt does not lead to constructive human behavior for the individual burdened by it. Similarly, misleading and polemical rhetoric which pretends that the issues are simple and starkly clear, such as "you're either part of the solution or part of the problem" or "they want everything their way," "kill whitey" or "stop the niggers," at best offers simple-minded solutions to complicated problems and at worst leads to non-rational behavior.

Conclusion

The increasing conservative trend in America is, in part, a yearning for a by-gone era of hard work, stability, authority, and equal opportunity. This era is exemplified by the tranquility and culture of the postwar years up to the 1950s. But then came the upheavals of the civil rights movement in the early 1960s and the rise of black power in the late 1960s and into the 1970s. It seemed as if American society was falling apart: black demands, riots, crime in the streets, drugs, welfare, and of course the war in Southeast Asia which split America. The biggest threat to the system came from the ghettos, from the blacks who had been shut out of the system in the past and merely wanted a piece of the action, who wanted to enter the system but on their own terms. Threatened by violent upheavals, to save their own vested interests, the people who run the system and who make the political and economic decisions merely gave in to (and are still giving in to) the demands of blacks with the glee and support of most liberals and at the expense of middle America. Rather than risk continued rioting, local and national policy makers made a false peace which pitted blacks against the white working and middle classes, the "have nots" against the "have littles."

Those on the top of the system, who run big government and big business, may deplore the attitudes and behaviors of blacks and may express this disdain in private conversation; but these people wish to protect the system and maintain their own status and wealth; therefore, they grudgingly cooperate with and surrender to the demands of blacks and other minorities. The next groups from below—the white working class and the middle class— must pay for these concessions, because the people on the top refuse.

We can conceive of middle Americans as running a rat race of their own, one that promises little advantage to them and offers little hope of see-ing their children rise to the apex of the system. They may be hard-working people who keep the system running and who live by American standards and believe in the American dream, but as a group they reap few of its rewards. Of course, a few of them manage to make it to the top by politics, luck, and one-upmanship. With the exception of the house "nigger," the super athlete, and the entertainer, we can conceive of most blacks as being shut out of the system until the late 1960s; once a perpetual under-class and now rapidly breaking into the system and approaching the economic level of middle Americans, with the younger and educated blacks surpassing their white counterparts. In the meantime, those on the apex of the system hold on to their privileged status by keeping the black-white conflict at no higher than the middle of the pyramid, away from the top.

A few politicians are beginning to recognize the grievances of the middle American, that his resentment of recent black gains can be traced to his sense of desertion by a government that appears preoccupied with black needs and inattentive to his own. Liberals and blacks have overused the ploy of "racism" to denounce the white response to the black revolution; they have oversimplified the impulses of the American mood and strengthened the impression of the man caught in the middle that the liberals neither understand nor sympathize with him while blacks duplicate the past errors of white racism.

It is true that intergroup negotiation and bargaining are important ingredients in the democratic process, but these must be undertaken with due regard for the rights and interests of various individuals and groups. There can be no simplistic slogans and solutions to complex problems, no equally simplistic appeals to the American creed or to race or ethnicity. There can be no viable social order, only a fragmented country whose tensions are stretched to the breaking point, unless groups depolarize and learn to communicate and cooperate. We will continue to fight each other for the same slice of pie, to seek gains at each other's expense, unless we become concerned with more than just disadvantaged and advantaged populations, unless the government and education establishments alike stop favoring the poor and rich, unless we address ourselves also to the grievances of the working and middle classes. A realistic economic and political policy that is just and fair for all, one that reduces inequalities and promotes a realistic domestic policy without overlooking the needs and concerns of any one group, minority or majority, is essential.

Postscript

a. There are several avenues of viewing the rise of ethnic consciousness. On the plus side is the fact that traditional discussions and research in social science analyze race relations and related social issues (e.g., income, crime, population movements, and schooling) in black-white terms. This conceptual framework, besides being tiresome, unwittingly adds to the polarization process because of the comparisons and the constant analyses of differences between the two groups.

Viewing America in black, brown and white groups—a relatively new phenomenon which coincides with the rise of Puerto Rican, Chicano, and Cuban consciousness and liberal reform—does little to depolarize society. A depolarization process is needed that transcends the barrier of race and discusses ethnic interrelations. Just as there are many differences and groups among black and brown people, we are rapidly learning there are many differences and groups among whites. The prime difference for social action and reform may not be income, education, or religion, but ethnicity—further divided into foreign born vs. American born.

On still another level, it would be refreshing and informative to analyze inter-ethnic competition. For example, coalitional and religio-ethnic groups in urban politics are a reality, yet they are rarely discussed or researched. How do various ethnic groups view each other? There is some data that suggests that there is friction among various ethnics, rooted in the "old" country as well as for today's jobs in America. There is other research which suggests strong correlations with ethnicity and a number of attitudinal and behavioral measures, even when income and education are controlled. How do various ethnics move up the socio-economic ladder? Without trying to stereotype, the Irish tend to enter the police and fire departments, law, and the foreign service. The Italians rely on construction and police jobs. The Jews enter medicine, law, and teaching. The Germans, Chinese, and Japanese go into science and mathematics. The Poles are found in the steel and metal trades. How do we create new jobs for disposed white ethnics, resulting from black power in the cities and affirmative-action policies, and cope with the intricately related competition for economic benefits? Studies of hospital behavior reveal that ethnic groups respond differently to pain in the hospital; the Italians tend to exaggerate, and the Irish deny it. Certain ethnics tend to intermarry more often than others, an example being the Irish and Germans. Some ethnics still live in ghetto areas on a voluntary basis—the Jews, Chinese, and Italians being prime examples—and are likely to reject intermarriage. It would be fascinating to learn how various ethnics provide for and treat aging parents and relatives, how parents relate to the young and vice-versa (Johnny might then understand mom and dad a little better.) The myth of suburbia fosters on image of a homogeneous and classless society without the trace of ethnicity and wide income differences. A breakdown of white income along ethnicity could possibly reveal that the Poles, Serbs, Chicanos, Croats, Ukranians, and Latvians have lower incomes than blacks, thus creating a whole new civil rights movement and affirmative-action policy.

The research of the 1960s correlated the teaching of black pride and culture with increased student achievement. One might expect the same correlation with the teaching of white ethnic pride, yet there is little or no research which provides us with these answers. It would be beneficial to learn how various ethnics reason on a cognitive-affective continuum and on a concrete-abstract continuum, also to learn their creative differences as well as attitudinal differences toward intergroup relations. The interaction effects of class, sex, age, language, foreign vs. American and Northern vs. Southern born could be held constant for purposes of planning curriculum and instruction, as well as for purposes of multi-ethnic education and school integration.

Rather than viewing the growing ethnicity as a political and social problem, we might analyze it as a positive model for studying community consciousness, urban renewal, social structure, and how various groups provide personal identity and group cohesion for their members—cultural richness and diversity, primary relationships, friendships, faith, and common origin. These communal ties tend to counteract the "lonely crowd" trend and "anomie" in urban society and could make fascinating reading for students of sociology and psychology.

All this is good, but it is not going to alleviate conflict, rather it is going to help groups define themselves—first for cultural and affective pride, then for political and social action. Ethnic consciousness on the part of blacks caught America by surprise in the 1960s. Ironically, it is the civil rights movement which has generated the rise of white ethnicity. The rationale for ethnicity in the 1970s is largely based on the view that whites are getting the short end of the stick while blacks are being favored. Whites are beginning to feel powerless and neglected, even victimized, as blacks have felt in the past. And because they view blacks as the chief beneficiary of social reform, the target for the new ethnic consciousness may become the blacks.

In another context, completion for political and economic benefits have pitted blacks against Puerto Ricans in New York City and to a lesser degree blacks against Chicanos in Chicago and Los Angeles. What is to prevent the Irish, Italians, and other white ethnics to fight for the remaining political slots and jobs? Few East European ethnics presently possess the political and community organizational skills similar to the Irish, Italians, and Jews. When these European groups gain similar insights under the banner of ethnic identity, how will they react, in what direction, and against whom, will they mobilize? Will they mobilize collectively against blacks or will they fight among one another, and further balkanize the cities. The "defense" organizations among Italian, Jewish, and Puerto Rican groups represent the extremist belief that it is necessary for ethnics to mobilize collectively in competition for civil rights, community preservation, political favors, and economic benefits; to some extent but on a less effective level, these organizations parallel the black militant position which also advocates "defensive" tactics.

While it is important for city and suburban residents to recognize the necessity for coalitions and intergroup relations beyond black-white distinctions, we can expect the growing ethnicity to go beyond cultural definition and pride and to increase hostilities. This will probably occur because of the anxiety-bred politics, the social aggression, and economic completion that permeates within our society which need only a trifling catalyst, a few irrational slogans, and some negative exchanges to stimulate a dog-eat-dog rivalry common among groups situated at the bottom of the heap or who feel they are ignored and castigated by the Establishment. Ethnicity creates the opportunity for social action and collective protest, and perhaps through no other route can these groups open the channels in which they may be heard. But the danger lies in encouraging a policy that elevates the rights of the group, while ignoring the rights of the individual and what is good for the entire country. As black power and affirmative-action become more interrelated and reverberate group rights, we can expect white ethnics to organize around cultural pride and group identity, then to demand their group rights—further splintering the country into various factions and intergroup conflict.

Notes

1. These two groups are often described as having separate life-styles and income, yet their family incomes tend to overlap at a certain range. In 1971, this overlap was around the $8,000 and $15,000 income range. In 1973, this overlap was around $9,000 and $16,500. Since attitudes and behaviors are in part functions of income, it is safe to say that much of their culture blurs and becomes indistinguishable at this income range. Also see table 7.1.

2. So-called assimilated second or third generation ethnics maintain some of their original identity and culture, especially as they approach middle age, get married and have children, experience subtle job biases, social interactions, and political coalitions and hear "harmless" ethnic jokes. Even the children of intermarried ethnics usually maintain allegiance to at least one group, and are aware of their dual identity.

3. The latest Gallup poll at the time of this writing reveals that only 9 percent of blacks and 4 percent of whites favor school busing. (*New York Times,* September 9, 1973).

4. The *New York Times* (May 6, 1973) reports that the Office of Education has estimated the average cost of a year at a private school, including tuition, room, and board but nothing else, will be $3,281 for the 1973–74 school year. The Ivy League schools cost about $1,000 more. Costs at public colleges average $1,492. No relief is in sight, and costs are expected to rise. Some university officials fear that college will be only for the rich who can afford to pay and for the poor who can qualify for scholarships.

5. The use of quotas was evident at the 1972 Democratic Convention and included blacks, women, and youth and at least nine members from the Gay Liberation Movement from the New York State delegation. No quotas were assigned for the ethnics, Catholics, middle-aged, aged, working class, even farmers from the mid-West, and these groups and interests were underrepresented. Also, it is questionable whether Jesse Jackson and the other militants really represented the black community; whether Shirley MacLaine, Gloria Steinem, and Bella Abzug really represented the women of the country, the millions of secretaries and housewives from middle America; or whether McGovern's "whiz kids" and Yale lawyers really represented the youth of America. This is one explanation for McGovern's overwhelming loss on November 7, 1972.

6. See chapter 7.

7. See chapter 2.

8. However, more than 80 percent of the nonwhite students are enrolled in segregated schools. In 1971, the Boston schools were charged by HEW with being in violation of the 1964 Civil Rights Act, the first such charge leveled against a major city in the North.

References

Alter, Robert
1972 "A Fever of Ethnicity." *Commentary*, June, pp. 68–73.
Baroni, Geno
1970 "I'm a Pig Too." *Washingtonian*, July, pp. 4–6.
1972 "Ethnicity and Public Policy." In *Pieces of a Dream*, ed. M. Wenk, S. M. Tomasi, and G. Baroni, pp. 1–12. New York: Center for Migration Studies.
Berger, Peter L., and Richard J. Neuhaus
1970 *On Revolution–Rhetorical and Real*. New York: Doubleday.
Brown, Judith L., and Otto Feinstein
1972 "Community Development and the Urban Ethnic Dimension." In *Pieces of a Dream*, ed. M. Wenk, S. M. Tomasi, and G. Baroni, pp. 31–52. New York: Center for Migration Studies.
Buckley, Tom
1973 "Running for the Unrunnable." *New York Times Magazine*, July 3, pp. 12, 60 ff.
Chicago Tribune
November 8, 1972.
November 9, 1972.
Corbally, John E., Jr.
1972 News article in the *Chicago Tribune*, November 8, p. 22.
Fein, Leonard J.
1970 "The Limits of Liberalism." *Saturday Review*, June 20, pp. 83–85, ff.
Friedman, Murray
1972 "Letter to the Editor." *Commentary*, June, pp. 8, 10. Reprinted from *Commentary*, by permission; Copyright © 1972 by the American Jewish Committee.
Galbraith, John K.
1958 *The Affluent Society*. Boston: Houghton Mifflin.
Gans, Herbert
1968 *People and Plans*. New York: Basic Books.
1972 "The New Egalitarianism." *Saturday Review*, May 6, pp. 43–46.
Gordon, Milton M.
1964 *Assimilation in American Life*. New York: Oxford University Press.
Greeley, Andrew M.
1972 "The New Ethnicity and Blue Collars." In *The World of the Blue Collar Worker*, ed. I. Howe, pp. 285–96. New York: Quadrangle.
Hamilton, Richard F.
1972 "Liberal Intelligentsia and White Backlash." In *The World of the Blue Collar Worker*, ed. I. Howe, pp. 227–38. New York: Quadrangle.
Hitchcock, James
1973 "The Intellectual and the People." *Commentary*, March, pp. 64–69. Reprinted from *Commentary*, by permission; Copyright © 1972 by the American Jewish Committee.
Hoffer, Eric
1972 Quote in A. Ribicoff, "The Alienation of the American Worker." *Saturday Review*, April 22, pp. 29–30.
Isaacs, Harold R.
1972 "The New Pluralists." *Commentary*, March pp. 75–79. Reprinted from *Commentary*, by permission; Copyright © 1972 by the American Jewish Committee.
Jonas, Gilbert
1970 News article in the *New York Times*, December 16, p. 17.

Levison, Andrew
 1972 "The Rebellion of the Blue Collar Youth." *Progressive,* October,
  pp. 38–42.
Lipset, Seymour M., and Earl Rabb
 1973 "The Election and the National Mood." *Commentary*, January, pp.
  43–50.
Mikulski, Barbara
 1972 "The Ethnic Neighborhood: Leave Room for a Boccie Ball." In
  Pieces of a Dream, ed. M. Wenk, S. M. Tomasi, and G. Baroni, pp.
  53–62. New York: Center for Migration Studies.
Moynihan, Daniel P.
 1969 *Maximum Feasible Misunderstanding.* New York: Free Press.
Newsweek
 1969 "The Troubled American." October 6, pp. 29–68.
New York Times
  November 8, 1972.
  November 9, 1972.
  November 12, 1972.
  December 10, 1972.
  December 14, 1972.
  May 6, 1973.
  September 9, 1973.
Novak, Michael
 1972 *The Rise of the Unmeltable Ethnics.* New York: Macmillan.
Ribicoff, Abraham
 1972 "The Alienation of the American Worker." *Saturday Review*,
  April 22, pp. 29–33. Adapted from A. Ribicoff, *America Can Make
  It*. New York: Atheneum.
Riesman, David
 1966 "Introduction." In R. Denney, *The Astonished Muse*. 2d ed. New
  York: Grosset.
Saturday Review **(The Editor)**
 1972 December 9, p. 26.
Scammon, Richard M.
 1972 "Ethnic Circumstance: America at the Polls." In *Pieces of a Dream*,
  ed. M. Wenk, S. M. Tomasi, and G. Baroni, pp. 113–20. New York:
  Center for Migration Studies.
Schrag, Peter
 1969 "The Forgotten American." *Harper's Magazine*, August, pp. 27–34.
Sennett, Richard, and Johnathan Cobb
 1972 *The Hidden Injuries of Class.* New York: Knopf.
Shils, Edward
 1972 *The Intellectuals and the Powers and Other Essays*. Chicago: Uni-
  versity of Chicago Press.
Steinhart, John S.
 1972 "Social Relations of Science." In *Scientific Institutions of the
  Future*, pp. 7–27. Washington, D.C.: Acropolis.
Toth, Csanad
 1972 "The Media and the Ethnics." In *Pieces of a Dream*, ed. M. Wenk,
  S. M. Tomasi, and G. Baroni, pp. 13–30. New York: Center for
  Migration Studies.
Quie, Albert H.
 1973 News article in *Phi Delta Kappan* 54:713.

chapter 7

The Rich

This chapter describes the rich, that stratum of society where life is comfortable and there is little concern about the black-white conflict. Among these privileged few, economic inequality in America is discussed as one reason blacks and whites are now fighting over a limited slice of the pie. Tax reform—without soaking the rich—is suggested as a way of raising the money needed to reduce inequality and, in turn, to help depolarize the country.

It's Fun to Be Rich

According to 1971 U. S. Department of Commerce figures, more than 90 percent of individual and 74 percent of family income is less than $15,000. Table 7.1 summarizes family income. The first column gives income class intervals; the second column gives the percentage of families in each income class; the third column gives the percentage of the total of all income that goes to the people in the given income class. Column four is based on computing the data in column two and shows what percentage of the total number of families belongs to each income class and below.

According to Samuelson (1973), the middle or median family income in 1971 was $10,285. The mean family income was $11,583, indicating that the income distribution is skewed above the mean. Single persons, of course, have lower mean incomes, $4,774. Combining both groups, the weighted income is $9,987.

In 1971, most families had incomes around $9,500. As many as 56 percent of the families had incomes between $5,000 and $15,000—what we would consider to be the bulk of middle America. For these people, fortunate enough to live in the working- and middle-income strata of America, there is just enough money, after taxes, insurance, and one or two installment payments, to pay for room, food, and clothing—nothing expensive, $150 for rent or monthly payment on a $20,000 mortgage, hamburgers, fish, and chicken on a routine basis, and a new suit every three or four years.

Table 7.1

DISTRIBUTION OF FAMILY INCOMES IN THE UNITED STATES, 1971

(1)	(2)	(3)	(4)
		Percentage of Total Income Received by Families in this Class	Percentage of Families in this Class and Lower Ones
	Percentage of all Families in this Class		
Income Class			
Under $ 2,500	6	1 (−)	6
$ 2,500 – 4,999	12	4	18
5,000 – 7,499	14	8	32
7,500 – 9,999	15	11	47
10,000 – 12,499	15	16	62
12,500 – 14,999	12	14	74
15,000 – 24,999	20	30	94
25,000 and up	6	16	100
Total	100	100	

The wage earner making between $5,000 and $15,000 per year saw his real income decline 4 percent between 1965 and 1970. Within this five-year period, monthly payments for the average new home went up 80 percent, hospital costs tripled, and college tuition at state universities increased 64 percent. These people were not poor enough to qualify for federal assistance and not fortunate enough to keep up with rising costs.

Between 1971 and mid-1973, the financial squeeze for the wage earner was even worse. Wage increases were enforced at a 5.5 percent annual increase. The price index rose 22 percent on all commodities and 95 percent on farm products—the most important commodity (*New York Times*, September 9, 1973). Inflation was out of control in 1973 and set records that dated back to 1943. Prices rose for the first quarter at the annual rate of 8.8 percent and 9.2 percent for the second quarter (*New York Times*, May 27, 1973). In the month of August alone, the consumer price index rose an extraordinary 1.9 percent; finished consumer goods rose at an annual rate of 16 percent in 3 months and food prices soared at an unbelievable rate of 43 percent (*New York Times*, August 26, September 23, 1973). The *Wall Street Journal* (August 29, 1973) pointed out that unless the individual's salary had risen more than 35 percent since 1966, his after-tax purchasing power had fallen. For example, a worker who had earned $10,000 in 1966 and earned 35 percent more in 1973—$1,350—actually lost a few hundred dollars after inflation and taxes. The actual loss was even greater because the tax calculations only included federal, state, and payroll taxes. John T. Dunlop (1973), director of the Cost of Living Council and in charge of administering wage and price controls under the Nixon administration, summed up the years between 1971 and 1973: "Wage increases have slowed markedly during the program while prices have soared" (p. 7). More frightening is the fact that the chief wage earner in this $15,000 or less income category tends to reach a permanent income plateau by his mid-thirties. As inflation and taxes increase his life becomes more of a downward treadmill.

The rich is the only group that has managed to keep up their incomes with growing inflation as a result of investments and tax loopholes. As a group, the rich have little conception of what it is like to be poor or even average in an era of extraordinary wealth. For the greater part, the rich are unconcerned with, or at least at the present unthreatened by, the conflict between the blacks and white middle Americans, between the "have nots" and the "have littles." Yet the rich, because they own an extraordinary share of the economic pie, are a major cause for this black-white conflict. Most of these people exploit the wealth of the country and live as if it were their private playground. These people, F. Scott Fitzgerald tried to convince Ernest Hemingway, "Are very much different from you and me. . . . Unless you were born rich, it is difficult to understand." Even if they loose their wealth and sink to our level or below us, "they still think they are better than we are."

The rich may be divided into three groups: (1) new rich, (2) safe rich, and (3) super-rich. The last two groups represent what I call the nation's aristocracy. Elaborating on each group, the new rich may be defined as those individuals who earned in 1968 at least $25,000 a year, equivalent to about $30,000 in 1973 dollars. They represent about 2 percent of the U. S. adult population. A nationwide survey conducted by Simmons & Associates and an in-depth interview of 53 people earning between $25,000 and $75,000 by Yankelovich, Inc., was condensed into a report by Main (1968) for *Fortune* magazine. Between the survey and interviews, an abundance of data about this group of rich was provided. As a group, these 2 percent made $56 billion annually, more than was earned by 30 percent of the entire population. With their buying power, they are three times more likely to own a color television or a hi-fi set than the person who earns $15,000 a year, five times more likely to drink scotch, seven times more likely to drink four or five glasses of imported wine in a week, and fifteen times more likely to buy a new car costing over $4,000. (This type of car in 1973 costs about $5,000.)

Many of these people use their money for purposes of ego gratification, for feeling important, and for conspicuous consumption. They are able to buy what they want when they want it as is illustrated by the interview which included such statements as: "I buy what I want when I need it . . . and when we want something we get it." "If something appeals to me, I buy it. I don't haggle." "I enjoy what I buy." "I am an acquirer of things." "I love new things." "I buy . . . for ownership" (p. 186).

Travel is one of their favorite diversions. As one businessman said, "When I travel, I travel deluxe" (p. 186). Most take two to four brief vacations a year, or at least one extended vacation. One west coast women expressed how life had become one big travel and shopping itinerary:

Two years ago we went to Europe and zipped about for five weeks. Last year we were in Europe for eight weeks.

We went to Istanbul and came back on a ship through
the Greek Islands. And I bought a fur coat in Germany.
And a topaz pin in London. We mostly buy jewelry and
paintings. And my husband has started collecting rare
books. I adore new things. I'm mad about them. I've always
felt this way. . . . If it's beautiful and within our means we'd
buy it. . . . I consider traveling first-class on ocean liners and
staying at the best hotels in Europe a luxury of which I
never tire. . . . When we are in New York, which we often
are, we hire a chauffeured limousine. . . . The things I look
forward to are trying to stay conscious and feeling alive. . . .
So few people are conscious. It's hard [p. 189].

Indeed, it is difficult to sympathize with this woman. She talks about the
problems of consciousness and living life to the fullest, almost as if she was
in a philosophy course, while most Americans—the poor and members of the
working and middle classes, not to mention the rest of mankind—are trying
to make ends meet on a daily basis.

While the woman interviewed uses her money to zip around the
world, most of the people in her income bracket seek to increase their wealth
with little regard for others. When asked what they would do with a $2,500
increase in income, the majority responded they would invest it; only one
person mentioned giving it to charity. Similarly, most of these people spoke
about making more money. Characteristic of their responses were such statements as: "I've reached the point where each dollar brings the desire for
more." "I have always felt the same way. It is very important to make a lot
of money. . . . It is a challenge." "I work hard and I want that big money. It
is important to me today as it ever was." "I'm making money for the sake of
making money" (p. 186). One might conclude from their statements about
spending and making money, from their desire to acquire things and enjoy
life, that they invariably must exploit others. To obtain more wealth and to
display this wealth, they often economically rape the majority of Americans.
Most of these people comprise the new rich, who are still in the stage of
showing others how important and rich they are.

A little less than 1 percent of the population enjoy annual incomes
of $100,000 or more; these are the safe rich. Most executives of the large
corporations earn more than $100,000, the president does; and while govern-
ors, congressmen, cabinet officials, and ambassadors earn half of that amount,
more than 50 percent of these people are worth more than $1 million. It goes
without saying that money is an avenue to political power, and traveled not
by Roosevelts, Kennedys, and Rockefellers alone. Most of our political
leaders, especially on the state and federal level, have had an inherited advantage of wealth. To a large extent, it is their money that led them into politics,
and through political legislation and associations they either maintain or increase their wealth.

In a survey of the top executives of the 500 largest corporations in
the country conducted by Yankelovich, Inc., and written by Diamond (1970)

for *Fortune* magazine, over 80 percent reported annual incomes between
$100,000 and $400,000, with another 10 percent enjoying still higher annual
incomes. Almost all of them owned their own homes, and 60 percent had
vacation or "get away" homes. As many as 48 percent collected original
works of art. Their most popular form of relaxation was golf (56 percent),
followed by fishing, boating, hunting, tennis, swimming, owning and racing
horses and sport cars, and flying private planes. Few preferred the "common"
relaxation of television or even the movies or plays. Pleasure trips were frequent, and more than 80 percent had made at least one vacation trip to a
foreign country.

    As for friendships, these people showed a distinct desire to segregate
themselves from others. Three out of five preferred to associate with other
executives, and only 12 percent associated with doctors, lawyers, and other
professionals on a regular basis. Their backgrounds reflected not only seclu-
sion but also the inequality inherent in the American system. Only 16 percent
are the sons of working-class or farm families, despite the fact they were born
at a time when these two categories of work accounted for more than 90 percent of the jobs. Most of them inherited money or received their start in
business from dad; in fact, 45 percent of the fathers stood at the top of the
business hierarchy either as founder, president of the corporation, chairman
of the board of directors, or owner. Ninety-four percent attended college
and 44 percent held graduate degrees, even though few of their age counterparts had gone to college at that time. More than 40 percent attended private
colleges, and another 35 percent went to Ivy League colleges. Over 80 percent were Protestant, and less than 10 percent each were Catholic or Jewish.
When it came to the top jobs in banking and insurance, 93 percent were of
Protestant faith. Episcopalians and Presbyterians dominated the top ranks
of business, although these two denominations together comprise less than
seven million people nationwide.

    When one thinks of the super-rich, one usually thinks about the
Mellons, Rockefellers, and Fords. But most members of this group are relatively obscure people. Parker (1972) tried to describe their wealth.

> In 1968, slightly more than 1,000 families reported an
> annual income of $1 million or more, and another 3,000
> reported earning between $500,000 and $1 million. The
> fact is that these people earned a good deal more. Even
> so, these 4,000 families together claimed a total income
> of nearly $4 billion dollars.

> Income of that magnitude is difficult to conceive, even
> in an age of multi-billion-dollar government and a tril-
> lion-dollar economy. In 1968, $4 billion was more than
> government expenditures for feeding the poor. . . . In
> that year $4 billion was more than what the federal
> government spent on education, and four times more
> than the federal government spent on all natural re-
> sources [pp. 130–31].

It is indeed hard to imagine 4,000 people sharing $4 billion dollars while
there is such a high level of poverty and hunger in the country and while
most Americans barely make ends meet. Lundberg (1968) also found it
difficult to make such large sums of money comprehensible:

> If a prudent hardworking, God-fearing, home-loving 100
> percent American saved $100,000 a year after taxes and
> expenses it would take him a full century to accumulate
> [10 million]. A self-incorporated film star who earned
> $1 million a year and paid a ten percent agent's fee, a
> rounded 50 percent corporation tax on the net and then
> withdrew $100,000 for his own use on which he also paid
> about 50 percent tax would need to be a box-office star
> for thirty-four unbroken years before he could save
> $10 million [pp. 35–36].

These people can be further divided into a select group of centimil-
lionaries. In 1968, 153 individuals were identified as belonging to this group.
Louis (1968) noted that most of them are unknown to the general public;
they show restraint and don't display their money or participate in conspicuous
consumption as do the new rich. Some of them try to avoid people, because
they are constantly approached to put up money for new business adventures
and to give to charities. (Actually, many of the centimillionaires donate sizable amounts to foundations and other charitable agencies, but for tax purposes.) Only a small portion of this select group are self-made men, illustrating
once more that there is a stable moneyed aristocracy which is capable of
surviving from one generation to another, while admitting few newcomers.

As a group the safe rich and super-rich, the families with annual
incomes of $100,000 or more as of 1968, belong to the American *aristocracy*,
a group that survives from generation to generation passing on its wealth to
its descendants. Most of these people and their descendants can be found in
the *Social Register*, which was first published in 1888 and is one of the best
guides to the membership of this national aristocracy. According to Domhoff
(1967), this is the group whose core of social institutions include private
schools, elite universities, the right fraternities and sororities, the right clubs,
exclusive summer resorts, charity balls, and restricted activities such as fox
hunts, polo matches, and yachting. Their economic institutions consist
mainly of corporation stock and corporation boards, the nature and control
of the economy. They dominate not only the large corporations but also the
major banks and insurance companies of the country, and own between 70
and 80 percent of all publicly owned stock. Intermarriage plays an important role in guarding and expanding their wealth and in restricting the boundaries of this inner group. They meet through their social secretaries, the
private schools, social clubs, charity balls, and summer resorts. Membership
in a gentlemen's club remains the essential proof that one is a gentleman or,
more accurately, a member of the nation's aristocracy. Many of these clubs

are anti-Jewish, anti-Catholic, and in some instances, even anti-ethnic: the old guard still remains reluctant to admit just "anybody" into the inner sanctum. For many, these clubs are essential gateways into the upper class. It usually takes money, clout, and the right education and religion to be admitted; they provide an informal atmosphere for relaxation, business, and the peaceful settling of economic and political differences. Indeed, these people are different from you and me: they are equipped with money, power, and prestige. They run the country. Many of them really do not care too much for the rest of us; many of them are unconcerned about the inequities of the system and the conflict over the rest of the economic pie.

Perhaps one way to understand the rich is to compare them with the unrich. According to the 1970 census estimate of "Income in 1969 of Families and Persons," the top 1 percent of the American population receives more money in one year than is received by all the people defined as poor; in fact, this 1 percent receives in one year more money than the poorest 50 million Americans. Even worse, this figure does not include the hidden income of the rich obtained through tax loopholes and business expense accounts such as meals, trips, entertainment, automobiles, and cash; it only includes their reported income. Just how well off the wealthy really are is illustrated by Lampman's (1960) study of the wealth holdings between 1922 and 1956. He pointed out that in 1953 the average estate of the richest 1.6 percent of the adult population was over $186,000, while the average estate of the remaining 98.4 percent was $7,900. He wrote:

> This group of 1.6 percent owned 32 percent of all privately owned wealth, consisting of 82.2 percent of the stock, 100 percent of the state and local (tax-exempt) bonds, 38.2 percent of federal bonds, 88.5 percent of other bonds, 29.1 percent of the cash, 36.2 percent of mortgages and notes, 13.3 percent of life insurance reserves, . . . 16.1 percent of real estate and 22.1 percent of debts and mortgages [pp. 192–93].

He also noted that the wealth is continually stratified: in 1956 the top 1 percent of the adult population owned 26 percent of the nation's wealth-holding, but the top 0.5 percent accounted for 25 percent of the private wealth-holdings. In other words the top 0.5 percent of the population accounts for most of the wealth of the 1.6 percent Lampman mentions. Lampman further showed that the top wealth holders were gaining a higher concentration of wealth, as evidenced by the trends beginning with the early 1950s into the 1960s; this data was supported ten years later by both Lundberg's (1968) analysis of *The Rich and the Super-Rich* and by Gans's discussion (1972) on inequality in the United States. Both author's point out that the situation had not changed since 1956; in fact, the concentration of wealth seems to have become even more lopsided. To avoid repetition, and since Gans used the 1970 census for his analysis, we will focus on his data; the poorest fifth of the population receives 4 percent of the nation's annual income; the next poorest fifth receives 11 percent, the richest fifth gets approximately 45 percent, and the top 5 percent, more than 20 percent. Inequality of assets is even greater: 1 percent of the people control more than 33 percent of the nation's wealth. Although many Americans own stock (about 32 million Americans in 1973, according to Bache stockbrokers), 2 percent of all individual stockholders own about two-thirds of the stock held by individuals. The same inequality exists in the business world. There are approximately 2 million corporations; one-tenth of 1 percent controls 55 percent of the total corporation assets; 1.1 percent controls 88 percent. At the other end of the continuum, 94 percent own only 9 percent of the total assets. Even the public economy is unequal. People who earn $2,000 or less pay half their incomes in indirect and direct taxes as compared with only 45 percent paid by people who earn $50,000 or more. Middle Americans are not much better off; those earning $8,000 to $10,000 a year paid 4 percent less of their incomes in taxes than those earning $25,000 to $50,000.

Using tax loopholes, inheritance trust fund loopholes, oil depletion allowances, crop supports, tax exemptions of municipal bond holders, and life insurance policies, this country has devised a reverse welfare program which provides the rich with the bulk of subsidies, the "have littles" or working and middle classes with a few hundred dollars, and the poor with a few dollars. While more and more people are coming to the realization that the rich do not pay their full share of taxes and that they have enormous political power, they do not appear resentful of this existing inequality. As Podhoretz (1973) points out, it is an intriguing feature of contemporary American society that so few people resent the rich and their concentration of money and power. Even radicals seem to spend more time criticizing the working and middle classes than criticizing the rich or corporate structure.

The extent of inequality is shameful and just surfacing to the consciousness of the American people. One of the earlier accounts of tax shelters, which perpetuate this inequality, was that by Stern (1964). He estimated that through tax privileges like those described above, a family that earns $1 million annually receives $720,000 in subsidies, the family earning $10,000 to 15,000 annually receives $650 in subsidies, and the family at the $3,000 level receives $16 in subsidies. Stern (1973) updated his analysis and maintained that the wonderful world of tax shelters had grown. A greater percentage of government officials, business executives, doctors, actors, and ball players were avoiding their share of taxes by investing in such tax dodges as real estate, oil, cattle, farming, and tax-exempt bonds. These people managed to eliminate the tax on their incomes altogether, or to reduce it to paltry amounts. Thus, the actual average tax rate for individuals with incomes between $100,000 and $1 million ranged between 29 and 33 percent, although it should have been between 45 and 70 percent. Moreover, many individuals with incomes over $100,000 paid no tax; many others paid less than 10 percent.

In this connection, Congressman Henry Reuss of Wisconsin has released 1970 statistics showing that the percentage of people who escaped federal taxes rose steadily as income increased. Only 0.12 percent of those earning between $15,000 and $20,000 paid no tax, but the percentage was almost four times as high (0.45 percent) in the $100,000 to $200,000 bracket, and nine times as high (1.07 percent) among those people reporting incomes between $500,000 and $1 million.[1] Senator Edmund S. Muskie revealed similar patterns among our corporations. The average tax for corporations was 35 percent: for the 50 largest, it was 25 percent, although it should have been 48 percent for all of them. Eight major corporations which earned a net of $651 million (after expenses) paid no federal income tax in either 1971 or 1972. Yet these eight companies paid a total of $418 million in dividends. At the same time, the federal government provided these eight corporations with $77 million in tax refunds and tax credits.

The outcome is, according to Stein (1973) and Tyler (1973), Uncle Sam loses about $50 to $60 billion a year through tax loopholes. The vast majority of Americans remain at the bottom of the heap, because the affluence of the nation is outside the reach of the people, concentrated among the top 1 to 2 percent of the populace. In fact, Tyler indicates that those in the top 2 percent income bracket have an annual income equal to that of all those in the bottom 40 percent,[2] and the top 10 percent of families report incomes equal to the bottom 60 percent.

How the system operates to maintain inequality is described in an angry analysis by Townsend (1972):

> America is run by and for about 5,000 people who are actively supported by 50,000 beavers eager to take their places. I arrive at this round figure this way: maybe 2,500 megacorporation executives, 500 politicians, lobbyists, and Congressional committee chairmen, 500 investment bankers, 500 commercial bankers, 500 partners in major accounting firms, 500 labor brokers. If you don't like my figures, make up your own. We won't be far apart in the context of a country with 210 million people. The 5,000 appoint their own successors, are responsible to nobody. They treat this nation as an exclusive whorehouse especially designed for their comfort and kicks. The President of these United States [no matter who he is], in their private view, is head towel boy [p. 24] [3].

So long as the wealth of this nation is locked up at the top, every decision to redistribute the remaining incomes becomes a battle among the "have nots" and "have littles," among the mass or lower 95 percent of the American people. In the past, Tyler (1973) points out that the U. S. avoided political upheaval because economic growth increased more rapidly than population growth. Without changing the distribution of the pie, the majority of Americans, which he refers to as the "Tribes," were able to obtain greater income and increase their standard of living. Now, however, several economists tell us that continued growth is highly inprobable, and it will probably taper off. Furthermore, there are a number of ecologists who claim that increased expansion must lead to the exhaustion of resources and minerals and the eventual economic decline of the world, including this country. With the expectations of the "have nots" and "have littles" increasing, some type of conflict, perhaps even upheaval, is probable unless the pie is redistributed and their share increased. The public may eventually become aware of the incredible discrepancies between the rich and unrich, between the aristocracy and the mass. Either the people will discover ways of getting the rich to pay their bill or they will rebel, not with guns but with votes.

Tax Reform is Needed

A genuine tax reform is needed, one that raises more revenue for the government without putting additional tax burdens on low- and middle-income groups. This would require corporations to pay at a higher rate more taxes than their maximum of 48 percent on profits, which they rarely pay in reality, and would eliminate tax shelters and deductions enjoyed by individuals who have substantial incomes from capital gains, inheritance, and depletion allowances from oil and other extractive industries, as well as from farm and real estate investments. Put in simple terms, Harrington (1972) claims, "We need to abolish every subsidy in the Internal Revenue Code" (p. 49). While this statement may be extreme, it describes the direction tax reform should take. Genuine tax reform must address itself to taxing all income on the same basis irrespective of the source of that income.

For example, on capital gains—or profit—of $50,000 or more made on the sale of stocks held for six months or longer, a corporation pays a flat 30 percent and an individual pays no more than 35 percent. (The highest percentage of tax an individual can pay is 70 percent; however, with capital gains the first 50 percent of profit is untaxed.) Capital gains made from the "arduous" work of buying and selling stock amount to $14 billion a year. The harried worker on the Chevy assembly line is taxed the maximum for every dollar, where the person selling GM stock pays tax on half his earnings if he waits for six months. In effect, the system deems the person sitting in his chair and calling his stockbroker to be more important and productive than the man who works on the assembly line.

According to Nader and Stanton (1972), in 1971 85 percent of capital gain loopholes benefited the wealthiest 5 percent of taxpayers. (Simply ask yourself—what is the distribution of wealth—that also will be a close distribution of capital gain.) On the other hand, the so-called progressive tax applies mainly to earned income, but special advantages are given to those who sell stock and other assets at a profit. The average wage earner with an annual income of $10,000 pays close to 30 percent in taxes to the federal government; in addition, he pays state and local taxes and social security tax, as well as other deductions toward union dues, health and life insurance, retirement, and the like, which other organizations invest, usually at a handsome profit.

In the case of tax-free municipal bonds, someone in the 50 percent income bracket who holds such bonds paying 5 percent actually achieves a 10 percent return on his investment. Moreover, taxes from the average citizen are used to pay the rich their dividends. True, the average wage earner usually has some savings in a bank. But interest derived from this source is not tax free, as with municipal bonds. A $10,000 wage earner watches his 5 percent bank interest dwindle to 3.3 percent after taxes, while the rich watch their 5 percent tax-free bonds soar to 10 to 14 percent after taxes. According to Brockman (1972), tax-free bonds are "a loophole enjoyed by the rich, for they have been buying these bonds at the expense of the average citizen" (p. 14). And Nader and Stanton (1972) point out that taxpayers whose annual adjusted gross incomes are $100,000 or more receive an average of $4,600 from this loophole, while middle-income groups or "have littles" in the $7,000 to $10,000 group receive an average of 39¢.

The wealthy, when they die, often leave their money in trust; in this way beneficiaries can enjoy the interest without touching the capital. Such a trust can be left not only to a son or daughter but also to a great-grandson or great-granddaughter not yet born. Under this system, called "generation skipping," tax is paid only once when the testator dies, and tax on growth in value of the estate as the years go on is avoided. Thus witness the wealth of the Kennedys and Rockefellers.

Considering depreciation allowances and the tax giveaways for property, particularly when a high leverage factor is involved, an individual can buy a building or part of a hotel for $500,00 by putting down $40,000 and borrowing the balance. All the interest paid on the loan and the operating expenses may be listed as tax deductions. The individual also may claim a depreciation allowance based on the purchase price of the building, even though the market value of the property may be rising. The result is, the individual who has invested only $40,000 has lowered his taxes on income from his own investment. A depreciation allowance over a ten-year period is common; this means that such an investor can have his gross income reduced $50,000 per year for ten years. If he earns $55,000 one year, he pays tax on $5,000. (This is a favorite scheme for the ever-popular slum landlord.) Writes Surrey (1972), as a result of this loophole "and others like it, persons with actual incomes in the hundreds of thousands, even millions, either pay no income tax or pay at a rate less than that of semiskilled construction workers" (p. 51).

Although the deduction of homeowners' property tax is called a middle-income tax preference, this is deceiving. The loophole is in effect a pittance for the man who has scraped and saved to buy a $25,000 home, but a princely gift for the person who can afford to buy a $150,000 home in Scarsdale or Winnetka. According to Nader and Stanton (1972), the taxpayer with an adjusted gross income of $100,000 or more obtains an average benefit of better than $1,700 per year from this deduction, while the taxpayer with an annual salary of $10,000 receives an average benefit of less than $21.

In effect, the tax deductions given for interest and property taxes confer the benefits to the owner of the more expensive home, the rich. In the same vein, deductions are given for property taxes and interest paid on mortgages, and the rental value of owner-occupied houses does not have to be declared as income; but no similar allowances are provided for renters, among the majority of low- and middle-income groups.

Wealthy farmers can write off $50,000 or whatever sum per year for five years; they show a profit on the fifth year but reinvest the profit immediately and start the deductions again. They are, in fact, increasing their assets through depreciation and claiming capital gains when they sell their cattle and grains. In particular, oil companies receive a generous tax shelter of 22 percent of their gross profit income as a depreciation allowance plus expenses for write-offs for drilling and exploratory work. In this way their real drilling costs are recovered many times over. Oil producers obtain a huge tax exemption on royalties paid to foreign countries. If, for example, they pay a 50 percent royalty on the value of the oil, the U. S. government allows them to deduct this figure, not from income, but from their taxes. Thus, someone in the 70 percent bracket can invest $100,000 in a drilling project without paying taxes on the money, knowing that even if no oil is struck, he stands to lose only $30,000—because had he kept the $100,000 he would be paying 70 percent to the government. Similar loopholes exist for other corporations. We know that the maximum tax rate on corporations, no matter how much profit they make, is 48 percent. Yet the real tax they pay, after depreciation allowances, cost-of-operations allowances, untaxed profits derived aboard, reduced taxes on income from exports, and write-offs for machinery averages about 30 to 35 percent, and for many corporations the effective rate is still lower. In this instance, and in the other examples described above, it is the "have littles" or middle Americans who make up the difference to Uncle Sam by paying their full share of taxes. (Thus the rich maintain most of their wealth while a greater proportion of the income of middle groups is paid in taxes and redistributed to the poor; there is reason, then, for middle America's desire to hold down federal spending to help the poor.)

Even the social security tax, which is supposed to help low- and middle-income groups, is becoming increasingly more unfair to the small wage earner and businessman; and the social security tax urgently needs reform that would be based on the individual's ability to pay. The maximum social security tax rose from $45 in 1950 to $174 in 1965 to $468 in 1972, then rose almost 40 percent to $632 in 1973 and to $772 in 1974—fully taxing everyone who earned as much as $13,200 per year in 1974. (Self-employed businessmen pay almost 50 percent more.) This means the person earning $50,000 per year pays the same social security tax as someone who earns $13,000, the former paying 1.4 percent of his annual income while the latter pays 5.9 percent of his earnings, with the small self-employed businessman who earns $13,000 paying as much as 9 percent. A family where both spouses work may pay as much as $1,544 in social security; in fact, if both spouses work and earn a total of $13,000, they wind up paying more federal tax and social security together than someone earning between $20,000 and $25,000. Granted, both spouses will collect a little more in benefits upon retirement, but this is not nearly equivalent to the extra income they had to pay into social security. Comparing the social security tax increase from 1950 to 1973, Dale (1973) writes, "The increase is far greater, proportionately, than any other tax. Even a state sales tax that was 1 cent in 1950 and is now 7 cents has not risen as much" (p. 8). He further points out that, for millions of wage earners, the "social security taxes are now larger than federal income taxes" (p. 40). Indeed, there is little resistance to this tax because taxpayers falsely feel that their payments are vested in their own names. As Miller (1972) contends, the social security tax, along with the sales taxes, entertainment taxes, and if I may add, the federal income tax,[4] are all regressive and bear "most heavily on the lowest 75 per cent of the population" (p. 66). Since 1950, "the taxes which have had the most spectacular increases are those which in their nature are regressive" (p. 68). As Brockman (1972) maintains, "There are many privileges and loopholes . . . enjoyed by the rich and not generally recognized" by the public. If the people were better informed about how the government gives away millions of dollars (the author feels it is billions) each year to the rich because of inequities in the tax system, they would demand reform and the financial position of most Americans would improve measurably" (p. 12).

In this connection, Harrington (1972) asserts that there should be no increased taxes on wages and salaries; rather, we should fully tax those who earn profits by speculating. He feels that the prediction about the Dow Jones plummeting is "self-righteous crap" promoted by Wall Street financiers. For example, only 5 percent of money used to meet corporation needs is derived from the stock market investors. The issue is simple: at present, the Internal Revenue Code operates to redistribute income from the unrich to the rich. Taxes need to be reversed, at least the burden "based on the ability to pay" (p. 49). Surrey (1972) points out that today's tax loopholes are not the product of evil governmental officials seeking to hide escape tunnels. The tax codes are written in the law for everyone to see; "they are the product of misguided attempts to use tax subsidies and incentives" to increase economic productivity and efficiency (p. 51). But the outcome is, the federal government ends up subsidizing the rich and helping them get still richer. Turning to the question of social reform, sweeping change in the tax system is needed to improve the quality of society, and to provide more opportunity for the majority of Americans. If government officials were honest with themselves, they would come to realize that tax preferences for the rich are neither morally fair nor needed; even worse, they put the tax burden on middle Americans. Unless these special tax privileges are repudiated, we can expect increasing dissatisfaction among Americans and growing polarization as the majority of people fight for a limited share of the economic pie.

What we need to do is to get rid of the capitalistic-gain preferences and special interest subsidies that favor large corporations (most of whose stock shares are owned by the wealthy) and wealthy individuals and make our tax laws simpler so that those who can afford private lawyers and accountants cannot take advantage of the loopholes. A genuine tax reform might include the following:

1. Tax *all* income on the same basis.
2. Eliminate the billions of dollars in revenues now lost through tax privileges which the low- and middle-income groups must make up by being overtaxed.
3. Reduce tax rates for the majority populace; increase them for the 2 percent in the highest income bracket.
4. Eliminate the privileges of the corporations without passing the effects on to the consumer.
5. Have public hearings on tax reform so lawyers and accountants who are paid by corporations or the rich cannot easily establish new loopholes behind closed doors.
6. Let the people know how they are being cheated; let them know which groups seek special privileges; let them vote for congressmen who will be committed to tax reform.

President Nixon's 1973 proposal for a "minimum taxable income" was an important step in the right direction. It required the taxpayer to pay at least 50 percent of his income by making it impossible to offset more than one half of the income from exclusions and item deductions. In effect, the proposal would reduce (not eliminate) many of the above tax shelters and limit the use of big deductions, such as interest charges and charity, as a means of offsetting most or all taxable income. No matter how many tax shelters and deductions a taxpayer could find in a given year, he would have to pay a minimum tax. He could not offset more than half of his income, and he would be required to pay tax on at least the balance. The *New York Times* (May 6, 1973) reported two actual examples provided by Treasury Secretary Shultz. In the first example, the "true" income of a couple is $350,000 per year; their tax is $71,000 now, and it would be $88,340 under the change. In the second example, the "true" income is $275,000; the tax is $45,358 now and would be $64,620 under the change. The aim of the plan was stated by Mr. Shultz, "to improve . . . the fairness in the tax system by reducing to zero if possible 'horror stories' about the wealthy whose tax returns show little or no tax" (p. 8).

On the other side of the coin, the elimination of these artificial tax losses could reduce investment in industry, especially in oil and gas which the nation needs. It might also reduce the motive to invest in a variety of construction, including low-income housing, which is also needed. Donations, upon which universities and other tax deductible agencies depend, would probably also be reduced. All these problems illustrate the clash of motives involved in our tax system: the desire to stimulate investment and donations to worthwhile agencies versus the need to make the tax system fairer to the majority of Americans. In the long run, however, we can expect Congress to water down almost any tax reform measure. But the next tax bill will probably address itself to those who earn large incomes and pay little or no tax. To what extent reform will be implemented will depend on the power of the wealthy versus the power of the public.

While some critics of domestic funding claim the programs were ineffective, and it was like funding a bottomless pit, another rationale for the turnabout in domestic funding was simply that the government could not afford the luxury of increased deficit spending. Whether viable social programs can be devised and implemented is a question the reformers must answer with honesty; however, the problem of deficit spending can easily be solved if the income of the rich is fully taxed and unneccessary deductions are eliminated. According to economist Joseph Peckman (1973) of the Brookings Institute and former Treasury Assistant Secretary Stanley Surrey (1972), it is possible to reduce taxes and deficit spending and still buy more public services by eliminating tax loopholes. Remember, the government loses $50 to $60 million a year in the game of tax exemptions to large corporations and wealthy individuals.

In the same vein, a closer working relationship between big government and big business is needed, one based on formulating a feasible social doctrine. It is becoming increasingly clear that the government does not seem big enough or smart enough to solve many of its domestic problems, such as providing adequate jobs, achieving quality education, rebuilding the cities, and providing quality air and water. Since the capacity of the private sector to invest is approximately six times greater than that of the federal government, a greater portion of the investment potential should be transferred from the average taxpayer and brought to bear on big business. What we need is a partnership between government and the private sector for the good of the country, not for the selfish interests of a few people. Private money will usually go in the direction of economic profit, and there are many instances—environmental control being a good example—where compliance is very expensive and jeopardizes profits, and only legally enforced governmental regulations will succeed.

While the federal government can choose to regulate and force big business to comply with national goals, a more suitable policy would be to recognize that the system of taxes is actually a system of incentives and to make a legitimate effort to align the tax incentives with the interest and goals of the nation. By this, this author does not mean to provide other tax loopholes, but rather to collect taxes which are fair and encourage business and individuals to act in accord with national interest and goals. In this connection, Miller (1972) points out that it is the job of government to define "the specifics of the national interest" and it is the role of business "to react in support of that interest" (p. 68).

Government in the future will have to be more sensitive to the needs of the majority and develop appropriate national planning. Business will have to be responsible to the public and manage every dollar with greater care and gear the spending of these dollars to national planning. Fusfeld (1972) declares that big government and big business have been coming together in a symbolic relationship. Big government needs big business because the large corporation has become the most important factor in the effective functioning of the economy. Big business, in turn, needs government because it provides the environment of economic growth in which corporations flourish and it provides the educational resources for managers and technicians that industry needs, maintains the framework for settling labor problems, and seeks international stability conductive for corporation growth. "Concentrated economic and political power are allies" (p. 38).

Tax reform, inflation, industrial growth, and international relations are serious problems that effect both government and business and that require cooperation between both systems. The roles of government and business are important and overlap in dealing with social issues such as ecology, race, militarism, and education. All these problems bring to surface the need for greater government-business cooperation and the need for humane economics. A humane economy requires change, the coming together of the government and private sector for the good of the country, and requires that the needs and concerns of the people be recognized. According to Fusfeld (1972), critics see the political and economic systems as essentially malign, antagonistic to the public. The problems of contemporary society indicate the path of the future. Government and big business "will have to move toward greater concern for human values toward a humane economy." Government and business that support the present disposition of power and wealth must be dispensed with for the good of the public. A humane economy is needed, one that enhances "compatability among man [with] his technology . . . and natural environment" (p. 39), and, if I may add, that also reduces racial tensions. Similarly Silk (1972) points out that political and economic institutions need to stress human welfare, and that the present arithmetic of economics does not provide adequate indicators of social conditions. We need a new economics that serves both as a measure of "well-being and as a guide to social policy" (p. 35).

Meyer (1972) puts it in these words: in the past "the slice of the pie was more important than how it was divided." The underlying assumptions in dealing with economic policy were to eliminate serious business recessions and increase economic growth at a respectable 3.5 percent per year, "and other economic and social problems would more or less solve themselves" (p. 5). Meyer points out the need for shifting the focus of economic research to include human capital, nonmarket activities such as the economics of families, and the impact of service industries such as health, education, and welfare. This means, for example, quantifying the study of crime and an analysis of the use of heroin or the demand for police protection, the relationship of poverty and health care, the relationship of education and economic return, or the relationship between quotas and productivity. According to Meyer, this translates into far greater use of sophisticated statistics, techniques that "provide greater opportunities for new insights into complex, multi-faceted problems" (p. 5).

Today's political and economic theories and systems seem incapable of dealing with many of the current issues: for example, how to make full employment compatible with reasonable price stability, how to deal with the demands and expectations of people, how to provide meaningful employment for people who wish to work, how to deal with the power of labor unions, the growth of large corporations, wage price standards, ecological and environmental balance, genuine tax reform, the various social problems that relate to education, medical care, race and racism, and urban growth,—or even what constitutes the well-being of all. What we need to do, according to Schultze (1972), is "to harness man's very human motivation to the public interest" (p. 57).

In general, there is confusion about the role of big business and big government, especially as it relates to the needs and concerns of the total populace. This role confusion seems very much in tune with the times. Generals and diplomats, senators and judges, university professors and teachers—all suffer from some confusion and uncertainty about their roles, not only in what they expect of themselves but in what society expects of them. Being out of date, being irrelevant, being confused is very much part of the times. What we need is a political and economic policy that is just and fair for all. It should consist of the right of each person to the most extensive liberties compatible with like liberties for others, a system based on merit and ability, where those who are favored by good fortune also work to improve the situation of the less fortunate.

Conclusion

Examining the most important and powerful economic and political institutions, there is sufficient evidence (Bainbridge 1961; Baltzell 1958; Dahl 1961; Domhoff 1967; Mills 1956; Parker 1972; Stern 1973) that the nation's rich own most of the wealth and run the country through the large corporations, interlocking interest groups, foundations, elite universities, political positions, and private associations. As an economic elite, they are mainly concerned with their own interests and sit back safely enjoying their money, status, and power while the "have nots" and "have littles" fight over the remaining dollars and a limited piece of the economic pie.

The problem is further compounded by the liberals who have alienated middle America so that the majority of the population has become more conservative, indirectly supporting the nation's aristocracy and embracing right wingism. Similarly, black Americans have threatened middle Americans to the extent that the political pendulum may swing back and strike them a harsh blow. What we need is a realistic political and economic framework that increases prosperity for as many Americans as possible, and forces members of the nation's aristocracy to pay less attention to gratifying their own needs and interests and to pay more attention to the remaining 98 percent of the country.

Notes

1. Even after these taxpayers take advantage of tax shelters, they often cheat on their tax returns. Treasury Secretary George P. Shultz reported that in 1971 as many as 106 taxpayers with incomes over $200,000 claimed they owed no tax. Of these taxpayers, 96 were audited and 41 had to cough up a total of $2.2 million.

2. It was reported earlier that the top 2 percent earned more than the bottom 30 percent. Now it is reported that the earning capacity of this 2 percent is equal to the bottom 40 percent. It is unclear as to what tax year each source is based on; however, the 1969 tax bill tightened tax reporting procedures. The economy has also expanded, and since the share of the pie is distributed in the same manner those who receive the largest percentage will also earn more money in absolute terms.

3. The bracketed statement, "no matter who he is," represents this author's view; Townsend was referring only to President Nixon.

4. Some tax experts claim the federal tax is mildly progressive. This may be true with earned income, and without considering the tax loopholes which favor the rich. In terms of the actual outcome of who pays how much tax, it is not even mildly progressive—rather mildly regressive.

References

Bainbridge, John
    1961 *The Super-Americans.* New York: Doubleday.
Baltzell, E. Digby
    1958 *An American Business Aristocracy.* New York: Free Press.
Brockman, David D.
    1972 Quote in S. Carr, "Tax Man Talks About Taxes." *Saturday Review,*
        October 14, p. 14.
Dahl, Robert A.
    1961 *Who Governs?* New Haven, Conn.: Yale University Press.
Dale, Edwin L., Jr.
    1973 "The Security of Social Security: The Young Pay for the Old."
        New York Times Magazine, January 14, pp. 8, 40–41 ff.
Diamond, Robert S.
    1970 "A Self-Portrait of the Chief Executive." *Fortune,* May, pp. 180–81,
        320–23.
Domhoff, G. William
    1967 *Who Runs America?* Englewood Cliffs, N.J.: Prentice-Hall.

Dunlop, John T.
1973 Quote in *New York Times*, August 12, sec. 3, p. 7.
Fusfeld, Daniel R.
1972 "Post-Post Keynes: The Scattered Synthesis." *Saturday Review*,
January 22, pp. 36–39.
Gans, Herbert
1972 "The New Egalitarianism." *Saturday Review*, May 6, pp. 43–46.
Harrington, Michael
1972 "Ideally, We Should Abolish Every Subsidy in the Internal Revenue
Code." *Saturday Review*, October 21, pp. 49–50.
Lampman, Robert
1960 *The Share of the Top Wealth-Holders in National Wealth, 1922–56.*
New York: National Bureau of Economic Research.
Louis, Arthur M.
1968 "America's Centimillionaires." *Fortune*, May, pp. 152–55 ff.
Lundberg, Ferdinand
1968 *The Rich and the Super-Rich.* New York: Lyle Stuart.
Main, Jerry
1968 "Good Living Begins at $25,000 a Year." *Fortune*, May, pp. 158–
61 ff.
Meyer, John R.
1972 News article in the *New York Times*, December 24, sec. 3, p. 5.
Miller, J. Irwin
1972 "What Business Can Expect in an Era of Change." *U. S. News &
World Report*, November 13, pp. 65–66, 68.
Mills, C. Wright
1956 *The Power Elite.* New York: Oxford University.
Nader, Ralph, and Tom Stanton
1972 "Our Tax Laws Favor the Rich and Complexity Makes it Worse."
Saturday Review, October 21, pp. 46–47.
New York Times
May 6, 1973.
May 27, 1973.
August 26, 1973.
September 9, 1973.
September 23, 1973.
Parker, Richard
1972 *The Myth of the Middle Class.* New York: Liveright.
Peckman, Joseph
1973 Quote in G. Tyler, "Debate: Nixon, the Great Society, and the
Future of Social Policy." *Commentary*, May, p. 57.
Podhoretz, Norman
1973 "The Intellectuals and the Pursuit of Happiness." *Commentary*,
February, pp. 7–8.
Samuelson, Paul A.
1973 *Economics* (9th ed.). New York: McGraw-Hill.
Schultze, Charles L.
1972 "Is Economics Absolute? No, Underemployed." *Saturday Review*,
January 22, pp. 50–52, 57.
Silk, Leonard
1972 "Wanted: A More Human, Less Dismal Science." *Saturday Review*,
January 22, pp. 34–35.
Stein, Herbert
1973 "Money Made by Money is Already Taxed More Than Money Made
by Men." *Saturday Review*, October 21, pp. 47–48.

Stern, Philip M.
   1964 *The Great Treasury Raid.* New York: Random House.
   1973 *The Rape of the Taxpayer.* New York: Random House.
Surrey, Stanley
   1972 "Taxes as a Moral Issue." *Saturday Review*, October 21, pp. 51–52.
Townsend, Robert
   1972 Review of L. Heilbroner. In "The Name of Profit." *New York Times Book Review*, April 30, pp. 5, 23–24.
Tyler, Gus
   1973 "Debate: Nixon, the Great Society, and the Future of Social Policy." *Commentary*, May, pp. 53–57.
U. S. Bureau of the Census
   1971 *Census Population, 1970.* Vol. 1. Washington, D.C.: U. S. Government Printing Office.
U. S. Department of Commerce
   1972 *Income Distribution, 1971.* Washington, D.C.: U. S. Government Printing Office.
Wall Street Journal
   August 29, 1973.

Afterword

Most likely there are some readers who have found this book to be antithetical to their views. I expect my critics to analyze the data in detail, marshaling their thinking against the facts, dissecting and damning the content wherever they can or wherever there may be another interpretation. I have taken a strong position, one that is unpopular in print, that forces me to be 101 percent right. On the other hand, someone else who voices a more popular position only needs to be 50 percent right. We have created a culture that does not permit criticism of a group that is deemed as a minority and claims to be "oppressed" by the majority. Indeed, the social scientist is losing his independent intellect when sensitive issues are raised. He gauges the estimate of the social worth of what he says, but also the personal consequences that may result.

One by one, definable groups have discovered that their so-called oppressed status provides certain advantages not provided to others. One of these advantages is the right to criticize and damn the so-called oppressor, while making it difficult to criticize them without being condemned. The almost inevitable law with each minority group that defines itself as oppressed has been the recent transformation in their respective movements from a "moderate" to "militant" point of view. The final stage of social protest has been in almost every case a sense of selfhood and *"we* ness" not accessible to any outsider, no matter how sympathetic. In obtaining this selfhood, one is required to view all the manifestations of the minority group as healthy. Apparent pathologies are either denied or considered appropriate behavior for dealing with the outside or alien group. Almost any criticism of an individual from the outside group is rejected and invites verbal attack and even possible physical harassment.

In this book, the terms "moderate" and "militant," "integrationist" and "nationalist" were frequently used. These are general terms, used because the dichotomies are easy to work with and operationalize. Also, people are familiar with these terms. I certainly recognize that it is difficult, if not impossible, to categorize the attitudes of blacks into opposing groups with only shades of differences in between. To be sure, it is no easy task to define the attitudes of a group that constitutes more than 22 million people with many diverse viewpoints. In the same vein, such opposing terms as "liberal" and "conservative" and such overlapping terms as "middle American," "silent majority," and "ethnic" were used to explain human behavior and human events. This lack of precision and exactitude in terms in part reflects a weakness in social science literature. Terms are often general and ill-defined to some extent. Pick up any piece of social science literature, popular or scholarly, and you will find similar terms. Only when dealing with scales and tests can we better define our terms.

If there are overriding issues in this book, they are: Blacks and minorities have been discriminated against in the past. Today, the words "prejudiceness," "bigotry," "racism," "victimization," and "oppression" have become ploys, part of a strategy for blacks to capitalize on. The civil rights movement caught America by surprise in the 1960s. The goal of integration on the part of blacks changed to black power and separatism. While all groups should maintain control over their own institutions, and as the group asserts its new power, there is a need to protect the rights of the individual. Similarly, there is a need to limit violence and extremist positions; otherwise, that society disintegrates. The civil rights movement also started with the theme of equal opportunity and progressed to the theme of equal results. The question is how to speed up progress for blacks and other minorities without reverse discrimination against whites, many of whom have had no part or have been in no position to discriminate. The present drive for equal results is a twisted form of racism. It is based on preferential treatment and quotas that permit incompetents to often beat out the most qualified. Due to the increased political clout of blacks, plus the threat of violence, the federal government has sanctioned and encouraged this new form of racism. Timetables and goals are terms used by the government, rather than quotas which are denied; preferential treatment is used, rather than reverse discrimination which is also denied. In either case, whatever terms are used, the outcome is similar, with the federal government increasing the pressure. While the majority of the population, black and white, fight for a few extra thousand dollars, while they battle over jobs and power, the rich remain generally untouched and basically secure with most of the money and power. Thus a small group of people manage to control most of the wealth of the nation, while the masses continue to scramble for the leftovers. This situation must cease.

And so we march into the future, and each day there seems to be another crisis, another problem that must be solved. Although there are serious defects in the American system and there are serious problems for which solutions must be found, one need not be apocalyptic in analyzing the future of this nation. None of our problems or defects need prove fatal.

As for the defects in the system, no one with good sense maintains that democracy is an easy form of government. Some of us think it is too flexible and unruly, too accommodating to compromise, and open to a great deal of error because the people are either ignorant or selfish. But consider the alternative—an efficient, rigid society that rules out the errors through governmental control and fear—an old-fashioned totalitarian state or perhaps some modern 1984 governmental system. Still others feel that the federal government has too much power, that it interferes with the rights of state and local governments, that it is involved in too many domestic functions and private agencies, that it is hampering business and free enterprise. Again consider the alternative, where cooperation and federation are replaced by self-interest and local prejudices, where collective force and large racial or ethnic groups and huge corporations have no restraints and dwarf the individual, where the world belongs to the strong when they no longer need any justification for their conquests or greed, and where the young, weak, and minority groups are gobbled up by nature's law of the survival of the fittest and strongest—indeed, old-fashioned laissez faire, which in today's industrial-political-racial system leads to a modern socio-economical jungle and complete chaos.

To be sure, the middle of the road is hard to find; it is elusive, intangible, and relative to one's biases. The critics of the system and the people who refuse to search for the middle road, whether they swerve to the Right or to the Left, whether they are for more controls or fewer controls, for a balanced budget or deficit spending, whether they represent the minority or majority viewpoint, tend to dismiss modern America as being too slow, too inefficient, too corrupt to implement genuine reform. There are many of us who would abridge freedom for the sake of order and efficiency, and there are others who would encourage rioting and violence for political and personal gain. Some of us do not care whether the hungry starve and prefer to ignore the painful existence of urban ghettos, and there are others that preach that quotas are justified, corporations must be dismantled, the rich must surrender their money to the poor, and those in power must surrender their authority or be prepared for urban warfare. And then there are the ordinary people, most of them overlooked, victimized and confused by the media, exploited by policy makers, and influenced by those on the Right and those on the Left.

There are no easy solutions to complex problems, and in a period of social turbulance it has become fashionable to distrust the democratic process. In *The Children of Light and the Children of Darkness,* Reinhold Niebuhr, the famous theologian, made his classic statement: "Man's capacity for justice makes democracy possible, but man's inclination to injustice makes democracy necessary." In today's troubled times, this is a good observation to keep in mind. A powerful government or "all power to the people," either one with unlimited constraints, is dangerous.

Index

Author

Subject